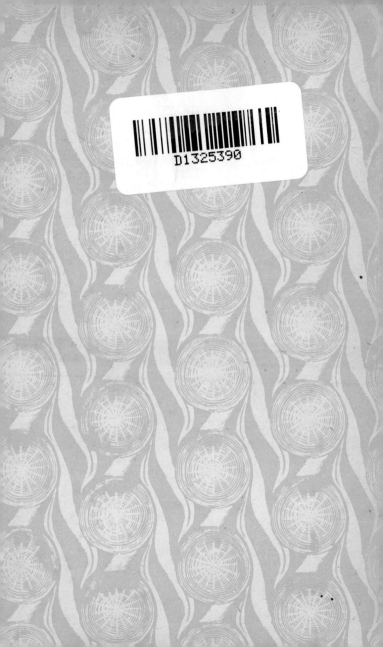

Everyman, I will go with thee, and be thy guide,
In thy most need to go by thy side.

EVERYMAN'S LIBRARY
EDITED BY ERNEST RHYS

POETRY

POEMS AND PROSE OF
ALGERNON CHARLES SWINBURNE
WITH AN INTRODUCTION BY
RICHARD CHURCH

ALGERNON CHARLES SWINBURNE. Son of Admiral Charles Henry and Lady Jane Swinburne. Born 5th April 1837, at 7 Chester St, Grosvenor Place, London. Died 10th April 1909, at The Pines, Putney Hill, London

SWINBURNE

Poems and Prose

LONDON: J. M. DENT & SONS LTD
NEW YORK: E. P. DUTTON & CO. INC.

All rights reserved
Made in Great Britain
at The Temple Press Letchworth
for
J. M. Dent & Sons Ltd.
Aldine House Bedford St. London
This selection first published 1940
Last reprinted 1946

TO GEORGES LAFOURCADE
PROFESSOR OF ENGLISH AT GRENOBLE
UNIVERSITY
AS A TRIBUTE TO HIS DEVOTION
TO SWINBURNE'S LIFE AND WORK

INTRODUCTION

ALGERNON CHARLES SWINBURNE, like the poet Shelley whom he adored, was a sort of social changeling. Both these singers of revolution and republicanism were born into aristocratic English families of feudal instincts and traditions. Both went to Eton and showed there a precocious and lonely genius for scholarship in the classics. Both had grandfathers of the eighteenth-century school of thought who slyly sympathized with and encouraged what were regarded as these family freaks. Both had fathers who were stern about the young apostates from caste. In a letter to W. M. Rossetti, written by Swinburne in 1870 at the age of thirty-three, the poet said: 'I think you are rather hard upon Shelley as to the filial relation. I have no more doubt that it may be said for Sir Timothy that his son was what Carlyle calls an "afflictive phenomenon" than that I was the same to my father before, during, and since my Oxford time; but I do not think you make allowance for the provocation given (as well as received) by a father who may be kindly and generous, to a boy or man between seventeen or twenty-one or thirty, with whom he has no deep or wide ground of sympathy beyond the animal relation or family tradition. You will allow me to say that I am sure you can never have felt at that age the irreparable, total, and inevitable isolation from all that had once been closest to the mind and thought, and was still closest to the flesh and memory, the solitude, into which one passes from separation to antagonism of spirit, without violent quarrel or open offence, but by pure logical necessity of consequences, the sense that where attraction gradually ends repulsion gradually begins, which many besides Shelley, and as affectionate and faithful by nature and temperament as he, *have* felt at that age.'

Psychologists and sociologists may be able to explain such aberrations of the so-called laws of heredity; and they may be left to do so. The fact remains that here are two of the major figures in the Romantic period, the one a generation later than the other, totally foreign in temperament, in physique, in intellect from their ancestors and from the contemporary members of their families. Both had high-pitched voices, an extreme volubility, a sort of fever of the intellect which made them live a degree or two above the thinking processes of the normal man and which thus removed them from contact with the sane reality that gives the best understanding of human nature and the most objective and dramatic poetry. Lacking in these qualities, Shelley and Swinburne, where they did not attract devotees, could inspire positive disgust. Charles Lamb's loathing for Shelley is notorious. Walt Whitman referred to Swinburne as 'that damned simulacrum.'

In some respects Whitman, himself a man of tumid conceptions, was right. Swinburne *was* a simulacrum, as Mr T. S. Eliot has pointed out in his study of this poet. But his vast range of historical, literary, and philological knowledge was none the less sincere and coherent for that. Swinburne created a universe of his own, as every powerful personality does. But something prevented him from putting it to the full and adult test of experience, so that he could inform it with the necessary contamination of flesh and blood, observed fact, acquired patience, and common sense.

To the end of his life, Swinburne remained fervent, a creature of extremes, hating or idolizing as a youth does, with an undisciplined extravagance of emotion. And where Swinburn *felt*, he sang, giving himself up to an intoxication quite primitive, Dionysiac in its force. It split his personality. Swinburne was two people in the one tadpole-like body. In his daily self he was diminutive, shy, bookish, and vague, with a high, squeaky voice. In the self that would, on provocative occasion, become suddenly fired with emotion, his great head, with its flame of red hair (see G. F. Watts's portrait), would seem to lift the little body off the ground, drawing with it some super-sexual vocal power that roared forth in a deep bass, loud and magnificent, out of the depths of his nature. During such moments of ecstatic possession, he would leap on and off sofas and chairs like a wild creature. And all that was needed to induce this condition was perhaps a reference to the poetry of Marlowe, or to the character of Mazzini.

Swinburne thus was in a greater social predicament than his beloved Shelley. The latter was unified in his war upon society. Swinburne the tadpole-scholar was a quiet member of his aristocratic family, aloof and retiring. But enrage him with drink, or poetry, and he would become poisoned with all possible forms of mental and emotional perversity, calling upon the ghost of the Marquis de Sade to initiate his imagination into the more exquisite forms of sensual indulgence, or evoking the lamian beauty of some Renaissance strumpet so that he might boast to his Victorian public of fictitious dallyings with her.

> I said, ' She must be swift and white,
> And subtly warm, and half perverse,
> And sweet like sharp soft fruit to bite,
> And like a snake's love lithe and fierce.'
> Men have guessed worse.

But had men guessed that in such verse as this Swinburne was dealing with a world of fact or personal experience in its more mundane sense, they would have guessed wrong. The raptures were reflected from the lives and writings of Baudelaire and Dante Gabriel Rossetti, and the roses with their emphasis of thorns were the flowers of alliteration rather than of vice.

Life did not repair this fissure in Swinburne's personality. Indeed, circumstances took a part in keeping the changeling half hostile to the legitimate half. A formal education, strictly supervised by his disciplinarian father and his highly cultivated mother, widened the cleavage. The two selves were further differentiated by the fact that Swinburne's life from earliest infancy was divided between one family seat in the Isle of Wight, in the warm south,

> . . . where the silver-sandalled shadows are,
> Too soft for arrows of the sun to mar,

and where he could watch the spring,

> With little unblown breasts and child-eyed looks
> Following, the very maid, the girl-child Spring,
> Lift windward her bright brows,
> Dip her light feet in warm and moving brooks,
> And kindle with her own mouth's colouring
> The fearful firstlings of the plumeless boughs,

and another family seat in Northumberland, a land of subtleties and hidden qualities, of austere moods in keeping with the proud young scholar-aristocrat wandering where

> Through fell and moorland,
> And salt-sea foreland,
> Our noisy norland
> Resounds and rings;
> Waste waves thereunder
> Are blown in sunder,
> And winds make thunder
> With cloudwide wings;

Sea-drift makes dimmer
The beacon's glimmer;
Nor sail nor swimmer
Can try the tides;
And snowdrifts thicken
Where, when leaves quicken,
Under the heather the sundew hides.

Thus, under the guidance of an unconscious conspiracy, the poet was reared. The result was one of the most odd and detached bodies of work in the whole of English literature. Although Swinburne, by his enthusiasms, can be placed as a typical example of the contemporary revolt from the materialism and substantiality of Victorian England, his work has no solid foundation in that revolt. He hovered on the fringe of the struggle, crying shrill encouragement to the zealots and fatalists whom he believed were reorganizing society and destroying both the theological and ethical structure in which Christianity had immured itself. We see now that much less happened than was expected by the reformers, just as much less is likely to happen from the violent convulsions that are tormenting Europe to-day. But enough was going on for Swinburne to drive himself into a frenzy. But then he did the same thing when he read a rag-and-sawdust melodrama by one of the more unreadable Elizabethan dramatists. Circumstances were really immaterial to him. He saw them, or heard them, through the clamour of his own mania.

And what was that mania? It was a divine insanity for words. He was a syllable-addict, a word-drunkard. He knew no temperance in self-expression. Indeed, his literary activity could hardly be called self-expression, because he never stopped to consider that self, or to consolidate it for commerce with the world around him.

Like the infant Coleridge, he could be mistaken, when walking along the Strand, into believing that he was swimming the Hellespont. It did not matter, that lack of correspondence between fact and fantasy. What *did* matter was the eloquence which either the fact or the fantasy must conjure from his depths as the moon conjures the tides.

An examination of any of his enormous output of poems will show the result of this lack of sobriety. We expect the poet's eye to roll in a fine frenzy; but that process was accelerated in Swinburne, and the reader has the conviction that behind the inspired eye a huge and intricate shop of machinery, with myriads of cogwheels, is set in motion. And once set in motion, it cannot be stopped easily. The beltings and wheels invariably go on slapping and grinding long after the poetic task has been done and the core of the poem shaped. As Swinburne grew older, that machinery creaked more, and its inertia carried it on for longer and longer periods after the poetic gesture had been made.

But this criticism is offered only in the certainty that Swinburne is a major poet, of enormous power, of divine skill. His work is saturated with his personality, and is immediately recognizable, even though by reason of the fact that it is often a parody of itself.

With all his prolixity, his metrical technique is impeccable. There is not a poet in our language with a more subtle ear for metre. He does with metre what Shelley did with rhythm, and what Milton did with cadence. It is the least of the three powers, but it is an essential one. And to this he added an exquisite skill in rhyming, one that never fell into the vulgar tricks which marred so much of Browning's audacities in this part of the poet's craft. And how unerringly, like Spenser, he could accumulate his rhyming pattern into a

xiv

stanza perfectly shaped to enhance the ring of the rhymes. Here is an example:

> The morning song beneath the stars that fled
> With twilight through the moonless mountain air,
> While youth with burning lips and wreathless hair
> Sang toward the sun that was to crown his head,
> Rising; the hopes that triumphed and fell dead,
> The sweet swift eyes and songs of hours that were;
> These may'st thou not give back for ever; these,
> As at the sea's heart all her wrecks lie waste,
> Lie deeper than the sea;
> But flowers thou may'st, and winds, and hours of ease,
> And all its April to the world thou may'st
> Give back, and half my April back to me.

Examples could be multiplied generously, with lovely instances of internal rhymes, and rhymes deliberately dropping to a solitary word at the verse-end, for an emphasis such as he developed with diabolical irony in the long lyric called *Félise*.

But these are matters of technique, toward which the general reader, if Swinburne is likely to attract the general reader, may show impatience, preferring rather to turn to the content of the work, to find out what 'message' it has for a later generation utterly foreign to the aesthetic and moral problems of the Victorian age. Such a younger reader, introduced by Mr Eliot's verse to a drearier weariness, and by Mr Dylan Thomas's to even more remote and perverse vices, will find Swinburne's lilies and languors and roses and raptures mere book-pressed blossoms, relics in a family album.

There is more still, however, to be found in Swinburne's poetry. Its very oddity of detachment, its self-rapt generation in a cosmos of words, its lack of contact with contemporary circumstance (in spite of the apostrophes to Victor Hugo, and its spittings at Russian Tsars), give it a dateless beauty, like the contrapuntal music of the eighteenth century.

In making a selection from Swinburne's enormous output, I could not avoid, on one or two occasions, pruning a poem that might have run on endlessly. The most glaring instance of this impertinence is in the poem *Laus Veneris*, which is the first in this volume. The other poem similarly handled is *Faustine*. Rather than attack *Tristram of Lyonesse* in this way, I have omitted it altogether. This long narrative shows Swinburne much diluted in the waters of Pre-Raphaelitism, and it is somewhat insipid reading, in which the inherent temptations of the heroic couplet have been too much for Swinburne's native predisposition.

This economy of space has enabled me to include intact the two classical dramas, *Atalanta in Calydon* and *Erechtheus*, which I had hoped to do for critical reasons. For my ear, *Erechtheus*, while less immediately appealing than the earlier *Atalanta*, shows Swinburne in his most austere and self-critical mood. The blank verse in this play has a movement and restrained force which Swinburne did not attain elsewhere, while the choruses are as finely chiselled as those of *Samson Agonistes*. Further, the theme of the play has an eternal application to our human struggle, and I would refer the twentieth-century reader to the final chorus:

From the depth of the springs of my spirit a fountain is poured of thanksgiving,
My country, my mother, for thee,
That thy dead for their death shall have life in thy sight and a name everliving
At heart of thy people to be
In the darkness of change on the waters of time they shall turn from afar
To the beam of this dawn for a beacon, the light of these pyres for a star.

xvi

*They shall see thee who love and take comfort, who hate thee shall
     see and take warning,*
Our mother that makest us free;
*And the sons of thine earth shall have help of the Waves that
     make war on the morning,*
And friendship and fame of the sea.

RICHARD CHURCH

The following is a list of the works of Algernon Charles
Swinburne:

The Queen Mother and *Rosamond,* 1860; *Atalanta in Calydon,*
1865; *Poems and Ballads,* 1866; *William Blake* (prose), 1868;
Songs before Sunrise, 1871; *Bothwell,* 1874; *Essays and Studies,*
1875; *Erechtheus,* 1876; *A Year's Letters,* 1877; *Poems and Ballads,*
Second Series, 1878; *A Study of Shakespeare,* 1880; *Mary Stuart*
1881; *Tristram of Lyonesse,* 1882; *Poems and Ballads,* Third Series,
1889; *Studies in Prose and Poetry,* 1894; *The Tale of Balen,* 1896;
First Collected Edition of Poems and Plays, 11 volumes, 1904.
There are also other publications. Swinburne's works are
published by William Heinemann Limited.

The principal works on Swinburne are the biographies by
Edmund Gosse (1917) and Georges Lafourcade (1932), both
excellent works; Earle Welby's *Study of Swinburne* (1926);
Harold Nicolson's *Swinburne* (1926); and Max Beerbohm's
essay in *And Even Now* (1926).

CONTENTS

Poems and Ballads : First Series

Songs before Sunrise

POEMS

POEMS AND BALLADS

First Series

Stanzas from 'Laus Veneris'

LO, this is she that was the world's delight;
  The old grey years were parcels of her might;
 The strewings of the ways wherein she trod
Were the twain seasons of the day and night.

Lo, she was thus when her clear limbs enticed
All lips that now grow sad with kissing Christ,
 Stained with blood fallen from the feet of God,
The feet and hands whereat our souls were priced.

Alas, Lord, surely thou art great and fair.
But lo her wonderfully woven hair!
 And thou didst heal us with thy piteous kiss;
But see now, Lord; her mouth is lovelier.

.   .   .

Behold, my Venus, my soul's body, lies
With my love laid upon her garment-wise,
 Feeling my love in all her limbs and hair
And shed between her eyelids through her eyes.

She holds my heart in her sweet open hands
Hanging asleep; hard by her head there stands,
 Crowned with gilt thorns and clothed with flesh like fire,
Love, wan as foam blown up the salt burnt sands.

Hot as the brackish waifs of yellow spume
That shift and steam—loose clots of arid fume
 From the sea's panting mouth of dry desire;
There stands he, like one labouring at a loom.

.   .   .

3

Ah yet would God this flesh of mine might be
Where air might wash and long leaves cover me,
    Where tides of grass break into foam of flowers,
Or where the wind's feet shine along the sea.

Ah yet would God that stems and roots were bred
Out of my weary body and my head,
    That sleep were sealed upon me with a seal,
And I were as the least of all his dead.

Would God my blood were dew to feed the grass,
Mine ears made deaf and mine eyes blind as glass,
    My body broken as a turning wheel,
And my mouth stricken ere it saith Alas!

Ah God, that love were as a flower or flame,
That life were as the naming of a name,
    That death were not more pitiful than desire,
That these things were not one thing and the same!

·   ·   ·

Outside it must be winter among men;
For at the gold bars of the gates again
    I heard all night and all the hours of it
The wind's wet wings and fingers drip with rain.

Knights gather, riding sharp for cold; I know
The ways and woods are strangled with the snow;
    And with short song the maidens spin and sit
Until Christ's birthnight, lily-like, arow.

The scent and shadow shed about me make
The very soul in all my senses ache;
    The hot hard night is fed upon my breath,
And sleep beholds me from afar awake.

4

Alas, but surely where the hills grow deep,
Or where the wild ways of the sea are steep,
   Or in strange places somewhere there is death,
And on death's face the scattered hair of sleep.

There lover-like with lips and limbs that meet
They lie, they pluck sweet fruit of life and eat;
   But me the hot and hungry days devour,
And in my mouth no fruit of theirs is sweet.

No fruit of theirs, but fruit of my desire,
For her love's sake whose lips through mine respire;
   Her eyelids on her eyes like flower on flower,
Mine eyelids on mine eyes like fire on fire.

So lie we, not as sleep that lies by death,
With heavy kisses and with happy breath;
   Not as man lies by woman, when the bride
Laughs low for love's sake and the words he saith.

For she lies, laughing low with love; she lies
And turns his kisses on her lips to sighs,
   To sighing sound of lips unsatisfied,
And the sweet tears are tender with her eyes.

Ah, not as they, but as the souls that were
Slain in the old time, having found her fair;
   Who, sleeping with her lips upon their eyes,
Heard sudden serpents hiss across her hair.

Their blood runs round the roots of time like rain:
She casts them forth and gathers them again;
   With nerve and bone she weaves and multiplies
Exceeding pleasure out of extreme pain.

Her little chambers drip with flower-like red,
Her girdles, and the chaplets of her head,
   Her armlets and her anklets; with her feet
She tramples all that winepress of the dead.

Her gateways smoke with fume of flowers and fires,
With loves burnt out and unassuaged desires;
   Between her lips the steam of them is sweet,
The languor in her ears of many lyres.

Her beds are full of perfume and sad sound,
Her doors are made with music, and barred round
   With sighing and with laughter and with tears,
With tears whereby strong souls of men are bound.

Ah God, that sleep with flower-sweet finger-tips
Would crush the fruit of death upon my lips;
   Ah God, that death would tread the grapes of sleep
And wring their juice upon me as it drips.

Sin, is it sin whereby men's souls are thrust
Into the pit? yet had I a good trust
   To save my soul before it slipped therein,
Trod under by the fire-shod feet of lust.

For if mine eyes fail and my soul takes breath,
I look between the iron sides of death
   Into sad hell where all sweet love hath end,
All but the pain that never finisheth.

There are the naked faces of great kings,
The singing-folk with all their lute-playings;
   There when one cometh he shall have to friend
The grave that covets and the worm that clings.

There sit the knights that were so great of hand,
The ladies that were queens of fair green land,
   Grown grey and black now, brought unto the dust,
Soiled, without raiment, clad about with sand.

There is one end for all of them; they sit
Naked and sad, they drink the dregs of it,
   Trodden as grapes in the wine-press of lust.
Trampled and trodden by the fiery feet.

I see the marvellous mouth whereby there fell
Cities and people whom the gods loved well,
   Yet for her sake on them the fire gat hold,
And for their sakes on her the fire of hell.

And softer than the Egyptian lote-leaf is,
The queen whose face was worth the world to kiss,
   Wearing at breast a suckling snake of gold;
And large pale lips of strong Semiramis,

Curled like a tiger's that curl back to feed;
Red only where the last kiss made them bleed;
   Her hair most thick with many a carven gem,
Deep in the mane, great-chested, like a steed.

Yea, with red sin the faces of them shine;
But in all these there was no sin like mine;
   No, not in all the strange great sins of them
That made the wine-press froth and foam with wine.

For I was of Christ's choosing, I God's knight,
No blinkard heathen stumbling for scant light;
   I can well see, for all the dusty days
Gone past, the clean great time of goodly fight.

I smell the breathing battle sharp with blows,
With shriek of shafts and snapping short of bows;
    The fair pure sword smites out in subtle ways,
Sounds and long lights are shed between the rows

Of beautiful mailed men; the edged light slips,
Most like a snake that takes short breath and dips
    Sharp from the beautifully bending head,
With all its gracious body lithe as lips

That curl in touching you; right in this wise
My sword doth, seeming fire in mine own eyes,
    Leaving all colours in them brown and red
And flecked with death; then the keen breaths like sighs,

The caught-up choked dry laughters following them,
When all the fighting face is grown a flame
    For pleasure, and the pulse that stuns the ears,
And the heart's gladness of the goodly game.

Ah, with blind lips I felt for you, and found
About my neck your hands and hair enwound,
    The hands that stifle and the hair that stings,
I felt them fasten sharply without sound.

Yea, for my sin I had great store of bliss:
Rise up, make answer for me, let thy kiss
    Seal my lips hard from speaking of my sin,
Lest one go mad to hear how sweet it is.

Yet I waxed faint with fume of barren bowers,
And murmuring of the heavy-headed hours;
    And let the dove's beak fret and peck within
My lips in vain, and Love shed fruitless flowers.

8

So that God looked upon me when your hands
Were hot about me; yea, God brake my bands
  To save my soul alive, and I came forth
Like a man blind and naked in strange lands

That hears men laugh and weep, and knows not whence
Nor wherefore, but is broken in his sense;
  Howbeit I met folk riding from the north
Towards Rome, to purge them of their souls' offence,

And rode with them, and spake to none; the day
Stunned me like lights upon some wizard way,
  And ate like fire mine eyes and mine eyesight;
So rode I, hearing all these chant and pray,

And marvelled; till before us rose and fell
White cursed hills, like outer skirts of hell
  Seen where men's eyes look through the day to night,
Like jagged shell's lips, harsh, untunable,

Blown in between by devils' wrangling breath;
Nathless we won well past that hell and death,
  Down to the sweet land where all airs are good,
Even unto Rome where God's grace tarrieth.

Then came each man and worshipped at his knees
Who in the Lord God's likeness bears the keys
  To bind or loose, and called on Christ's shed blood,
And so the sweet-souled father gave him ease.

But when I came I fell down at his feet,
Saying, 'Father, though the Lord's blood be right sweet,
  The spot it takes not off the panther's skin,
Nor shall an Ethiop's stain be bleached with it.

'Lo, I have sinned and have spat out at God,
Wherefore his hand is heavier and his rod
     More sharp because of mine exceeding sin,
And all his raiment redder than bright blood

'Before mine eyes; yea, for my sake I wot
The heat of hell is waxen seven times hot
     Through my great sin.' Then spake he some sweet
          word,
Giving me cheer; which thing availed me not.

Yea, scarce I wist if such indeed were said;
For when I ceased—lo, as one newly dead
     Who hears a great cry out of hell, I heard
The crying of his voice across my head.

'Until this dry shred staff, that hath no whit
Of leaf nor bark, bear blossom and smell sweet,
     Seek thou not any mercy in God's sight,
For so long shalt thou be cast out from it.'

For I came home right heavy, with small cheer,
And lo my love, mine own soul's heart, more dear
     Than mine own soul, more beautiful than God,
Who hath my being between the hands of her—

Fair still, but fair for no man saving me,
As when she came out of the naked sea
     Making the foam as fire whereon she trod,
And as the inner flower of fire was she.

Yea, she laid hold upon me, and her mouth
Clove unto mine as soul to body doth,
     And, laughing, made her lips luxurious;
Her hair had smells of all the sunburnt south,

10

Strange spice and flower, strange savour of crushed fruit,
And perfume the swart kings tread underfoot
  For pleasure when their minds wax amorous,
Charred frankincense and grated sandal-root.

And I forgot fear and all weary things,
All ended prayers and perished thanksgivings,
  Feeling her face with all her eager hair
Cleave to me, clinging as a fire that clings

To the body and to the raiment, burning them;
As after death I know that such-like flame
  Shall cleave to me for ever; yea, what care,
Albeit I burn then, having felt the same?

Ah love, there is no better life than this;
To have known love, how bitter a thing it is,
  And afterwards be cast out of God's sight;
Yea, these that know not, shall they have such bliss

High up in barren heaven before his face
As we twain in the heavy-hearted place,
  Remembering love and all the dead delight,
And all that time was sweet with for a space?

For till the thunder in the trumpet be,
Soul may divide from body, but not we
  One from another; I hold thee with my hand,
I let mine eyes have all their will of thee,

I seal myself upon thee with my might,
Abiding alway out of all men's sight
  Until God loosen over sea and land
The thunder of the trumpets of the night.

The Triumph of Time

BEFORE our lives divide for ever,
    While time is with us and hands are free,
(Time, swift to fasten and swift to sever
    Hand from hand, as we stand by the sea)
I will say no word that a man might say
Whose whole life's love goes down in a day;
For this could never have been; and never,
    Though the gods and the years relent, shall be.

Is it worth a tear, is it worth an hour,
    To think of things that are well outworn?
Of fruitless husk and fugitive flower,
    The dream forgone and the deed forborne?
Though joy be done with and grief be vain,
Time shall not sever us wholly in twain;
Earth is not spoilt for a single shower;
    But the rain has ruined the ungrown corn.

It will not grow again, this fruit of my heart,
    Smitten with sunbeams, ruined with rain.
The singing seasons divide and depart,
    Winter and summer depart in twain.
It will grow not again, it is ruined at root,
The bloodlike blossom, the dull red fruit;
Though the heart yet sickens, the lips yet smart,
    With sullen savour of poisonous pain.

I have given no man of my fruit to eat;
    I trod the grapes, I have drunken the wine.
Had you eaten and drunken and found it sweet,
    This wild new growth of the corn and vine,
This wine and bread without lees or leaven,
We had grown as gods, as the gods in heaven,
Souls fair to look upon, goodly to greet,
    One splendid spirit, your soul and mine.

In the change of years, in the coil of things,
  In the clamour and rumour of life to be,
We, drinking love at the furthest springs,
  Covered with love as a covering tree,
We had grown as gods, as the gods above,
Filled from the heart to the lips with love,
Held fast in his hands, clothed warm with his wings,
  O love, my love, had you loved but me!

We had stood as the sure stars stand, and moved
  As the moon moves, loving the world; and seen
Grief collapse as a thing disproved,
  Death consume as a thing unclean.
Twain halves of a perfect heart, made fast
Soul to soul while the years fell past;
Had you loved me once, as you have not loved;
  Had the chance been with us that has not been.

I have put my days and dreams out of mind,
  Days that are over, dreams that are done.
Though we seek life through, we shall surely find
  There is none of them clear to us now, not one.
But clear are these things; the grass and the sand,
Where, sure as the eyes reach, ever at hand,
With lips wide open and face burnt blind,
  The strong sea-daisies feast on the sun.

The low downs lean to the sea; the stream,
  One loose thin pulseless tremulous vein,
Rapid and vivid and dumb as a dream,
  Works downward, sick of the sun and the rain;
No wind is rough with the rank rare flowers;
The sweet sea, mother of loves and hours,
Shudders and shines as the grey winds gleam,
  Turning her smile to a fugitive pain.

Mother of loves that are swift to fade,
 Mother of mutable winds and hours.
A barren mother, a mother-maid,
 Cold and clean as her faint salt flowers.
I would we twain were even as she,
Lost in the night and the light of the sea,
Where faint sounds falter and wan beams wade,
 Break, and are broken, and shed into showers.

The love and hours of the life of a man,
 They are swift and sad, being born of the sea.
Hours that rejoice and regret for a span,
 Born with a man's breath, mortal as he;
Loves that are lost ere they come to birth,
Weeds of the wave, without fruit upon earth.
I lose what I long for, save what I can,
 My love, my love, and no love for me!

It is not much that a man can save
 On the sands of life, in the straits of time,
Who swims in sight of the great third wave
 That never a swimmer shall cross or climb.
Some waif washed up with the strays and spars
That ebb-tide shows to the shore and the stars;
Weed from the water, grass from a grave,
 A broken blossom, a ruined rhyme.

There will no man do for your sake, I think,
 What I would have done for the least word said.
I had wrung life dry for your lips to drink,
 Broken it up for your daily bread:
Body for body and blood for blood,
As the flow of the full sea risen to flood
That yearns and trembles before it sink,
 I had given, and lain down for you, glad and dead.

Yea, hope at highest and all her fruit,
    And time at fullest and all his dower,
I had given you surely, and life to boot,
    Were we once made one for a single hour.
But now, you are twain, you are cloven apart,
Flesh of his flesh, but heart of my heart;
And deep in one is the bitter root,
    And sweet for one is the lifelong flower.

To have died if you cared I should die for you, clung
    To my life if you bade me, played my part
As it pleased you—these were the thoughts that stung
    The dreams that smote with a keener dart
Than shafts of love or arrows of death;
These were but as fire is, dust, or breath,
Or poisonous foam on the tender tongue
    Of the little snakes that eat my heart.

I wish we were dead together to-day,
    Lost sight of, hidden away out of sight,
Clasped and clothed in the cloven clay,
    Out of the world's way, out of the light,
Out of the ages of worldly weather,
Forgotten of all men altogether.
As the world's first dead, taken wholly away,
    Made one with death, filled full of the night.

How we should slumber, how we should sleep,
    Far in the dark with the dreams and the dews!
And dreaming, grow to each other, and weep,
    Laugh low, live softly, murmur and muse;
Yea, and it may be, struck through by the dream,
Feel the dust quicken and quiver, and seem
Alive as of old to the lips, and leap
    Spirit to spirit as lovers use.

Sick dreams and sad of a dull delight;
  For what shall it profit when men are dead
To have dreamed, to have loved with the whole soul's might,
  To have looked for day when the day was fled?
Let come what will, there is one thing worth,
To have had fair love in the life upon earth:
To have held love safe till the day grew night,
  While skies had colour and lips were red.

Would I lose you now? would I take you then,
  If I lose you now that my heart has need?
And come what may after death to men,
  What thing worth this will the dead years breed?
Lose life, lose all; but at least I know,
O sweet life's love, having loved you so,
Had I reached you on earth, I should lose not again,
  In death nor life, nor in dream or deed.

Yea, I know this well: were you once sealed mine.
  Mine in the blood's beat, mine in the breath,
Mixed into me as honey in wine,
  Not time, that sayeth and gainsayeth,
Nor all strong things had severed us then;
Not wrath of gods, nor wisdom of men,
Nor all things earthly, nor all divine,
  Nor joy nor sorrow, nor life nor death.

I had grown pure as the dawn and the dew,
  You had grown strong as the sun or the sea.
But none shall triumph a whole life through:
  For death is one, and the fates are three.
At the door of life, by the gate of breath,
There are worse things waiting for men than death;
Death could not sever my soul and you,
  As these have severed your soul from me.

You have chosen and clung to the chance they sent you,
  Life sweet as perfume and pure as prayer.
But will it not one day in heaven repent you?
  Will they solace you wholly, the days that were?
Will you lift up your eyes between sadness and bliss,
Meet mine, and see where the great love is,
And tremble and turn and be changed?   Content you;
  The gate is strait; I shall not be there.

But you, had you chosen, had you stretched hand,
  Had you seen good such a thing were done,
I too might have stood with the souls that stand
  In the sun's sight, clothed with the light of the sun;
But who now on earth need care how I live?
Have the high gods anything left to give,
Save dust and laurels and gold and sand?
  Which gifts are goodly; but I will none.

O all fair lovers about the world,
  There is none of you, none, that shall comfort me.
My thoughts are as dead things, wrecked and whirled
  Round and round in a gulf of the sea;
And still, through the sound and the straining stream,
Through the coil and chafe, they gleam in a dream,
The bright fine lips so cruelly curled,
  And strange swift eyes where the soul sits free.

Free, without pity, withheld from woe,
  Ignorant; fair as the eyes are fair.
Would I have you change now, change at a blow
  Startled and stricken, awake and aware?
Yea, if I could, would I have you see
My very love of you filling me,
And know my soul to the quick, as I know
  The likeness and look of your throat and hair?

I shall not change you.   Nay, though I might,
  Would I change my sweet one love with a word?
I had rather your hair should change in a night,
  Clear now as the plume of a black bright bird;
Your face fail suddenly, cease, turn grey,
Die as a leaf that dies in a day.
I will keep my soul in a place out of sight,
  Far off, where the pulse of it is not heard.

Far off it walks, in a bleak blown space,
  Full of the sound of the sorrow of years.
I have woven a veil for the weeping face,
  Whose lips have drunken the wine of tears;
I have found a way for the failing feet,
A place for slumber and sorrow to meet;
There is no rumour about the place,
  Nor light, nor any that sees or hears.

I have hidden my soul out of sight, and said
  'Let none take pity upon thee, none
Comfort thy crying: for lo, thou art dead,
  Lie still now, safe out of sight of the sun.
Have I not built thee a grave, and wrought
Thy grave-clothes on thee of grievous thought,
With soft spun verses and tears unshed,
  And sweet light visions of things undone?

'I have given thee garments and balm and myrrh,
  And gold, and beautiful burial things.
But thou, be at peace now, make no stir;
  Is not thy grave as a royal king's?
Fret not thyself though the end were sore;
Sleep, be patient, vex me no more.
Sleep; what hast thou to do with her?
  The eyes that weep, with the mouth that sings?'

Where the dead red leaves of the years lie rotten,
    The cold old crimes and the deeds thrown by,
The misconceived and the misbegotten,
    I would find a sin to do ere I die,
Sure to dissolve and destroy me all through,
That would set you higher in heaven, serve you
And leave you happy, when clean forgotten,
    As a dead man out of mind, am I.

Your lithe hands draw me, your face burns through me,
    I am swift to follow you, keen to see;
But love lacks might to redeem or undo me;
    As I have been, I know I shall surely be;
'What should such fellows as I do?' Nay,
My part were worse if I chose to play;
For the worst is this after all; if they knew me,
    Not a soul upon earth would pity me.

And I play not for pity of these; but you,
    If you saw with your soul what man am I,
You would praise me at least that my soul all through
    Clove to you, loathing the lives that lie;
The souls and lips that are bought and sold,
The smiles of silver and kisses of gold,
The lapdog loves that whine as they chew,
    The little lovers that curse and cry.

There are fairer women, I hear; that may be;
    But I, that I love you and find you fair,
Who are more than fair in my eyes if they be,
    Do the high gods know or the great gods care?
Though the swords in my heart for one were seven,
Should the iron hollow of doubtful heaven,
That knows not itself whether night-time or day be,
    Reverberate words and a foolish prayer?

I will go back to the great sweet mother,
  Mother and lover of men, the sea.
I will go down to her, I and none other,
  Close with her, kiss her and mix her with me;
Cling to her, strive with her, hold her fast:
O fair white mother, in days long past
Born without sister, born without brother,
  Set free my soul as thy soul is free.

O fair green-girdled mother of mine,
  Sea, that art clothed with the sun and the rain,
Thy sweet hard kisses are strong like wine,
  Thy large embraces are keen like pain.
Save me and hide me with all thy waves,
Find me one grave of thy thousand graves,
Those pure cold populous graves of thine
  Wrought without hand in a world without stain.

I shall sleep, and move with the moving ships,
  Change as the winds change, veer in the tide;
My lips will feast on the foam of thy lips,
  I shall rise with thy rising, with thee subside;
Sleep, and not know if she be, if she were,
Filled full with life to the eyes and hair,
As a rose is fulfilled to the roseleaf tips
  With splendid summer and perfume and pride.

This woven raiment of nights and days,
  Were it once cast off and unwound from me,
Naked and glad would I walk in thy ways,
  Alive and aware of thy ways and thee;
Clear of the whole world, hidden at home,
Clothed with the green and crowned with the foam,
A pulse of the life of thy straits and bays,
  A vein in the heart of the streams of the sea.

Fair mother, fed with the lives of men,
    Thou art subtle and cruel of heart, men say.
Thou hast taken, and shalt not render again;
    Thou art full of thy dead, and cold as they.
But death is the worst that comes of thee;
Thou art fed with our dead, O mother, O sea,
But when hast thou fed on our hearts? or when,
    Having given us love, hast thou taken away?

O tender-hearted, O perfect lover,
    Thy lips are bitter, and sweet thine heart.
The hopes that hurt and the dreams that hover,
    Shall they not vanish away and apart?
But thou, thou art sure, thou art older than earth;
Thou art strong for death and fruitful of birth;
Thy depths conceal and thy gulfs discover;
    From the first thou wert; in the end thou art.

And grief shall endure not for ever, I know.
    As things that are not shall these things be;
We shall live through seasons of sun and of snow,
    And none be grievous as this to me.
We shall hear, as one in a trance that hears,
The sound of time, the rhyme of the years;
Wrecked hope and passionate pain will grow
    As tender things of a spring-tide sea.

Sea-fruit that swings in the waves that hiss,
    Drowned gold and purple and royal rings.
And all time past, was it all for this?
    Times unforgotten, and treasures of things?
Swift years of liking and sweet long laughter,
That wist not well of the years thereafter
Till love woke, smitten at heart by a kiss,
    With lips that trembled and trailing wings?

There lived a singer in France of old
    By the tideless dolorous midland sea.
In a land of sand and ruin and gold
    There shone one woman, and none but she.
And finding life for her love's sake fail,
Being fain to see her, he bade set sail,
Touched land, and saw her as life grew cold,
    And praised God, seeing; and so died he.

Died, praising God for his gift and grace:
    For she bowed down to him weeping, and said
'Live'; and her tears were shed on his face
    Or ever the life in his face was shed.
The sharp tears fell through her hair, and stung
Once, and her close lips touched him and clung
Once, and grew one with his lips for a space;
    And so drew back, and the man was dead.

O brother, the gods were good to you.
    Sleep, and be glad while the world endures.
Be well content as the years wear through;
    Give thanks for life, and the loves and lures;
Give thanks for life, O brother, and death,
For the sweet last sound of her feet, her breath,
For gifts she gave you, gracious and few,
    Tears and kisses, that lady of yours.

Rest, and be glad of the gods; but I,
    How shall I praise them, or how take rest?
There is not room under all the sky
    For me that know not of worst or best,
Dream or desire of the days before,
Sweet things or bitterness, any more.
Love will not come to me now though I die,
    As love came close to you, breast to breast.

I shall never be friends again with roses;
    I shall loathe sweet tunes, where a note grown strong
Relents and recoils, and climbs and closes,
    As a wave of the sea turned back by song.
There are sounds where the soul's delight takes fire,
Face to face with its own desire;
A delight that rebels, a desire that reposes;
    I shall hate sweet music my whole life long.

The pulse of war and passion of wonder,
    The heavens that murmur, the sounds that shine,
The stars that sing and the loves that thunder,
    The music burning at heart like wine,
An armed archangel whose hands raise up
All senses mixed in the spirit's cup
Till flesh and spirit are molten in sunder—
    These things are over, and no more mine.

These were a part of the playing I heard
    Once, ere my love and my heart were at strife;
Love that sings and hath wings as a bird,
    Balm of the wound and heft of the knife.
Fairer than earth is the sea, and sleep
Than overwatching of eyes that weep,
Now time has done with his one sweet word,
    The wine and leaven of lovely life.

I shall go my ways, tread out my measure,
    Fill the days of my daily breath
With fugitive things not good to treasure,
    Do as the world doth, say as it saith;
But if we had loved each other—O sweet,
Had you felt, lying under the palms of your feet,
The heart of my heart, beating harder with pleasure
    To feel you tread it to dust and death—

Ah, had I not taken my life up and given
   All that life gives and the years let go,
The wine and honey, the balm and leaven,
   The dreams reared high and the hopes brought low?
Come life, come death, not a word be said;
Should I lose you living, and vex you dead?
I never shall tell you on earth; and in heaven,
   If I cry to you then, will you hear or know?

LET us go hence, my songs; she will not hear.
　　Let us go hence together without fear;
Keep silence now, for singing-time is over,
And over all old things and all things dear.
She loves not you nor me as all we love her.
Yea, though we sang as angels in her ear,
　　　　She would not hear.

Let us rise up and part; she will not know.
Let us go seaward as the great winds go,
Full of blown sand and foam; what help is here?
There is no help, for all these things are so,
And all the world is bitter as a tear.
And how these things are, though ye strove to show,
　　　　She would not know.

Let us go home and hence; she will not weep.
We gave love many dreams and days to keep,
Flowers without scent, and fruits that would not grow,
Saying 'If thou wilt, thrust in thy sickle and reap.'
All is reaped now; no grass is left to mow;
And we that sowed, though all we fell on sleep,
　　　　She would not weep.

Let us go hence and rest; she will not love,
She shall not hear us if we sing hereof,
Nor see love's ways, how sore they are and steep.
Come hence, let be, lie still; it is enough.
Love is a barren sea, bitter and deep;
And though she saw all heaven in flower above,
　　　　She would not love.

Let us give up, go down; she will not care.
Though all the stars made gold of all the air,
And the sea moving saw before it move
One moon-flower making all the foam-flowers fair;
Though all those waves went over us, and drove
Deep down the stifling lips and drowning hair,
        She would not care.

Let us go hence, go hence; she will not see.
Sing all once more together; surely she,
She too, remembering days and words that were,
Will turn a little toward us, sighing; but we,
We are hence, we are gone, as though we had not been
        there.
Nay, and though all men seeing had pity on me,
        She would not see.

Itylus

SWALLOW, my sister, O sister swallow,
How can thine heart be full of the spring?
A thousand summers are over and dead.
What hast thou found in the spring to follow?
What hast thou found in thine heart to sing?
What wilt thou do when the summer is shed?

O swallow, sister, O fair swift swallow,
Why wilt thou fly after spring to the south,
The soft south whither thine heart is set?
Shall not the grief of the old time follow?
Shall not the song thereof cleave to thy mouth?
Hast thou forgotten ere I forget?

Sister, my sister, O fleet sweet swallow,
Thy way is long to the sun and the south;
But I, fulfilled of my heart's desire,
Shedding my song upon height, upon hollow,
From tawny body and sweet small mouth
Feed the heart of the night with fire.

I the nightingale all spring through,
O swallow, sister, O changing swallow,
All spring through till the spring be done,
Clothed with the light of the night on the dew,
Sing, while the hours and the wild birds follow,
Take flight and follow and find the sun.

Sister, my sister, O soft light swallow,
Though all things feast in the spring's guest-
chamber,
How hast thou heart to be glad thereof yet?

27

For where thou fliest I shall not follow,
    Till life forget and death remember,
      Till thou remember and I forget.

Swallow, my sister, O singing swallow,
    I know not how thou hast heart to sing.
      Hast thou the heart? is it all past over?
Thy lord the summer is good to follow,
    And fair the feet of thy lover the spring:
      But what wilt thou say to the spring thy lover?

O swallow, sister, O fleeting swallow,
    My heart in me is a molten ember
      And over my head the waves have met.
But thou wouldst tarry or I would follow,
    Could I forget or thou remember,
      Couldst thou remember and I forget.

O sweet stray sister, O shifting swallow,
    The heart's division divideth us.
      Thy heart is light as a leaf of a tree;
But mine goes forth among sea-gulfs hollow
    To the place of the slaying of Itylus,
      The feast of Daulis, the Thracian sea.

O swallow, sister, O rapid swallow,
    I pray thee sing not a little space.
      Are not the roofs and the lintels wet?
The woven web that was plain to follow,
    The small slain body, the flowerlike face,
      Can I remember if thou forget?

O sister, sister, thy first-begotten!
  The hands that cling and the feet that follow,
  The voice of the child's blood crying yet
Who hath remembered me? who hath forgotten?
  Thou hast forgotten, O summer swallow,
  But the world shall end when I forget.

Hymn to Proserpine

After the Proclamation in Rome of the Christian Faith

VICISTI, GALILAEE

I HAVE lived long enough, having seen one thing, that
   love hath an end;
Goddess and maiden and queen, be near me now and
   befriend.
Thou art more than the day or the morrow, the seasons that
   laugh or that weep;
For these give joy and sorrow; but thou, Proserpina, sleep.
Sweet is the treading of wine, and sweet the feet of the
   dove;
But a goodlier gift is thine than foam of the grapes or love.
Yea, is not even Apollo, with hair and harpstring of gold,
A bitter God to follow, a beautiful God to behold?
I am sick of singing: the bays burn deep and chafe: I am
   fain
To rest a little from praise and grievous pleasure and pain.
For the Gods we know not of, who give us our daily breath,
We know they are cruel as love or life, and lovely as death.
O Gods dethroned and deceased, cast forth, wiped out in a
   day!
From your wrath is the world released, redeemed from your
   chains, men say.
New Gods are crowned in the city; their flowers have
   broken your rods;
They are merciful, clothed with pity, the young com‑
   passionate Gods.
But for me their new device is barren, the days are bare;
Things long past over suffice, and men forgotten that were.
Time and the Gods are at strife; ye dwell in the midst
   thereof,
Draining a little life from the barren breasts of love.

I say to you, cease, take rest; yea, I say to you all, be at
peace,
Till the bitter milk of her breast and the barren bosom shall
cease.
Wilt thou yet take all, Galilean? but these thou shalt not
take,
The laurel, the palms and the paean, the breasts of the
nymphs in the brake;
Breasts more soft than a dove's, that tremble with tenderer
breath;
And all the wings of the Loves, and all the joy before death;
All the feet of the hours that sound as a single lyre,
Dropped and deep in the flowers, with strings that flicker
like fire.
More than these wilt thou give, things fairer than all these
things?
Nay, for a little we live, and life hath mutable wings.
A little while and we die; shall life not thrive as it may?
For no man under the sky lives twice, outliving his day.
And grief is a grievous thing, and a man hath enough of
his tears:
Why should he labour, and bring fresh grief to blacken his
years?
Thou hast conquered, O pale Galilean; the world has
grown grey from thy breath;
We have drunken of things Lethean, and fed on the fullness
of death.
Laurel is green for a season, and love is sweet for a day;
But love grows bitter with treason, and laurel outlives not
May.
Sleep, shall we sleep after all? for the world is not sweet in
the end;
For the old faiths loosen and fall, the new years ruin and
rend.
Fate is a sea without shore, and the soul is a rock that abides;

But her ears are vexed with the roar and her face with the
   foam of the tides.
O lips that the live blood faints in, the leavings of racks and
   rods!
O ghastly glories of saints, dead limbs of gibbeted Gods!
Though all men abase them before you in spirit, and all
   knees bend,
I kneel not neither adore you, but standing, look to the end.
All delicate days and pleasant, all spirits and sorrows are cast
Far out with the foam of the present that sweeps to the surf
   of the past:
Where beyond the extreme sea-wall, and between the
   remote sea-gates,
Waste water washes, and tall ships founder, and deep death
   waits:
Where, mighty with deepening sides, clad about with the
   seas as with wings,
And impelled of invisible tides, and fulfilled of unspeakable
   things,
White-eyed and poisonous-finned, shark-toothed and ser-
   pentine-curled,
Rolls, under the whitening wind of the future, the wave of
   the world.
The depths stand naked in sunder behind it, the storms flee
   away;
In the hollow before it the thunder is taken and snared as
   a prey;
In its sides is the north-wind bound; and its salt is of all
   men's tears;
With light of ruin, and sound of changes, and pulse of
   years:
With travail of day after day, and with trouble of hour
   upon hour;
And bitter as blood is the spray; and the crests are as fangs
   that devour:

And its vapour and storm of its steam as the sighing of
    spirits to be;
And its noise as the noise in a dream; and its depth as the
    roots of the sea:
And the height of its heads as the height of the utmost
    stars of the air:
And the ends of the earth at the might thereof tremble,
    and time is made bare.
Will ye bridle the deep sea with reins, will ye chasten the
    high sea with rods?
Will ye take her to chain her with chains, who is older
    than all ye Gods?
All ye as a wind shall go by, as a fire shall ye pass and be past;
Ye are Gods, and behold, ye shall die, and the waves be
    upon you at last.
In the darkness of time, in the deeps of the years, in the
    changes of things,
Ye shall sleep as a slain man sleeps, and the world shall
    forget you for kings.
Though the feet of thine high priests tread where thy lords
    and our forefathers trod,
Though these that were Gods are dead, and thou being
    dead art a God,
Though before thee the throned Cytherean be fallen, and
    hidden her head,
Yet thy kingdom shall pass, Galilean, thy dead shall go
    down to thee dead.
Of the maiden thy mother men sing as a goddess with
    grace clad around;
Thou art throned where another was king; where another
    was queen she is crowned.
Yea, once we had sight of another: but now she is queen,
    say these.
Not as thine, not as thine was our mother, a blossom of
    flowering seas,

33

Clothed round with the world's desire as with raiment, and
fair as the foam,
And fleeter than kindled fire, and a goddess, and mother
of Rome.
For thine came pale and a maiden, and sister to sorrow; but
ours,
Her deep hair heavily laden with odour and colour of
flowers,
White rose of the rose-white water, a silver splendour, a
flame,
Bent down unto us that besought her, and earth grew sweet
with her name.
For thine came weeping, a slave among slaves, and rejected;
but she
Came flushed from the full-flushed wave, and imperial,
her foot on the sea.
And the wonderful waters knew her, the winds and the
viewless ways,
And the roses grew rosier, and bluer the sea-blue stream of
the bays.
Ye are fallen, our lords, by what token? we wist that ye
should not fall.
Ye were all so fair that are broken; and one more fair than
ye all.
But I turn to her still, having seen she shall surely abide in
the end;
Goddess and maiden and queen, be near me now and
befriend.
O daughter of earth, of my mother, her crown and blossom
of birth,
I am also, I also, thy brother; I go as I came unto earth.
In the night where thine eyes are as moons are in heaven,
the night where thou art,
Where the silence is more than all tunes, where sleep over-
flows from the heart,

Where the poppies are sweet as the rose in our world, and the red rose is white,

And the wind falls faint as it blows with the fume of the flowers of the night,

And the murmur of spirits that sleep in the shadow of Gods from afar

Grows dim in thine ears and deep as the deep dim soul of a star,

In the sweet low light of thy face, under heavens untrod by the sun,

Let my soul with their souls find place, and forget what is done and undone.

Thou art more than the Gods who number the days of our temporal breath;

For these give labour and slumber; but thou, Proserpina, death.

Therefore now at thy feet I abide for a season in silence. I know

I shall die as my fathers died, and sleep as they sleep; even so.

For the glass of the years is brittle wherein we gaze for a span;

A little soul for a little bears up this corpse which is man.[1]

So long I endure, no longer; and laugh not again, neither weep.

For there is no God found stronger than death; and death is a sleep.

[1] ψυχάριον εἶ βαστάζον νεκρόν.—EPICTETUS.

A Match

IF love were what the rose is,
    And I were like the leaf,
Our lives would grow together
In sad or singing weather,
Blown fields or flowerful closes,
    Green pleasure or grey grief;
If love were what the rose is,
    And I were like the leaf.

If I were what the words are,
    And love were like the tune,
With double sound and single
Delight our lips would mingle,
With kisses glad as birds are
    That get sweet rain at noon;
If I were what the words are,
    And love were like the tune.

If you were life, my darling,
    And I your love were death,
We'd shine and snow together
Ere March made sweet the weather
With daffodil and starling
    And hours of fruitful breath;
If you were life, my darling,
    And I your love were death.

If you were thrall to sorrow,
    And I were page to joy,
We'd play for lives and seasons
With loving looks and treasons
And tears of night and morrow
    And laughs of maid and boy;
If you were thrall to sorrow,
    And I were page to joy.

If you were April's lady,
  And I were lord in May,
We 'd throw with leaves for hours
And draw for days with flowers,
Till day like night were shady
  And night were bright like day;
If you were April's lady,
  And I were lord in May.

If you were queen of pleasure,
  And I were king of pain,
We 'd hunt down love together,
Pluck out his flying feather,
And teach his feet a measure,
  And find his mouth a rein;
If you were queen of pleasure,
  And I were king of pain.

Stanzas from 'Faustine'

Ave Faustina Imperatrix, morituri te salutant.

LEAN back, and get some minutes' peace;
    Let your head lean
Back to the shoulder with its fleece
    Of locks, Faustine.

The shapely silver shoulder stoops,
    Weighed over clean
With state of splendid hair that droops
    Each side, Faustine.

Let me go over your good gifts
    That crown you queen;
A queen whose kingdom ebbs and shifts
    Each week, Faustine.

Bright heavy brows well gathered up:
    White gloss and sheen;
Carved lips that make my lips a cup
    To drink, Faustine,

Wine and rank poison, milk and blood,
    Being mixed therein
Since first the devil threw dice with God
    For you, Faustine.

Your naked new-born soul, their stake,
    Stood blind between;
God said 'let him that wins her take
    And keep Faustine.'

But this time Satan throve, no doubt;
    Long since, I ween,
God's part in you was battered out;
    Long since, Faustine.

The die rang sideways as it fell,
    Rang cracked and thin,
Like a man's laughter heard in hell
    Far down, Faustine,

A shadow of laughter like a sigh,
    Dead sorrow's kin;
So rang, thrown down, the devil's die
    That won Faustine.

A suckling of his breed you were,
    One hard to wean;
But God, who lost you, left you fair,
    We see, Faustine.

You have the face that suits a woman
    For her soul's screen—
The sort of beauty that's called human
    In hell, Faustine.

You could do all things but be good
    Or chaste of mien;
And that you would not if you could,
    We know, Faustine.

Even he who cast seven devils out
    Of Magdalene
Could hardly do as much, I doubt,
    For you, Faustine.

Did Satan make you to spite God?
    Or did God mean
To scourge with scorpions for a rod
    Our sins, Faustine?

.   .   .

Your drenched loose hands were stretched to hold
    The vine's wet green,
Long ere they coined in Roman gold
    Your face, Faustine.

Then after change of soaring feather
    And winnowing fin,
You woke in weeks of feverish weather,
    A new Faustine.

A star upon your birthday burned,
    Whose fierce serene
Red pulseless planet never yearned
    In heaven, Faustine.

Stray breaths of Sapphic song that blew
    Through Mitylene
Shook the fierce quivering blood in you
    By night, Faustine.

The shameless nameless love that makes
    Hell's iron gin
Shut on you like a trap that breaks
    The soul, Faustine.

And when your veins were void and dead,
    What ghosts unclean
Swarmed round the straitened barren bed
    That hid Faustine?

What sterile growths of sexless root
    Or epicene?
What flower of kisses without fruit
    Of love, Faustine?

What adders came to shed their coats?
  What coiled obscene
Small serpents with soft stretching throats
  Caressed Faustine?

But the time came of famished hours,
  Maimed loves and mean,
This ghastly thin-faced time of ours,
  To spoil Faustine.

You seem a thing that hinges hold,
  A love-machine
With clockwork joints of supple gold—
  No more, Faustine.

Not godless, for you serve one God,
  The Lampsacene,
Who metes the gardens with his rod;
  Your lord, Faustine.

If one should love you with real love
  (Such things have been,
Things your fair face knows nothing of,
  It seems, Faustine);

That clear hair heavily bound back,
  The lights wherein
Shift from dead blue to burnt-up black;
  Your throat, Faustine,

Strong, heavy, throwing out the face
  And hard bright chin
And shameful scornful lips that grace
  Their shame, Faustine,

Curled lips, long since half kissed away
    Still sweet and keen;
You 'd give him—poison shall we say?
    Or what, Faustine?

TAKE hands and part with laughter;
 Touch lips and part with tears;
Once more and no more after,
 Whatever comes with years.
We twain shall not remeasure
 The ways that left us twain;
Nor crush the lees of pleasure
 From sanguine grapes of pain.

We twain once well in sunder,
 What will the mad gods do
For hate with me, I wonder,
 Or what for love with you?
Forget them till November,
 And dream there's April yet;
Forget that I remember,
 And dream that I forget.

Time found our tired love sleeping,
 And kissed away his breath;
But what should we do weeping,
 Though light love sleep to death?
We have drained his lips at leisure,
 Till there's not left to drain
A single sob of pleasure,
 A single pulse of pain.

Dream that the lips once breathless
 Might quicken if they would;
Say that the soul is deathless;
 Dream that the gods are good;
Say March may wed September,
 And time divorce regret;
But not that you remember,
 And not that I forget.

43

We have heard from hidden places
    What love scarce lives and hears:
We have seen on fervent faces
    The pallor of strange tears:
We have trod the wine-vat's treasure,
    Whence, ripe to steam and stain,
Foams round the feet of pleasure
    The blood-red must of pain.

Remembrance may recover
    And time bring back to time
The name of your first lover,
    The ring of my first rhyme;
But rose-leaves of December
    The frosts of June shall fret,
The day that you remember,
    The day that I forget.

The snake that hides and hisses
    In heaven we twain have known;
The grief of cruel kisses,
    The joy whose mouth makes moan;
The pulse's pause and measure,
    Where in one furtive vein
Throbs through the heart of pleasure
    The purpler blood of pain.

We have done with tears and treasons
    And love for treason's sake;
Room for the swift new seasons,
    The years that burn and break,
Dismantle and dismember
    Men's days and dreams, Juliette;
For love may not remember,
    But time will not forget.

Life treads down love in flying,
    Time withers him at root;
Bring all dead things and dying,
    Reaped sheaf and ruined fruit,
Where, crushed by three days' pressure,
    Our three days' love lies slain;
And earlier leaf of pleasure,
    And latter flower of pain.

Breathe close upon the ashes,
    It may be flame will leap;
Unclose the soft close lashes,
    Lift up the lids, and weep.
Light love's extinguished ember,
    Let one tear leave it wet
For one that you remember
    And ten that you forget.

A Ballad of Burdens

THE burden of fair women. Vain delight,
  And love self-slain in some sweet shameful way,
And sorrowful old age that comes by night
  As a thief comes that has no heart by day,
  And change that finds fair cheeks and leaves them grey,
And weariness that keeps awake for hire,
  And grief that says what pleasure used to say;
This is the end of every man's desire.

The burden of bought kisses. This is sore,
  A burden without fruit in childbearing;
Between the nightfall and the dawn threescore,
  Threescore between the dawn and evening.
  The shuddering in thy lips, the shuddering
In thy sad eyelids tremulous like fire,
  Makes love seem shameful and a wretched thing.
This is the end of every man's desire.

The burden of sweet speeches. Nay, kneel down,
  Cover thy head, and weep; for verily
These market-men that buy thy white and brown
  In the last days shall take no thought for thee.
  In the last days like earth thy face shall be,
Yea, like sea-marsh made thick with brine and mire,
  Sad with sick leavings of the sterile sea.
This is the end of every man's desire.

The burden of long living. Thou shalt fear
  Waking, and sleeping mourn upon thy bed;
And say at night 'Would God the day were here,'
  And say at dawn 'Would God the day were dead.'
  With weary days thou shalt be clothed and fed,
And wear remorse of heart for thine attire,
  Pain for thy girdle and sorrow upon thine head;
This is the end of every man's desire.

The burden of bright colours.   Thou shalt see
   Gold tarnished, and the grey above the green;
And as the thing thou seest thy face shall be,
   And no more as the thing beforetime seen.
   And thou shalt say of mercy 'It hath been,'
And living, watch the old lips and loves expire,
   And talking, tears shall take thy breath between;
This is the end of every man's desire.

The burden of sad sayings.   In that day
   Thou shalt tell all thy days and hours, and tell
Thy times and ways and words of love, and say
   How one was dear and one desirable,
   And sweet was life to hear and sweet to smell,
But now with lights reverse the old hours retire
   And the last hour is shod with fire from hell;
This is the end of every man's desire.

The burden of four seasons.   Rain in spring,
   White rain and wind among the tender trees;
A summer of green sorrows gathering,
   Rank autumn in a mist of miseries,
   With sad face set towards the year, that sees
The charred ash drop out of the dropping pyre,
   And winter wan with many maladies;
This is the end of every man's desire.

The burden of dead faces.   Out of sight
   And out of love, beyond the reach of hands,
Changed in the changing of the dark and light,
   They walk and weep about the barren lands
   Where no seed is nor any garner stands,
Where in short breaths the doubtful days respire,
   And time's turned glass lets through the sighing sands;
This is the end of every man's desire.

The burden of much gladness.   Life and lust
    Forsake thee, and the face of thy delight;
And underfoot the heavy hour strews dust,
    And overhead strange weathers burn and bite;
    And where the red was, lo the bloodless white,
And where truth was, the likeness of a liar,
    And where day was, the likeness of the night;
This is the end of every man's desire.

L'ENVOY

Princes, and ye whom pleasure quickeneth,
    Heed well this rhyme before your pleasure tire;
For life is sweet, but after life is death.
    This is the end of every man's desire.

PUSH hard across the sand,
 For the salt wind gathers breath;
Shoulder and wrist and hand,
 Push hard as the push of death.

The wind is as iron that rings,
 The foam-heads loosen and flee;
It swells and welters and swings,
 The pulse of the tide of the sea.

And up on the yellow cliff
 The long corn flickers and shakes;
Push, for the wind holds stiff,
 And the gunwale dips and rakes.

Good hap to the fresh fierce weather,
 The quiver and beat of the sea!
While three men hold together,
 The kingdoms are less by three.

Out to the sea with her there,
 Out with her over the sand;
Let the kings keep the earth for their share!
 We have done with the sharers of land.

They have tied the world in a tether,
 They have bought over God with a fee;
While three men hold together,
 The kingdoms are less by three.

We have done with the kisses that sting,
 The thief's mouth red from the feast,
The blood on the hands of the king
 And the lie at the lips of the priest.

Will they tie the winds in a tether,
  Put a bit in the jaws of the sea?
While three men hold together,
  The kingdoms are less by three.

Let our flag run out straight in the wind!
  The old red shall be floated again
When the ranks that are thin shall be thinned,
  When the names that were twenty are ten;

When the devil's riddle is mastered
  And the galley-bench creaks with a Pope,
We shall see Bonaparte the bastard
  Kick heels with his throat in a rope.

While the shepherd sets wolves on his sheep
  And the emperor halters his kine,
While Shame is a watchman asleep
  And Faith is a keeper of swine,

Let the wind shake our flag like a feather,
  Like the plumes of the foam of the sea!
While three men hold together,
  The kingdoms are less by three.

All the world has its burdens to bear,
  From Cayenne to the Austrian whips;
Forth, with the rain in our hair
  And the salt sweet foam in our lips;

In the teeth of the hard glad weather,
  In the blown wet face of the sea;
While three men hold together,
  The kingdoms are less by three.

Dolores

Notre-Dame des sept douleurs

COLD eyelids that hide like a jewel
   Hard eyes that grow soft for an hour;
The heavy white limbs, and the cruel
   Red mouth like a venomous flower;
When these are gone by with their glories,
   What shall rest of thee then, what remain,
O mystic and sombre Dolores,
   Our Lady of Pain?

Seven sorrows the priests give their Virgin;
   But thy sins, which are seventy times seven,
Seven ages would fail thee to purge in,
   And then they would haunt thee in heaven:
Fierce midnights and famishing morrows,
   And the loves that complete and control
All the joys of the flesh, all the sorrows
   That wear out the soul.

O garment not golden but gilded,
   O garden where all men may dwell,
O tower not of ivory, but builded
   By hands that reach heaven from hell;
O mystical rose of the mire,
   O house not of gold but of gain,
O house of unquenchable fire,
   Our Lady of Pain!

O lips full of lust and of laughter,
   Curled snakes that are fed from my breast,
Bite hard, lest remembrance come after
   And press with new lips where you pressed.

For my heart too springs up at the pressure,
　　Mine eyelids too moisten and burn;
Ah, feed me and fill me with pleasure,
　　Ere pain come in turn.

In yesterday's reach and to-morrow's,
　　Out of sight though they lie of to-day,
There have been and there yet shall be sorrows
　　That smite not and bite not in play.
The life and the love thou despisest,
　　These hurt us indeed, and in vain,
O wise among women, and wisest,
　　Our Lady of Pain.

Who gave thee thy wisdom? what stories
　　That stung thee, what visions that smote?
Wert thou pure and a maiden, Dolores,
　　When desire took thee first by the throat?
What bud was the shell of a blossom
　　That all men may smell to and pluck?
What milk fed thee first at what bosom?
　　What sins gave thee suck?

We shift and bedeck and bedrape us,
　　Thou art noble and nude and antique;
Libitina thy mother, Priapus
　　Thy father, a Tuscan and Greek.
We play with light loves in the portal,
　　And wince and relent and refrain;
Loves die, and we know thee immortal,
　　Our Lady of Pain.

Fruits fail and love dies and time ranges;
　　Thou art fed with perpetual breath,
And alive after infinite changes,
　　And fresh from the kisses of death;

Of languors rekindled and rallied,
  Of barren delights and unclean,
Things monstrous and fruitless, a pallid
  And poisonous queen.

Could you hurt me, sweet lips, though I hurt you?
  Men touch them, and change in a trice
The lilies and languors of virtue
  For the raptures and roses of vice;
Those lie where thy foot on the floor is,
  These crown and caress thee and chain,
O splendid and sterile Dolores,
  Our Lady of Pain.

There are sins it may be to discover,
  There are deeds it may be to delight.
What new work wilt thou find for thy lover,
  What new passions for daytime or night?
What spells that they know not a word of
  Whose lives are as leaves overblown?
What tortures undreamt of, unheard of,
  Unwritten, unknown?

An beautiful passionate body
  That never has ached with a heart!
On thy mouth though the kisses are bloody,
  Though they sting till it shudder and smart,
More kind than the love we adore is,
  They hurt not the heart or the brain,
O bitter and tender Dolores,
  Our Lady of Pain.

As our kisses relax and redouble,
  From the lips and the foam and the fangs
Shall no new sin be born for men's trouble,
  No dream of impossible pangs?

With the sweet of the sins of old ages
    Wilt thou satiate thy soul as of yore?
Too sweet is the rind, say the sages,
    Too bitter the core.

Hast thou told all thy secrets the last time,
    And bared all thy beauties to one?
Ah, where shall we go then for pastime,
    If the worst that can be has been done?
But sweet as the rind was the core is;
    We are fain of thee still, we are fain,
O sanguine and subtle Dolores,
    Our Lady of Pain.

By the hunger of change and emotion,
    By the thirst of unbearable things,
By despair, the twin-born of devotion,
    By the pleasure that winces and stings,
The delight that consumes the desire,
    The desire that outruns the delight,
By the cruelty deaf as a fire
    And blind as the night,

By the ravenous teeth that have smitten
    Through the kisses that blossom and bud,
By the lips intertwisted and bitten
    Till the foam has a savour of blood,
By the pulse as it rises and falters,
    By the hands as they slacken and strain,
I adjure thee, respond from thine altars,
    Our Lady of Pain.

Wilt thou smile as a woman disdaining
    The light fire in the veins of a boy?
But he comes to thee sad, without feigning,
    Who has wearied of sorrow and joy;

Less careful of labour and glory
  Than the elders whose hair has uncurled;
And young, but with fancies as hoary
  And grey as the world.

I have passed from the outermost portal
  To the shrine where a sin is a prayer;
What care though the service be mortal?
  O our Lady of Torture, what care?
All thine the last wine that I pour is,
  The last in the chalice we drain,
O fierce and luxurious Dolores,
  Our Lady of Pain.

All thine the new wine of desire,
  The fruit of four lips as they clung
Till the hair and the eyelids took fire,
  The foam of a serpentine tongue,
The froth of the serpents of pleasure,
  More salt than the foam of the sea,
Now felt as a flame, now at leisure
  As wine shed for me.

Ah thy people, thy children, thy chosen,
  Marked cross from the womb and perverse!
They have found out the secret to cozen
  The gods that constrain us and curse;
They alone, they are wise, and none other;
  Give me place, even me, in their train,
O my sister, my spouse, and my mother,
  Our Lady of Pain.

For the crown of our life as it closes
  Is darkness, the fruit thereof dust;
No thorns go as deep as a rose's,
  And love is more cruel than lust.

Time turns the old days to derision,
    Our loves into corpses or wives;
And marriage and death and division
    Make barren our lives.

And pale from the past we draw nigh thee,
    And satiate with comfortless hours;
And we know thee, how all men belie thee,
    And we gather the fruit of thy flowers;
The passion that slays and recovers,
    The pangs and the kisses that rain
On the lips and the limbs of thy lovers,
    Our Lady of Pain.

The desire of thy furious embraces
    Is more than the wisdom of years,
On the blossom though blood lie in traces,
    Though the foliage be sodden with tears.
For the lords in whose keeping the door is
    That opens on all who draw breath
Gave the cypress to love, my Dolores,
    The myrtle to death.

And they laughed, changing hands in the measure
    And they mixed and made peace after strife;
Pain melted in tears, and was pleasure;
    Death tingled with blood, and was life.
Like lovers they melted and tingled,
    In the dusk of thine innermost fane;
In the darkness they murmured and mingled,
    Our Lady of Pain.

In a twilight where virtues are vices,
    In thy chapels, unknown of the sun,
To a tune that enthralls and entices,
    They were wed, and the twain were as one.

For the tune from thine altar hath sounded
    Since God bade the world's work begin,
And the fume of thine incense abounded,
    To sweeten the sin.

Love listens, and paler than ashes,
    Through his curls as the crown on them slips,
Lifts languid wet eyelids and lashes,
    And laughs with insatiable lips.
Thou shalt hush him with heavy caresses,
    With music that scares the profane;
Thou shalt darken his eyes with thy tresses,
    Our Lady of Pain.

Thou shalt blind his bright eyes though he wrestle,
    Thou shalt chain his light limbs though he strive;
In his lips all thy serpents shall nestle,
    In his hands all thy cruelties thrive.
In the daytime thy voice shall go through him,
    In his dreams he shall feel thee and ache;
Thou shalt kindle by night and subdue him
    Asleep and awake.

Thou shalt touch and make redder his roses
    With juice not of fruit nor of bud;
When the sense in the spirit reposes,
    Thou shalt quicken the soul through the blood.
Thine, thine the one grace we implore us,
    Who would live and not languish or feign,
O sleepless and deadly Dolores,
    Our Lady of Pain.

Dost thou dream, in a respite of slumber,
    In a lull of the fires of thy life,
Of the days without name, without number,
    When thy will stung the world into strife;

When, a goddess, the pulse of thy passion
    Smote kings as they revelled in Rome;
And they hailed thee re-risen, O Thalassian,
    Foam-white, from the foam?

When thy lips had such lovers to flatter;
    When the city lay red from thy rods,
And thine hands were as arrows to scatter
    The children of change and their gods;
When the blood of thy foemen made fervent
    A sand never moist from the main,
As one smote them, their lord and thy servant,
    Our Lady of Pain.

On sands by the storm never shaken,
    Nor wet from the washing of tides;
Nor by foam of the waves overtaken,
    Nor winds that the thunder bestrides;
But red from the print of thy paces,
    Made smooth for the world and its lords,
Ringed round with a flame of fair faces,
    And splendid with swords.

There the gladiator, pale for thy pleasure,
    Drew bitter and perilous breath;
There torments laid hold on the treasure
    Of limbs too delicious for death;
When thy gardens were lit with live torches;
    When the world was a steed for thy rein;
When the nations lay prone in thy porches,
    Our Lady of Pain.

When, with flame all around him aspirant,
    Stood flushed, as a harp-player stands,
The implacable beautiful tyrant,
    Rose-crowned, having death in his hands;

And a sound as the sound of loud water
  Smote far through the flight of the fires,
And mixed with the lightning of slaughter
  A thunder of lyres.

Dost thou dream of what was and no more is,
  The old kingdoms of earth and the kings?
Dost thou hunger for these things, Dolores,
  For these, in a world of new things?
But thy bosom no fasts could emaciate,
  No hunger compel to complain
Those lips that no bloodshed could satiate,
  Our Lady of Pain.

As of old when the world's heart was lighter,
  Through thy garments the grace of thee glows,
The white wealth of thy body made whiter
  By the blushes of amorous blows,
And seamed with sharp lips and fierce fingers,
  And branded by kisses that bruise;
When all shall be gone that now lingers,
  Ah, what shall we lose?

Thou wert fair in the fearless old fashion,
  And thy limbs are as melodies yet,
And move to the music of passion
  With lithe and lascivious regret.
What ailed us, O gods, to desert you
  For creeds that refuse and restrain?
Come down and redeem us from virtue,
  Our Lady of Pain.

All shrines that were Vestal are flameless,
  But the flame has not fallen from this;
Though obscure be the god, and though nameless
  The eyes and the hair that we kiss;

Low fires that love sits by and forges
  Fresh heads for his arrows and thine;
Hair loosened and soiled in mid orgies
  With kisses and wine.

Thy skin changes country and colour,
  And shrivels or swells to a snake's.
Let it brighten and bloat and grow duller,
  We know it, the flames and the flakes,
Red brands on it smitten and bitten,
  Round skies where a star is a stain,
And the leaves with thy litanies written,
  Our Lady of Pain.

On thy bosom though many a kiss be,
  There are none such as knew it of old.
Was it Alciphron once or Arisbe,
  Male ringlets or feminine gold,
That thy lips met with under the statue,
  Whence a look shot out sharp after thieves
From the eyes of the garden-god at you
  Across the fig-leaves?

Then still, through dry seasons and moister,
  One god had a wreath to his shrine;
Then love was the pearl of his oyster,[1]
  And Venus rose red out of wine.
We have all done amiss, choosing rather
  Such loves as the wise gods disdain;
Intercede for us thou with thy father,
  Our Lady of Pain.

[1] Nam te praecipuè in suis urbibus colit ora
  Hellespontia, caeteris ostreosior oris.
                    CATULL. *Carm.* xviii.

In spring he had crowns of his garden,
  Red corn in the heat of the year,
Then hoary green olives that harden
  When the grape-blossom freezes with fear;
And milk-budded myrtles with Venus
  And vine-leaves with Bacchus he trod;
And ye said, 'We have seen, he hath seen us,
  A visible God.'

What broke off the garlands that girt you?
  What sundered you spirit and clay?
Weak sins yet alive are as virtue
  To the strength of the sins of that day.
For dried is the blood of thy lover,
  Ipsithilla, contracted the vein;
Cry aloud, 'Will he rise and recover,
  Our Lady of Pain?'

Cry aloud; for the old world is broken:
  Cry out; for the Phrygian is priest,
And rears not the bountiful token
  And spreads not the fatherly feast.
From the midmost of Ida, from shady
  Recesses that murmur at morn,
They have brought and baptized her, Our Lady,
  A goddess new-born.

And the chaplets of old are above us,
  And the oyster-bed teems out of reach;
Old poets outsing and outlove us,
  And Catullus makes mouths at our speech.
Who shall kiss, in thy father's own city,
  With such lips as he sang with, again?
Intercede for us all of thy pity,
  Our Lady of Pain.

Out of Dindymus heavily laden
   Her lions draw bound and unfed
A mother, a mortal, a maiden,
   A queen over death and the dead.
She is cold, and her habit is lowly,
   Her temple of branches and sods;
Most fruitful and virginal, holy,
   A mother of gods.

She hath wasted with fire thine high places,
   She hath hidden and marred and made sad
The fair limbs of the Loves, the fair faces
   Of gods that were goodly and glad.
She slays, and her hands are not bloody;
   She moves as a moon in the wane,
White-robed, and thy raiment is ruddy,
   Our Lady of Pain.

They shall pass and their places be taken,
   The gods and the priests that are pure.
They shall pass, and shalt thou not be shaken?
   They shall perish, and shalt thou endure?
Death laughs, breathing close and relentless
   In the nostrils and eyelids of lust,
With a pinch in his fingers of scentless
   And delicate dust.

But the worm shall revive thee with kisses;
   Thou shalt change and transmute as a god,
As the rod to a serpent that hisses,
   As the serpent again to a rod.
Thy life shall not cease though thou doff it;
   Thou shalt live until evil be slain,
And good shall die first, said thy prophet,
   Our Lady of Pain.

Did he lie? did he laugh? does he know it,
  Now he lies out of reach, out of breath,
Thy prophet, thy preacher, thy poet,
  Sin's child by incestuous Death?
Did he find out in fire at his waking,
  Or discern as his eyelids lost light,
When the bands of the body were breaking
  And all came in sight?

Who has known all the evil before us,
  Or the tyrannous secrets of time?
Though we match not the dead men that bore
  At a song, at a kiss, at a crime—
Though the heathen outface and outlive us,
  And our lives and our longings are twain—
Ah, forgive us our virtues, forgive us,
  Our Lady of Pain.

Who are we that embalm and embrace thee
  With spices and savours of song?
What is time, that his children should face thee;
  What am I, that my lips do thee wrong?
I could hurt thee—but pain would delight thee;
  Or caress thee—but love would repel;
And the lovers whose lips would excite thee
  Are serpents in hell.

Who now shall content thee as they did,
  Thy lovers, when temples were built
And the hair of the sacrifice braided
  And the blood of the sacrifice spilt,
In Lampsacus fervent with faces,
  In Aphaca red from thy reign,
Who embraced thee with awful embraces,
  Our Lady of Pain?

Where are they, Cotytto or Venus,
    Astarte or Ashtaroth, where?
Do their hands as we touch come between us?
    Is the breath of them hot in thy hair?
From their lips have thy lips taken fever,
    With the blood of their bodies grown red?
Hast thou left upon earth a believer
    If these men are dead?

They were purple of raiment and golden,
    Filled full of thee, fiery with wine,
Thy lovers, in haunts unbeholden,
    In marvellous chambers of thine.
They are fled, and their footprints escape us,
    Who appraise thee, adore, and abstain,
O daughter of Death and Priapus,
    Our Lady of Pain.

What ails us to fear overmeasure,
    To praise thee with timorous breath,
O mistress and mother of pleasure,
    The one thing as certain as death?
We shall change as the things that we cherish,
    Shall fade as they faded before,
As foam upon water shall perish,
    As sand upon shore.

We shall know what the darkness discovers,
    If the grave-pit be shallow or deep;
And our fathers of old, and our lovers,
    We shall know if they sleep not or sleep.
We shall see whether hell be not heaven,
    Find out whether tares be not grain,
And the joys of thee seventy times seven,
    Our Lady of Pain.

The Garden of Proserpine

Here, where the world is quiet;
  Here, where all trouble seems
Dead winds' and spent waves' riot
  In doubtful dreams of dreams;
I watch the green field growing
For reaping folk and sowing,
For harvest-time and mowing,
  A sleepy world of streams.

I am tired of tears and laughter,
  And men that laugh and weep;
Of what may come hereafter
  For men that sow to reap:
I am weary of days and hours,
Blown buds of barren flowers,
Desires and dreams and powers
  And everything but sleep.

Here life has death for neighbour,
  And far from eye or ear
Wan waves and wet winds labour,
  Weak ships and spirits steer;
They drive adrift, and whither
They wot not who make thither;
But no such winds blow hither,
  And no such things grow here.

No growth of moor or coppice,
  No heather-flower or vine,
But bloomless buds of poppies,
  Green grapes of Proserpine,
Pale beds of blowing rushes
Where no leaf blooms or blushes
Save this whereout she crushes
  For dead men deadly wine.

Pale, without name or number,
In fruitless fields of corn,
They bow themselves and slumber
All night till light is born;
And like a soul belated,
In hell and heaven unmated,
By cloud and mist abated
Comes out of darkness morn.

Though one were strong as seven,
He too with death shall dwell,
Nor wake with wings in heaven,
Nor weep for pains in hell;
Though one were fair as roses,
His beauty clouds and closes;
And well though love reposes,
In the end it is not well.

Pale, beyond porch and portal,
Crowned with calm leaves, she stands
Who gathers all things mortal
With cold immortal hands;
Her languid lips are sweeter
Than love's who fears to greet her
To men that mix and meet her
From many times and lands.

She waits for each and other,
She waits for all men born:
Forgets the earth her mother;
The life of fruits and corn;
And spring and seed and swallow
Take wing for her and follow
Where summer song rings hollow
And flowers are put to scorn.

There go the loves that wither,
  The old loves with wearier wings;
And all dead years draw thither,
  And all disastrous things;
Dead dreams of days forsaken,
Blind buds that snows have shaken,
Wild leaves that winds have taken,
  Red strays of ruined springs.

We are not sure of sorrow,
  And joy was never sure;
To-day will die to-morrow;
  Time stoops to no man's lure;
And love, grown faint and fretful,
With lips but half regretful
Sighs, and with eyes forgetful
  Weeps that no loves endure.

From too much love of living,
  From hope and fear set free,
We thank with brief thanksgiving
  Whatever gods may be
That no life lives for ever;
That dead men rise up never;
That even the weariest river
  Winds somewhere safe to sea.

Then star nor sun shall waken,
  Nor any change of light:
Nor sound of waters shaken,
  Nor any sound or sight:
Nor wintry leaves nor vernal,
Nor days nor things diurnal;
Only the sleep eternal
  In an eternal night.

OUT of the golden remote wild west where the sea
  without shore is,
  Full of the sunset, and sad, if at all, with the fullness of joy,
As a wind sets in with the autumn that blows from the
  region of stories,
  Blows with a perfume of songs and of memories beloved
  from a boy,
Blows from the capes of the past oversea to the bays of the
  present,
  Filled as with shadow of sound with the pulse of invisible
  feet,
Far out to the shallows and straits of the future, by rough
  ways or pleasant,
  Is it thither the wind's wings beat? is it hither to me, O
  my sweet?
For thee, in the stream of the deep tide-wind blowing in
  with the water,
  Thee I behold as a bird borne in with the wind from the
  west,
Straight from the sunset, across white waves whence rose
  as a daughter
  Venus thy mother, in years when the world was a water
  at rest.
Out of the distance of dreams, as a dream that abides after
  slumber,
  Strayed from the fugitive flock of the night, when the
  moon overhead
Wanes in the wan waste heights of the heaven, and stars
  without number
  Die without sound, and are spent like lamps that are
  burnt by the dead,
Comes back to me, stays by me, lulls me with touch of
  forgotten caresses,

One warm dream clad about with a fire as of life that
endures;
The delight of thy face, and the sound of thy feet, and the
wind of thy tresses,
And all of a man that regrets, and all of a maid that
allures.
But thy bosom is warm for my face and profound as a
manifold flower,
Thy silence as music, thy voice as an odour that fades in
a flame;
Not a dream, not a dream is the kiss of thy mouth, and the
bountiful hour
That makes me forget what was sin, and would make me
forget were it shame.
Thine eyes that are quiet, thine hands that are tender, thy
lips that are loving,
Comfort and cool me as dew in the dawn of a moon like
a dream;
And my heart yearns baffled and blind, moved vainly
toward thee, and moving
As the refluent seaweed moves in the languid exuberant
stream,
Fair as a rose is on earth, as a rose under water in
prison,
That stretches and swings to the slow passionate pulse
of the sea,
Closed up from the air and the sun, but alive, as a ghost
rearisen,
Pale as the love that revives as a ghost rearisen in me.
From the bountiful infinite west, from the happy memorial
places
Full of the stately repose and the lordly delight of the
dead,
Where the fortunate islands are lit with the light of ineffable
faces,

And the sound of a sea without wind is about them, and
    sunset is red,
Come back to redeem and release me from love that recalls
    and represses,
    That cleaves to my flesh as a flame, till the serpent has
      eaten his fill;
From the bitter delights of the dark, and the feverish, the
    furtive caresses
    That murder the youth in a man or ever his heart have
      its will.
Thy lips cannot laugh and thine eyes cannot weep; thou
    art pale as a rose is,
    Paler and sweeter than leaves that cover the blush of the bud;
And the heart of the flower is compassion, and pity the core
    it encloses,
    Pity, not love, that is born of the breath and decays with
      the blood.
As the cross that a wild nun clasps till the edge of it bruises
    her bosom,
    So love wounds as we grasp it, and blackens and burns
      as a flame;
I have loved overmuch in my life; when the live bud bursts
    with the blossom,
    Bitter as ashes or tears is the fruit, and the wine thereof
      shame.
As a heart that its anguish divides is the green bud cloven
    asunder,
    As the blood of a man self-slain is the flush of the leaves
      that allure;
And the perfume as poison and wine to the brain, a delight
    and a wonder;
    And the thorns are too sharp for a boy, too slight for a
      man, to endure.
Too soon did I love it, and lost love's rose; and I cared not
    for glory's:

Only the blossoms of sleep and of pleasure were mixed in
my hair.
Was it myrtle or poppy thy garland was woven with, O
my Dolores?
Was it pallor of slumber, or blush as of blood, that I
found in thee fair?
For desire is a respite from love, and the flesh not the heart
is her fuel;
She was sweet to me once, who am fled and escaped from
the rage of her reign;
Who behold as of old time at hand as I turn, with her
mouth growing cruel,
And flushed as with wine with the blood of her lovers,
Our Lady of Pain.
Low down where the thicket is thicker with thorns than
with leaves in the summer,
In the brake is a gleaming of eyes and a hissing of tongues
that I knew;
And the lithe long throats of her snakes reach round her,
their mouths overcome her,
And her lips grow cool with their foam, made moist as
a desert with dew.
With the thirst and the hunger of lust though her beautiful
lips be so bitter,
With the cold foul foam of the snakes they soften and
redden and smile;
And her fierce mouth sweetens, her eyes wax wide and her
eyelashes glitter,
And she laughs with a savour of blood in her face, and a
savour of guile.
She laughs, and her hands reach hither, her hair blows
hither and hisses,
As a low-lit flame in a wind, back-blown till it shudder
and leap;

Let her lips not again lay hold on my soul, nor her poisonous
kisses,
To consume it alive and divide from thy bosom, Our
Lady of Sleep.
Ah daughter of sunset and slumber, if now it return into
prison,
Who shall redeem it anew? but we, if thou wilt, let us fly;
Let us take to us, now that the white skies thrill with a
moon unarisen,
Swift horses of fear or of love, take flight and depart and
not die.
They are swifter than dreams, they are stronger than death;
there is none that hath ridden,
None that shall ride in the dim strange ways of his life
as we ride;
By the meadows of memory, the highlands of hope, and
the shore that is hidden,
Where life breaks loud and unseen, a sonorous invisible
tide;
By the sands where sorrow has trodden, the salt pools bitter
and sterile,
By the thundering reef and the low sea-wall and the
channel of years,
Our wild steeds press on the night, strain hard through
pleasure and peril,
Labour and listen and pant not or pause for the peril
that nears;
And the sound of them trampling the way cleaves night as
an arrow asunder,
And slow by the sand-hill and swift by the down with
its glimpses of grass,
Sudden and steady the music, as eight hoofs trample and
thunder,
Rings in the ear of the low blind wind of the night as we
pass;

Shrill shrieks in our faces the blind bland air that was mute
    as a maiden,
  Stung into storm by the speed of our passage, and deaf
    where we past;
And our spirits too burn as we bound, thine holy but mine
    heavy-laden,
  As we burn with the fire of our flight; ah love, shall we
    win at the last?

The Sundew

A LITTLE marsh-plant, yellow green,
   And pricked at lip with tender red.
Tread close, and either way you tread
Some faint black water jets between
Lest you should bruise the curious head.

A live thing maybe; who shall know?
The summer knows and suffers it;
For the cool moss is thick and sweet
Each side, and saves the blossom so
That it lives out the long June heat.

The deep scent of the heather burns
About it; breathless though it be,
Bow down and worship; more than we
Is the least flower whose life returns,
Least weed renascent in the sea.

We are vexed and cumbered in earth's sight
With wants, with many memories;
These see their mother what she is,
Glad-growing, till August leave more bright
The apple-coloured cranberries.

Wind blows and bleaches the strong grass,
Blown all one way to shelter it
From trample of strayed kine, with feet
Felt heavier than the moorhen was,
Strayed up past patches of wild wheat.

You call it sundew: how it grows,
If with its colour it have breath,
If life taste sweet to it, if death
Pain its soft petal, no man knows:
Man has no sight or sense that saith.

My sundew, grown of gentle days,
In these green miles the spring begun
Thy growth ere April had half done
With the soft secret of her ways
Or June made ready for the sun.

O red-lipped mouth of marsh-flower,
I have a secret halved with thee.
The name that is love's name to me
Thou knowest, and the face of her
Who is my festival to see.

The hard sun, as thy petals knew,
Coloured the heavy moss-water:
Thou wert not worth green midsummer
Nor fit to live to August blue,
O sundew, not remembering her.

Mais où sont les neiges d'antan?

WHAT shall be said between us here
  Among the downs, between the trees,
In fields that knew our feet last year,
 In sight of quiet sands and seas,
 This year, Félise?

Who knows what word were best to say?
 For last year's leaves lie dead and red
On this sweet day, in this green May,
 And barren corn makes bitter bread.
 What shall be said?

Here as last year the fields begin,
 A fire of flowers and glowing grass;
The old fields we laughed and lingered in,
 Seeing each our souls in last year's glass,
 Félise, alas!

Shall we not laugh, shall we not weep,
 Not we, though this be as it is?
For love awake or love asleep
 Ends in a laugh, a dream, a kiss,
 A song like this.

I that have slept awake, and you
 Sleep, who last year were well awake.
Though love do all that love can do,
 My heart will never ache or break
 For your heart's sake.

The great sea, faultless as a flower,
 Throbs, trembling under beam and breeze,
And laughs with love of the amorous hour.
 I found you fairer once, Félise,
 Than flowers or seas.

We played at bondsman and at queen;
  But as the days change men change too;
I find the grey sea's notes of green,
  The green sea's fervent flakes of blue,
  More fair than you.

Your beauty is not over fair
  Now in mine eyes, who am grown up wise.
The smell of flowers in all your hair
  Allures not now; no sigh replies
  If your heart sighs.

But you sigh seldom, you sleep sound,
  You find love's new name good enough.
Less sweet I find it than I found
  The sweetest name that ever love
  Grew weary of.

My snake with bright bland eyes, my snake
  Grown tame and glad to be caressed,
With lips athirst for mine to slake
  Their tender fever! who had guessed
  You loved me best?

I had died for this last year, to know
  You loved me. Who shall turn on fate?
I care not if love come or go
  Now, though your love seek mine for mate.
  It is too late.

The dust of many strange desires
  Lies deep between us; in our eyes
Dead smoke of perishable fires
  Flickers, a fume in air and skies,
  A steam of sighs.

You loved me and you loved me not;
　A little, much, and overmuch.
Will you forget as I forgot?
　Let all dead things lie dead; none such
　Are soft to touch.

I love you and I do not love,
　Too much, a little, not at all;
Too much, and never yet enough.
　Birds quick to fledge and fly at call
　Are quick to fall.

And these love longer now than men,
　And larger loves than ours are these.
No diver brings up love again
　Dropped once, my beautiful Félise,
　In such cold seas.

Gone deeper than all plummets sound,
　Where in the dim green dayless day
The life of such dead things lies bound
　As the sea feeds on, wreck and stray
　And castaway.

Can I forget? yea, that can I,
　And that can all men; so will you,
Alive, or later, when you die.
　Ah, but the love you plead was true?
　Was mine not too?

I loved you for that name of yours
　Long ere we met, and long enough.
Now that one thing of all endures—
　The sweetest name that ever love
　Waxed weary of.

Like colours in the sea, like flowers,
  Like a cat's splendid circled eyes
That wax and wane with love for hours,
  Green as green flame, blue-grey like skies,
  And soft like sighs—

And all these only like your name,
  And your name full of all of these.
I say it, and it sounds the same—
  Save that I say it now at ease,
  Your name, Félise.

I said 'she must be swift and white,
  And subtly warm, and half perverse,
And sweet like sharp soft fruit to bite,
  And like a snake's love lithe and fierce.'
  Men have guessed worse.

What was the song I made of you
  Here where the grass forgets our feet
As afternoon forgets the dew?
  Ah that such sweet things should be fleet,
  Such fleet things sweet!

As afternoon forgets the dew,
  As time in time forgets all men,
As our old place forgets us two,
  Who might have turned to one thing then,
  But not again.

  O lips that mine have grown into
    Like April's kissing May,
  O fervent eyelids letting through
  Those eyes the greenest of things blue,
    The bluest of things grey,

If you were I and I were you,
  How could I love you, say?
How could the roseleaf love the rue,
The day love nightfall and her dew,
  Though night may love the day?

You loved it may be more than I;
  We know not; love is hard to seize.
And all things are not good to try;
  And lifelong loves the worst of these
  For us, Félise.

Ah, take the season and have done,
  Love well the hour and let it go:
Two souls may sleep and wake up one,
  Or dream they wake and find it so,
  And then—you know.

Kiss me once hard as though a flame
  Lay on my lips and made them fire;
The same lips now, and not the same;
  What breath shall fill and re-inspire
  A dead desire?

The old song sounds hollower in mine ear
  Than thin keen sounds of dead men's speech—
A noise one hears and would not hear;
  Too strong to die, too weak to reach
  From wave to beach.

We stand on either side the sea,
  Stretch hands, blow kisses, laugh and lean
I toward you, you toward me;
  But what hears either save the keen
  Grey sea between?

A year divides us, love from love,
  Though you love now, though I loved then.
The gulf is strait, but deep enough;
  Who shall recross, who among men
  Shall cross again?

Love was a jest last year, you said,
  And what lives surely, surely dies.
Even so; but now that love is dead,
  Shall love rekindle from wet eyes,
  From subtle sighs?

For many loves are good to see;
  Mutable loves, and loves perverse;
But there is nothing, nor shall be,
  So sweet, so wicked, but my verse
  Can dream of worse.

For we that sing and you that love
  Know that which man may, only we.
The rest live under us; above,
  Live the great gods in heaven, and see
  What things shall be.

So this thing is and must be so;
  For man dies, and love also dies.
Though yet love's ghost moves to and fro
  The sea-green mirrors of your eyes,
  And laughs, and lies.

Eyes coloured like a water-flower,
  And deeper than the green sea's glass;
Eyes that remember one sweet hour—
  In vain we swore it should not pass;
  In vain, alas!

Ah my Félise, if love or sin,
    If shame or fear could hold it fast,
Should we not hold it?   Love wears thin,
    And they laugh well who laugh the last.
    Is it not past?

The gods, the gods are stronger; time
    Falls down before them, all men's knees
Bow, all men's prayers and sorrows climb
    Like incense towards them; yea, for these
    Are gods, Félise.

Immortal are they, clothed with powers,
    Not to be comforted at all;
Lords over all the fruitless hours;
    Too great to appease, too high to appal,
    Too far to call.

For none shall move the most high gods,
    Who are most sad, being cruel; none
Shall break or take away the rods
    Wherewith they scourge us, not as one
    That smites a son.

By many a name of many a creed
    We have called upon them, since the sands
Fell through time's hour-glass first, a seed
    Of life; and out of many lands
    Have we stretched hands.

When have they heard us? who hath known
    Their faces, climbed unto their feet,
Felt them and found them?   Laugh or groan,
    Doth heaven remurmur and repeat
    Sad sounds or sweet?

Do the stars answer? in the night
  Have ye found comfort? or by day
Have ye seen gods?   What hope, what light,
  Falls from the farthest starriest way
  On you that pray?

Are the skies wet because we weep,
  Or fair because of any mirth?
Cry out; they are gods; perchance they sleep;
  Cry; thou shalt know what prayers are worth,
  Thou dust and earth.

O earth, thou art fair; O dust, thou art great;
  O laughing lips and lips that mourn,
Pray, till ye feel the exceeding weight
  Of God's intolerable scorn,
  Not to be borne.

Behold, there is no grief like this;
  The barren blossom of thy prayer,
Thou shalt find out how sweet it is.
  O fools and blind, what seek ye there,
  High up in the air?

Ye must have gods, the friends of men,
  Merciful gods, compassionate,
And these shall answer you again.
  Will ye beat always at the gate,
  Ye fools of fate?

Ye fools and blind; for this is sure,
  That all ye shall not live, but die.
Lo, what thing have ye found endure?
  Or what thing have ye found on high
  Past the blind sky?

The ghosts of words and dusty dreams,
  Old memories, faiths infirm and dead.
Ye fools; for which among you deems
  His prayer can alter green to red
  Or stones to bread?

Why should ye bear with hopes and fears
  Till all these things be drawn in one,
The sound of iron-footed years,
  And all the oppression that is done
  Under the sun?

Ye might end surely, surely pass
  Out of the multitude of things,
Under the dust, beneath the grass,
  Deep in dim death, where no thought stings,
  No record clings.

No memory more of love or hate,
  No trouble, nothing that aspires,
No sleepless labour thwarting fate,
  And thwarted; where no travail tires,
  Where no faith fires.

All passes, nought that has been is,
  Things good and evil have one end.
Can anything be otherwise
  Though all men swear all things would mend
  With God to friend?

Can ye beat off one wave with prayer,
  Can ye move mountains? bid the flower
Take flight and turn to a bird in the air?
  Can ye hold fast for shine or shower
  One wingless hour?

Ah sweet, and we too, can we bring
   One sigh back, bid one smile revive?
Can God restore one ruined thing,
   Or he who slays our souls alive
   Make dead things thrive?

Two gifts perforce he has given us yet,
   Though sad things stay and glad things fly;
Two gifts he has given us, to forget
   All glad and sad things that go by,
   And then to die.

We know not whether death be good,
   But life at least it will not be:
Men will stand saddening as we stood,
   Watch the same fields and skies as we
   And the same sea.

Let this be said between us here,
   One love grows green when one turns grey;
This year knows nothing of last year;
   To-morrow has no more to say
   To yesterday.

Live and let live, as I will do,
   Love and let love, and so will I.
But, sweet, for me no more with you:
   Not while I live, not though I die.
   Good night, good-bye.

ALL the night sleep came not upon my eyelids,
   Shed not dew, nor shook nor unclosed a feather,
Yet with lips shut close and with eyes of iron
   Stood and beheld me.

Then to me so lying awake a vision
Came without sleep over the seas and touched me,
Softly touched mine eyelids and lips; and I too,
   Full of the vision,

Saw the white implacable Aphrodite,
Saw the hair unbound and the feet unsandalled
Shine as fire of sunset on western waters;
   Saw the reluctant

Feet, the straining plumes of the doves that drew her,
Looking always, looking with necks reverted,
Back to Lesbos, back to the hills whereunder
   Shone Mitylene;

Heard the flying feet of the Loves behind her
Make a sudden thunder upon the waters,
As the thunder flung from the strong unclosing
   Wings of a great wind.

So the goddess fled from her place, with awful
Sound of feet and thunder of wings around her;
While behind a clamour of singing women
   Severed the twilight.

Ah the singing, ah the delight, the passion!
All the Loves wept, listening; sick with anguish,
Stood the crowned nine Muses about Apollo;
   Fear was upon them,

While the tenth sang wonderful things they knew not.
Ah the tenth, the Lesbian! the nine were silent,
None endured the sound of her song for weeping;
    Laurel by laurel,

Faded all their crowns; but about her forehead,
Round her woven tresses and ashen temples
White as dead snow, paler than grass in summer,
    Ravaged with kisses,

Shone a light of fire as a crown for ever.
Yea, almost the implacable Aphrodite
Paused, and almost wept; such a song was that song.
    Yea, by her name too

Called her, saying, 'Turn to me, O my Sappho';
Yet she turned her face from the Loves, she saw not
Tears for laughter darken immortal eyelids,
    Heard not about her

Fearful fitful wings of the doves departing,
Saw not how the bosom of Aphrodite
Shook with weeping, saw not her shaken raiment,
    Saw not her hands wrung;

Saw the Lesbians kissing across their smitten
Lutes with lips more sweet than the sound of lute-strings,
Mouth to mouth and hand upon hand, her chosen,
    Fairer than all men;

Only saw the beautiful lips and fingers,
Full of songs and kisses and little whispers,
Full of music; only beheld among them
    Soar, as a bird soars

Newly fledged, her visible song, a marvel,
Made of perfect sound and exceeding passion,
Sweetly shapen, terrible, full of thunders,
    Clothed with the wind's wings.

Then rejoiced she, laughing with love, and scattered
Roses, awful roses of holy blossom;
Then the Loves thronged sadly with hidden faces
    Round Aphrodite,

Then the Muses, stricken at heart, were silent;
Yea, the gods waxed pale; such a song was that song.
All reluctant, all with a fresh repulsion,
    Fled from before her.

All withdrew long since, and the land was barren,
Full of fruitless women and music only.
Now perchance, when winds are assuaged at sunset,
    Lulled at the dewfall,

By the grey sea-side, unassuaged, unheard of,
Unbeloved, unseen in the ebb of twilight,
Ghosts of outcast women return lamenting,
    Purged not in Lethe,

Clothed about with flame and with tears, and singing
Songs that move the heart of the shaken heaven,
Songs that break the heart of the earth with pity,
    Hearing, to hear them.

UNDER green apple-boughs
　　That never a storm will rouse,
My lady hath her house
　　Between two bowers;
In either of the twain
Red roses full of rain;
She hath for bondwomen
　　All kind of flowers.

She hath no handmaid fair
To draw her curled gold hair
Through rings of gold that bear
　　Her whole hair's weight;
She hath no maids to stand
Gold-clothed on either hand;
In all the great green land
　　None is so great.

She hath no more to wear
But one white hood of vair
Drawn over eyes and hair,
　　Wrought with strange gold,
Made for some great queen's head,
Some fair great queen since dead;
And one strait gown of red
　　Against the cold.

Beneath her eyelids deep
Love lying seems asleep,
Love, swift to wake, to weep,
　　To laugh, to gaze;
Her breasts are like white birds,
And all her gracious words
As water-grass to herds
　　In the June-days.

To her all dews that fall
And rains are musical;
Her flowers are fed from all,
   Her joy from these;
In the deep-feathered firs
Their gift of joy is hers,
In the least breath that stirs
   Across the trees.

She grows with greenest leaves,
Ripens with reddest sheaves,
Forgets, remembers, grieves,
   And is not sad;
The quiet lands and skies
Leave light upon her eyes;
None knows her, weak or wise,
   Or tired or glad.

None knows, none understands,
What flowers are like her hands;
Though you should search all lands
   Wherein time grows,
What snows are like her feet,
Though his eyes burn with heat
Through gazing on my sweet,
   Yet no man knows.

Only this thing is said;
That white and gold and red,
God's three chief words, man's bread
   And oil and wine,
Were given her for dowers,
And kingdom of all hours,
And grace of goodly flowers
   And various vine.

This is my lady's praise:
God after many days
Wrought her in unknown ways,
  In sunset lands;
This was my lady's birth;
God gave her might and mirth
And laid his whole sweet earth
  Between her hands.

Under deep apple-boughs
My lady hath her house;
She wears upon her brows
  The flower thereof;
All saying but what God saith
To her is as vain breath;
She is more strong than death,
  Being strong as love.

ATALANTA IN CALYDON

A TRAGEDY

The Argument

ALTHAEA, daughter of Thestius and Eurythemis, queen of Calydon, being with child of Meleager her first-born son, dreamed that she brought forth a brand burning; and upon his birth came the three Fates and prophesied of him three things, namely these; that he should have great strength of his hands, and good fortune in this life, and that he should live no longer when the brand then in the fire were consumed: wherefore his mother plucked it forth and kept it by her. And the child being a man grown sailed with Jason after the fleece of gold, and won himself great praise of all men living; and when the tribes of the north and west made war upon Aetolia, he fought against their army and scattered it. But Artemis, having at the first stirred up these tribes to war against Oeneus king of Calydon, because he had offered sacrifice to all the gods saving her alone, but her he had forgotten to honour, was yet more wroth because of the destruction of this army, and sent upon the land of Calydon a wild boar which slew many and wasted all their increase, but him could none slay, and many went against him and perished. Then were all the chief men of Greece gathered together, and among them Atalanta daughter of Iasius the Arcadian, a virgin; for whose sake Artemis let slay the boar, seeing she favoured the maiden greatly; and Meleager having dispatched it gave the spoil thereof to Atalanta, as one beyond measure enamoured of her; but the brethren of Althaea his mother, Toxeus and Plexippus, with such others as misliked that she only should bear off the praise whereas many had borne the labour, laid wait for her to take away her spoil; but Meleager fought against them and slew them: whom when Althaea their sister beheld and knew to be slain of her son, she waxed for wrath and sorrow like as one mad, and taking the brand whereby the measure of her son's life was meted to him, she cast it upon a fire; and with the wasting thereof his life likewise wasted away, that being brought back to his father's house he died in a brief space; and his mother also endured not long after for very sorrow; and this was his end, and the end of that hunting.

The Persons

Chief Huntsman	Atalanta
Chorus	Toxeus
Althaea	Plexippus
Meleager	Herald
Oeneus	Messenger
Second Messenger	

ἴστω δ' ὅστις οὐχ ὑπόπτερος
φροντίσιν δαεὶς,
τὰν ἁ παιδολύμας τάλαινα Θεστιὰς μήσατο
πυρδαῆ τινα πρόνοιαν,
καταίθουσα παιδὸς δαφοινὸν
δαλὸν ἥλικ', ἐπεὶ μολὼν
ματρόθεν κελάδησε·
σύμμετρόν τε διαὶ βίου
μοιρόκραντον ἐς ἆμαρ.

AESCH. *Cho.* 602–12.

CHIEF HUNTSMAN

MAIDEN, and mistress of the months and stars
  Now folded in the flowerless fields of heaven,
Goddess whom all gods love with threefold heart,
Being treble in thy divided deity,
A light for dead men and dark hours, a foot
Swift on the hills as morning, and a hand
To all things fierce and fleet that roar and range
Mortal, with gentler shafts than snow or sleep;
Hear now and help and lift no violent hand,
But favourable and fair as thine eye's beam
Hidden and shown in heaven; for I all night
Amid the king's hounds and the hunting men
Have wrought and worshipped toward thee; nor shall
     man
See goodlier hounds or deadlier edge of spears;
But for the end, that lies unreached at yet
Between the hands and on the knees of gods.
O fair-faced sun, killing the stars and dews
And dreams and desolation of the night!
Rise up, shine, stretch thine hand out, with thy bow
Touch the most dimmest height of trembling heaven,
And burn and break the dark about thy ways,
Shot through and through with arrows; let thine hair
Lighten as flame above that flameless shell
Which was the moon, and thine eyes fill the world
And thy lips kindle with swift beams; let earth
Laugh, and the long sea fiery from thy feet
Through all the roar and ripple of streaming springs
And foam in reddening flakes and flying flowers
Shaken from hands and blown from lips of nymphs
Whose hair or breast divides the wandering wave
With salt close tresses cleaving lock to lock,

All gold, or shuddering and unfurrowed snow;
And all the winds about thee with their wings,
And fountain-heads of all the watered world;
Each horn of Acheloüs, and the green
Euenus, wedded with the straitening sea.
For in fair time thou comest; come also thou,
Twin-born with him, and virgin, Artemis,
And give our spears their spoil, the wild boar's hide,
Sent in thine anger against us for sin done
And bloodless altars without wine or fire.
Him now consume thou; for thy sacrifice
With sanguine-shining steam divides the dawn,
And one, the maiden rose of all thy maids,
Arcadian Atalanta, snowy-souled,
Fair as the snow and footed as the wind,
From Ladon and well-wooded Maenalus
Over the firm hills and the fleeting sea
Hast thou drawn hither, and many an armèd king,
Heroes, the crown of men, like gods in fight.
Moreover out of all the Aetolian land,
From the full-flowered Lelantian pasturage
To what of fruitful field the son of Zeus
Won from the roaring river and labouring sea
When the wild god shrank in his horn and fled
And foamed and lessened through his wrathful fords,
Leaving clear lands that steamed with sudden sun,
These virgins with the lightening of the day
Bring thee fresh wreaths and their own sweeter hair,
Luxurious locks and flower-like mixed with flowers,
Clean offering, and chaste hymns; but me the time
Divides from these things; whom do thou not less
Help and give honour, and to mine hounds good speed,
And edge to spears, and luck to each man's hand.

When the hounds of spring are on winter's traces,
  The mother of months in meadow or plain
Fills the shadows and windy places
  With lisp of leaves and ripple of rain;
And the brown bright nightingale amorous
Is half assuaged for Itylus,
For the Thracian ships and the foreign faces,
  The tongueless vigil, and all the pain.

Come with bows bent and with emptying of quivers,
  Maiden most perfect, lady of light,
With a noise of winds and many rivers,
  With a clamour of waters, and with might;
Bind on thy sandals, O thou most fleet,
Over the splendour and speed of thy feet;
For the faint east quickens, the wan west shivers,
  Round the feet of the day and the feet of the night.

Where shall we find her, how shall we sing to her,
  Fold our hands round her knees, and cling?
O that man's heart were as fire and could spring to her,
  Fire, or the strength of the streams that spring!
For the stars and the winds are unto her
As raiment, as songs of the harp-player;
For the risen stars and the fallen cling to her,
  And the south-west wind and the west wind sing.

For winter's rains and ruins are over,
  And all the season of snows and sins;
The days dividing lover and lover,
  The light that loses, the night that wins;
And time remembered is grief forgotten,
And frosts are slain and flowers begotten,
And in green underwood and cover
  Blossom by blossom the spring begins.

The full streams feed on flower of rushes,
    Ripe grasses trammel a travelling foot,
The faint fresh flame of the young year flushes
    From leaf to flower and flower to fruit;
And fruit and leaf are as gold and fire,
And the oat is heard above the lyre,
And the hoofèd heel of a satyr crushes
    The chestnut-husk at the chestnut-root.

And Pan by noon and Bacchus by night,
    Fleeter of foot than the fleet-foot kid,
Follows with dancing and fills with delight
    The Maenad and the Bassarid;
And soft as lips that laugh and hide
The laughing leaves of the trees divide,
And screen from seeing and leave in sight
    The god pursuing, the maiden hid.

The ivy falls with the Bacchanal's hair
    Over her eyebrows hiding her eyes;
The wild vine slipping down leaves bare
    Her bright breast shortening into sighs;
The wild vine slips with the weight of its leaves,
But the berried ivy catches and cleaves
To the limbs that glitter, the feet that scare
    The wolf that follows, the fawn that flies.

ALTHAEA

What do ye singing? what is this ye sing?

CHORUS

Flowers bring we, and pure lips that please the gods,
And raiment meet for service: lest the day
Turn sharp with all its honey in our lips.

97

ALTHAEA

Night, a black hound, follows the white fawn day,
Swifter than dreams the white flown feet of sleep;
Will ye pray back the night with any prayers?
And though the spring put back a little while
Winter, and snows that plague all men for sin,
And the iron time of cursing, yet I know
Spring shall be ruined with the rain, and storm
Eat up like fire the ashen autumn days.
I marvel what men do with prayers awake
Who dream and die with dreaming; any god,
Yea the least god of all things called divine,
Is more than sleep and waking; yet we say,
Perchance by praying a man shall match his god.
For if sleep have no mercy, and man's dreams
Bite to the blood and burn into the bone,
What shall this man do waking?   By the gods,
He shall not pray to dream sweet things to-night,
Having dreamt once more bitter things than death.

CHORUS

Queen, but what is it that hath burnt thine heart?
For thy speech flickers like a blown-out flame.

ALTHAEA

Look, ye say well, and know not what ye say;
For all my sleep is turned into a fire,
And all my dreams to stuff that kindles it.

CHORUS

Yet one doth well being patient of the gods.

ALTHAEA

Yea, lest they smite us with some four-foot plague.

CHORUS

But when time spreads find out some herb for it.

ALTHAEA

And with their healing herbs infect our blood.

CHORUS

What ails thee to be jealous of their ways?

ALTHAEA

What if they give us poisonous drinks for wine?

CHORUS

They have their will; much talking mends it not.

ALTHAEA

And gall for milk, and cursing for a prayer?

CHORUS

Have they not given life, and the end of life?

ALTHAEA

Lo, where they heal, they help not; thus they do,
They mock us with a little piteousness,
And we say prayers, and weep; but at the last,
Sparing awhile, they smite and spare no whit.

CHORUS

Small praise man gets dispraising the high gods:
What have they done that thou dishonourest them?

ALTHAEA

First Artemis for all this harried land
I praise not, and for wasting of the boar

That mars with tooth and tusk and fiery feet
Green pasturage and the grace of standing corn
And meadow and marsh with springs and unblown
    leaves,
Flocks and swift herds and all that bite sweet grass,
I praise her not; what things are these to praise?

CHORUS

But when the king did sacrifice, and gave
Each god fair dues of wheat and blood and wine,
Her not with bloodshed nor burnt offering
Revered he, nor with salt or cloven cake;
Wherefore being wroth she plagued the land; but now
Takes off from us fate and her heavy things.
Which deed of these twain were not good to praise?
For a just deed looks always either way
With blameless eyes, and mercy is no fault.

ALTHAEA

Yea, but a curse she hath sent above all these
To hurt us where she healed us; and hath lit
Fire where the old fire went out, and where the wind
Slackened, hath blown on us with deadlier air.

CHORUS

What storm is this that tightens all our sail?

ALTHAEA

Love, a thwart sea wind full of rain and foam.

CHORUS

Whence blown, and born under what stormier star?

ALTHAEA

Southward across Euenus from the sea.

Thy speech turns toward Arcadia like blown wind.

ALTHAEA

Sharp as the north sets when the snows are out.

CHORUS

Nay, for this maiden hath no touch of love.

ALTHAEA

I would she had sought in some cold gulf of sea
Love, or in dens where strange beasts lurk, or fire,
Or snows on the extreme hills, or iron land
Where no spring is; I would she had sought therein
And found, or ever love had found her here.

CHORUS

She is holier than all holy days or things,
The sprinkled water or fume of perfect fire;
Chaste, dedicated to pure prayers, and filled
With higher thoughts than heaven; a maiden clean,
Pure iron, fashioned for a sword; and man
She loves not; what should one such do with love?

ALTHAEA

Look you, I speak not as one light of wit,
But as a queen speaks, being heart-vexed; for oft
I hear my brothers wrangling in mid hall,
And am not moved; and my son chiding them,
And these things nowise move me, but I know
Foolish and wise men must be to the end,
And feed myself with patience; but this most,
This moves me, that for wise men as for fools
Love is one thing, an evil thing, and turns

Choice words and wisdom into fire and air.
And in the end shall no joy come, but grief,
Sharp words and soul's division and fresh tears
Flower-wise upon the old root of tears brought forth,
Fruit-wise upon the old flower of tears sprung up,
Pitiful sighs, and much regrafted pain.
These things are in my presage, and myself
Am part of them and know not; but in dreams
The gods are heavy on me, and all the fates
Shed fire across my eyelids mixed with night,
And burn me blind, and disilluminate
My sense of seeing, and my perspicuous soul
Darken with vision; seeing I see not, hear
And hearing am not holpen, but mine eyes
Stain many tender broideries in the bed
Drawn up about my face that I may weep
And the king wake not; and my brows and lips
Tremble and sob in sleeping, like swift flames
That tremble, or water when it sobs with heat
Kindled from under; and my tears fill my breast
And speck the fair dyed pillows round the king
With barren showers and salter than the sea,
Such dreams divide me dreaming; for long since
I dreamed that out of this my womb had sprung
Fire and a firebrand; this was ere my son,
Meleager, a goodly flower in fields of fight,
Felt the light touch him coming forth, and wailed
Childlike; but yet he was not; and in time
I bare him, and my heart was great; for yet
So royally was never strong man born,
Nor queen so nobly bore as noble a thing
As this my son was: such a birth God sent
And such a grace to bear it.   Then came in
Three weaving women, and span each a thread,
Saying This for strength and That for luck, and one

Saying Till the brand upon the hearth burn down,
So long shall this man see good days and live.
And I with gathered raiment from the bed
Sprang, and drew forth the brand, and cast on it
Water, and trod the flame bare-foot, and crushed
With naked hand spark beaten out of spark
And blew against and quenched it; for I said,
These are the most high Fates that dwell with us,
And we find favour a little in their sight,
A little, and more we miss of, and much time
Foils us; howbeit they have pitied me, O son,
And thee most piteous, thee a tenderer thing
Than any flower of fleshly seed alive.
Wherefore I kissed and hid him with my hands,
And covered under arms and hair, and wept,
And feared to touch him with my tears, and laughed;
So light a thing was this man, grown so great
Men cast their heads back, seeing against the sun
Blaze the armed man carven on his shield, and hear
The laughter of little bells along the brace
Ring, as birds singing or flutes blown, and watch,
High up, the cloven shadow of either plume
Divide the bright light of the brass, and make
His helmet as a windy and wintering moon
Seen through blown cloud and plume-like drift, when
    ships
Drive, and men strive with all the sea, and oars
Break, and the beaks dip under, drinking death;
Yet was he then but a span long, and moaned
With inarticulate mouth inseparate words,
And with blind lips and fingers wrung my breast
Hard, and thrust out with foolish hands and feet,
Murmuring; but those grey women with bound hair
Who fright the gods frighted not him; he laughed
Seeing them, and pushed out hands to feel and haul

Distaff and thread, intangible; but they
Passed, and I hid the brand, and in my heart
Laughed likewise, having all my will of heaven.
But now I know not if to left or right
.The gods have drawn us hither; for again
I dreamt, and saw the black brand burst on fire
As a branch bursts in flower, and saw the flame
Fade flower-wise, and Death came and with dry lips
Blew the charred ash into my breast; and Love
Trampled the ember and crushed it with swift feet.
This I have also at heart; that not for me,
Not for me only or son of mine, O girls,
The gods have wrought life, and desire of life,
Heart's love and heart's division; but for all
There shines one sun and one wind blows till night.
And when night comes the wind sinks and the sun,
And there is no light after, and no storm,
But sleep and much forgetfulness of things.
In such wise I gat knowledge of the gods
Years hence, and heard high sayings of one most wise,
Eurythemis my mother, who beheld
With eyes alive and spake with lips of these
As one on earth disfleshed and disallied
From breath or blood corruptible; such gifts
Time gave her, and an equal soul to these
And equal face to all things; thus she said.
But whatsoever intolerable or glad
The swift hours weave and unweave, I go hence
Full of mine own soul, perfect of myself,
Toward mine and me sufficient; and what chance
The gods cast lots for and shake out on us,
That shall we take, and that much bear withal.
And now, before these gather to the hunt,
I will go arm my son and bring him forth,
Lest love or some man's anger work him harm.

Before the beginning of years
  There came to the making of man
Time, with a gift of tears;
  Grief, with a glass that ran;
Pleasure, with pain for leaven;
  Summer, with flowers that fell;
Remembrance fallen from heaven,
  And madness risen from hell;
Strength without hands to smite;
  Love that endures for a breath:
Night, the shadow of light,
  And life, the shadow of death.

And the high gods took in hand
  Fire, and the falling of tears,
And a measure of sliding sand
  From under the feet of the years;
And froth and drift of the sea;
  And dust of the labouring earth;
And bodies of things to be
  In the houses of death and of birth;
And wrought with weeping and laughter,
  And fashioned with loathing and love
With life before and after
  And death beneath and above,
For a day and a night and a morrow,
  That his strength might endure for a span
With travail and heavy sorrow,
  The holy spirit of man.

From the winds of the north and the south
  They gathered as unto strife;
They breathed upon his mouth,
  They filled his body with life;

Eyesight and speech they wrought
    For the veils of the soul therein,
A time for labour and thought,
    A time to serve and to sin;
They gave him light in his ways,
    And love, and a space for delight,
And beauty and length of days,
    And night, and sleep in the night.
His speech is a burning fire;
    With his lips he travaileth;
In his heart is a blind desire,
    In his eyes foreknowledge of death;
He weaves, and is clothed with derision;
    Sows, and he shall not reap;
His life is a watch or a vision
    Between a sleep and a sleep.

MELEAGER

O sweet new heaven and air without a star,
Fair day, be fair and welcome, as to men
With deeds to do and praise to pluck from thee.
Come forth a child, born with clear sound and light,
With laughter and swift limbs and prosperous looks;
That this great hunt with heroes for the hounds
May leave thee memorable and us well sped.

ALTHAEA

Son, first I praise thy prayer, then bid thee speed;
But the gods hear men's hands before their lips,
And heed beyond all crying and sacrifice
Light of things done and noise of labouring men.
But thou, being armed and perfect for the deed,
Abide; for like rain-flakes in a wind they grow,
The men thy fellows, and the choice of the world,
Bound to root out the tuskèd plague, and leave
Thanks and safe days and peace in Calydon.

For the whole city and all the low-lying land
Flames, and the soft air sounds with them that come;
The gods give all these fruit of all their works.

ALTHAEA

Set thine eye thither and fix thy spirit and say
Whom there thou knowest; for sharp mixed shadow and
    wind
Blown up between the morning and the mist,
With steam of steeds and flash of bridle or wheel,
And fire, and parcels of the broken dawn,
And dust divided by hard light, and spears
That shine and shift as the edge of wild beasts' eyes,
Smite upon mine; so fiery their blind edge
Burns, and bright points break up and baffle day.

MELEAGER

The first, for many I know not, being far off,
Pelcus the Larissaean, couched with whom
Sleeps the white sea-bred wife and silver-shod,
Fair as fled foam, a goddess; and their son
Most swift and splendid of men's children born,
Most like a god, full of the future fame.

ALTHAEA

Who are these shining like one sundered star?

MELEAGER

Thy sister's sons, a double flower of men.

ALTHAEA

O sweetest kin to me in all the world,
O twin-born blood of Leda, gracious heads

Like kindled lights in untempestuous heaven,
Fair flower-like stars on the iron foam of fight,
With what glad heart and kindliness of soul,
Even to the staining of both eyes with tears
And kindling of warm eyelids with desire,
A great way off I greet you, and rejoice
Seeing you so fair, and moulded like as gods.
Far off ye come, and least in years of these,
But lordliest, but worth love to look upon.

MELEAGER

Even such (for sailing hither I saw far hence,
And where Eurotas hollows his moist rock
Nigh Sparta with a strenuous-hearted stream)
Even such I saw their sisters; one swan-white,
The little Helen, and less fair than she
Fair Clytaemnestra, grave as pasturing fawns
Who feed and fear some arrow; but at whiles,
As one smitten with love or wrung with joy,
She laughs and lightens with her eyes, and then
Weeps; whereat Helen, having laughed, weeps too,
And the other chides her, and she being chid speaks
     nought,
But cheeks and lips and eyelids kisses her,
Laughing; so fare they, as in their bloomless bud
And full of unblown life, the blood of gods.

ALTHAEA

Sweet days befall them and good loves and lords,
And tender and temperate honours of the hearth,
Peace, and a perfect life and blameless bed.
But who shows next an eagle wrought in gold,
That flames and beats broad wings against the sun
And with void mouth gapes after emptier prey?

MELEAGER

Know by that sign the reign of Telamon
Between the fierce mouths of the encountering brine
On the strait reefs of twice-washed Salamis.

ALTHAEA

For like one great of hand he bears himself,
Vine-chapleted, with savours of the sea,
Glittering as wine and moving as a wave.
But who girt round there roughly follows him?

MELEAGER

Ancaeus, great of hand, an iron bulk,
Two-edged for fight as the axe against his arm,
Who drives against the surge of stormy spears
Full-sailed; him Cepheus follows, his twin-born,
Chief name next his of all Arcadian men.

ALTHAEA

Praise be with men abroad; chaste lives with us,
Home-keeping days and household reverences.

MELEAGER

Next by the left unsandalled foot know thou
The sail and oar of this Aetolian land,
Thy brethren, Toxeus and the violent-souled
Plexippus, over-swift with hand and tongue;
For hands are fruitful, but the ignorant mouth
Blows and corrupts their work with barren breath.

ALTHAEA

Speech too bears fruit, being worthy; and air blows down
Things poisonous, and high-seated violences,
And with charmed words and songs have men put out
Wild evil, and the fire of tyrannies.

MELEAGER

Yea, all things have they, save the gods and love.

ALTHAEA

Love thou the law and cleave to things ordained.

MELEAGER

Law lives upon their lips whom these applaud.

ALTHAEA

How sayest thou these? what god applauds new things?

MELEAGER

Zeus, who hath fear and custom under foot.

ALTHAEA

But loves not laws thrown down and lives awry.

MELEAGER

Yet is not less himself than his own law.

ALTHAEA

Nor shifts and shuffles old things up and down.

MELEAGER

But what he will remoulds and discreates.

ALTHAEA

Much, but not this, that each thing live its life.

MELEAGER

Nor only live, but lighten and lift up higher.

110

Pride breaks itself, and too much gained is gone.

MELEAGER

Things gained are gone, but great things done endure.

ALTHAEA

Child, if a man serve law through all his life
And with his whole heart worship, him all gods
Praise; but who loves it only with his lips,
And not in heart and deed desiring it
Hides a perverse will with obsequious words,
Him heaven infatuates and his twin-born fate
Tracks, and gains on him, scenting sins far off,
And the swift hounds of violent death devour.
Be man at one with equal-minded gods,
So shall he prosper; not through laws torn up,
Violated rule and a new face of things.
A woman armed makes war upon herself,
Unwomanlike, and treads down use and wont
And the sweet common honour that she hath,
Love, and the cry of children, and the hand
Trothplight and mutual mouth of marriages,
This doth she, being unloved; whom if one love,
Not fire nor iron and the wide-mouthed wars
Are deadlier than her lips or braided hair.
For of the one comes poison, and a curse
Falls from the other and burns the lives of men.
But thou, son, be not filled with evil dreams,
Nor with desire of these things; for with time
Blind love burns out; but if one feed it full
Till some discolouring stain dyes all his life,
He shall keep nothing praiseworthy, nor die
The sweet wise death of old men honourable,

Who have lived out all the length of all their years
Blameless, and seen well-pleased the face of gods,
And without shame and without fear have wrought
Things memorable, and while their days held out
In sight of all men and the sun's great light
Have gat them glory and given of their own praise
To the earth that bare them and the day that bred,
Home friends and far-off hospitalities,
And filled with gracious and memorial fame
Lands loved of summer or washed by violent seas,
Towns populous and many unfooted ways,
And alien lips and native with their own.
But when white age and venerable death
Mow down the strength and life within their limbs,
Drain out the blood and darken their clear eyes,
Immortal honour is on them, having past
Through splendid life and death desirable
To the clear seat and remote throne of souls,
Lands indiscoverable in the unheard-of west,
Round which the strong stream of a sacred sea
Rolls without wind for ever, and the snow
There shows not her white wings and windy feet,
Nor thunder nor swift rain saith anything,
Nor the sun burns, but all things rest and thrive;
And these, filled full of days, divine and dead,
Sages and singers fiery from the god,
And such as loved their land and all things good
And, best beloved of best men, liberty,
Free lives and lips, free hands of men free-born,
And whatsoever on earth was honourable
And whosoever of all the ephemeral seed,
Live there a life no liker to the gods
But nearer than their life of terrene days.
Love thou such life and look for such a death.
But from the light and fiery dreams of love

Spring heavy sorrows and a sleepless life,
Visions not dreams, whose lids no charm shall close
Nor song assuage them waking; and swift death
Crushes with sterile feet the unripening ear,
Treads out the timeless vintage; whom do thou
Eschewing embrace the luck of this thy life,
Not without honour; and it shall bear to thee
Such fruit as men reap from spent hours and wear,
Few men, but happy; of whom be thou, O son,
Happiest, if thou submit thy soul to fate,
And set thine eyes and heart on hopes high-born
And divine deeds and abstinence divine.
So shalt thou be toward all men all thy days
As light and might communicable, and burn
From heaven among the stars above the hours,
And break not as a man breaks nor burn down:
For to whom other of all heroic names
Have the gods given his life in hand as thine?
And gloriously hast thou lived, and made thy life
To me that bare thee and to all men born
Thankworthy, a praise for ever; and hast won fame
When wild wars broke all round thy father's house,
And the mad people of windy mountain ways
Laid spears against us like a sea, and all
Aetolia thundered with Thessalian hoofs;
Yet these, as wind baffles the foam, and beats
Straight back the relaxed ripple, didst thou break
And loosen all their lances, till undone
And man from man they fell; for ye twain stood
God against god, Ares and Artemis,
And thou the mightier; wherefore she unleashed
A sharp-toothed curse thou too shalt overcome;
For in the greener blossom of thy life
Ere the full blade caught flower, and when time gave
Respite, thou didst not slacken soul nor sleep,

But with great hand and heart seek praise of men
Out of sharp straits and many a grievous thing.
Seeing the strange foam of undivided seas
On channels never sailed in, and by shores
Where the old winds cease not blowing, and all the night
Thunders, and day is no delight to men.

Meleager, a noble wisdom and fair words
The gods have given this woman; hear thou these.

MELEAGER

O mother, I am not fain to strive in speech
Nor set my mouth against thee, who art wise
Even as they say and full of sacred words.
But one thing I know surely, and cleave to this;
That though I be not subtle of wit as thou
Nor womanlike to weave sweet words, and melt
Mutable minds of wise men as with fire,
I too, doing justly and reverencing the gods,
Shall not want wit to see what things be right.
For whom they love and whom reject, being gods,
There is no man but seeth, and in good time
Submits himself, refraining all his heart.
And I too as thou sayest have seen great things;
Seen otherwhere, but chiefly when the sail
First caught between stretched ropes the roaring west,
And all our oars smote eastward, and the wind
First flung round faces of seafaring men
White splendid snow-flakes of the sundering foam,
And the first furrow in virginal green sea
Followed the plunging ploughshare of hewn pine,
And closed, as when deep sleep subdues man's breath
Lips close and heart subsides; and closing, shone
Sunlike with many a Nereid's hair, and moved

114

Round many a trembling mouth of doubtful gods,
Risen out of sunless and sonorous gulfs
Through waning water and into shallow light,
That watched us; and when flying the dove was snared
As with men's hands, but we shot after and sped
Clear through the irremeable Symplegades;
And chiefliest when hoar beach and herbless cliff
Stood out ahead from Colchis, and we heard
Clefts hoarse with wind, and saw through narrowing reefs
The lightning of the intolerable wave
Flash, and the white wet flame of breakers burn
Far under a kindling south wind, as a lamp
Burns and bends all its blowing flame one way;
Wild heights untravelled of the wind, and vales
Cloven seaward by their violent streams, and white
With bitter flowers and bright salt scurf of brine;
Heard sweep their sharp swift gales, and bowing birdwise
Shriek with birds' voices, and with furious feet
Tread loose the long skirts of a storm; and saw
The whole white Euxine clash together and fall
Full-mouthed, and thunderous from a thousand throats:
Yet we drew thither and won the fleece and won
Medea, deadlier than the sea; but there
Seeing many a wonder and fearful things to men
I saw not one thing like this one seen here,
Most fair and fearful, feminine, a god,
Faultless; whom I that love not, being unlike,
Fear, and give honour, and choose from all the gods.

OENEUS

Lady, the daughter of Thestius, and thou, son,
Not ignorant of your strife nor light of wit,
Scared with vain dreams and fluttering like spent fire,
I come to judge between you, but a king
Full of past days and wise from years endured.

Nor thee I praise, who art fain to undo things done:
Nor thee, who art swift to esteem them overmuch.
For what the hours have given is given, and this
Changeless; howbeit these change, and in good time
Devise new things and good, not one thing still.
Us have they sent now at our need for help
Among men armed a woman, foreign born,
Virgin, not like the natural flower of things
That grows and bears and brings forth fruit and dies;
Unlovable, no light for a husband's house,
Espoused; a glory among unwedded girls,
And chosen of gods who reverence maidenhood.
These too we honour in honouring her; but thou,
Abstain thy feet from following, and thine eyes
From amorous touch; nor set toward hers thine heart,
Son, lest hate bear no deadlier fruit than love.

ALTHAEA

O king, thou art wise, but wisdom halts; and just,
But the gods love not justice more than fate,
And smite the righteous and the violent mouth,
And mix with insolent blood the reverent man's,
And bruise the holier as the lying lips.
Enough; for wise words fail me, and my heart
Takes fire and trembles flamewise, O my son,
O child, for thine head's sake; mine eyes wax thick,
Turning toward thee, so goodly a weaponed man,
So glorious; and for love of thine own eyes
They are darkened, and tears burn them, fierce as fire,
And my lips pause and my soul sinks with love.
But by thine hand, by thy sweet life and eyes,
By thy great heart and these clasped knees, O son,
I pray thee that thou slay me not with thee.
For there was never a mother woman-born
Loved her sons better; and never a queen of men

More perfect in her heart toward whom she loved.
For what lies light on many and they forget,
Small things and transitory as a wind o' the sea,
I forget never; I have seen thee all thine years
A man in arms, strong and a joy to men
Seeing thine head glitter and thine hand burn its way
Through a heavy and iron furrow of sundering spears;
But always also a flower of three suns old,
The small one thing that lying drew down my life
To lie with thee and feed thee; a child and weak,
Mine, a delight to no man, sweet to me.
Who then sought to thee? who gat help? who knew
If thou wert goodly? nay, no man at all.
Or what sea saw thee, or sounded with thine oar,
Child? or what strange land shone with war through thee?
But fair for me thou wert, O little life,
Fruitless, the fruit of mine own flesh, and blind,
More than much gold, ungrown, a foolish flower.
For silver nor bright snow nor feather of foam
Was whiter, and no gold yellower than thine hair,
O child, my child; and now thou art lordlier grown,
Not lovelier, nor a new thing in mine eyes,
I charge thee by thy soul and this my breast,
Fear thou the gods and me and thine own heart,
Lest all these turn against thee; for who knows
What wind upon what wave of altering time
Shall speak a storm and blow calamity?
And there is nothing stabile in the world
But the gods break it; yet not less, fair son,
If but one thing be stronger, if one endure,
Surely the bitter and the rooted love
That burns between us, going from me to thee,
Shall more endure than all things. What dost thou,
Following strange loves? why wilt thou kill mine heart?
Lo, I talk wild and windy words, and fall

From my clear wits, and seem of mine own self
Dethroned, dispraised, disseated; and my mind,
That was my crown, breaks, and mine heart is gone,
And I am naked of my soul, and stand
Ashamed, as a mean woman; take thou thought:
Live if thou wilt, and if thou wilt not, look,
The gods have given thee life to lose or keep,
Thou shalt not die as men die, but thine end
Fallen upon thee shall break me unaware.

MELEAGER

Queen, my whole heart is molten with thy tears,
And my limbs yearn with pity of thee, and love
Compels with grief mine eyes and labouring breath;
For what thou art I know thee, and this thy breast
And thy fair eyes I worship, and am bound
Toward thee in spirit and love thee in all my soul.
For there is nothing terribler to men
Than the sweet face of mothers, and the might.
But what shall be let be; for us the day
Once only lives a little, and is not found.
Time and the fruitful hour are more than we,
And these lay hold upon us; but thou, God,
Zeus, the sole steersman of the helm of things,
Father, be swift to see us, and as thou wilt
Help: or if adverse, as thou wilt, refrain.

CHORUS

We have seen thee, O Love, thou art fair; thou art goodly,
  O Love;
Thy wings make light in the air as the wings of a dove.
Thy feet are as winds that divide the stream of the sea;
Earth is thy covering to hide thee, the garment of thee.
Thou art swift and subtle and blind as a flame of fire;

Before thee the laughter, behind thee the tears of desire;
And twain go forth beside thee, a man with a maid;
Her eyes are the eyes of a bride whom delight makes afraid;
As the breath in the buds that stir is her bridal breath:
But Fate is the name of her; and his name is Death.

        For an evil blossom was born
            Of sea-foam and the frothing of blood,
                Blood-red and bitter of fruit,
                    And the seed of it laughter and tears,
        And the leaves of it madness and scorn;
            A bitter flower from the bud,
                Sprung of the sea without root,
                    Sprung without graft from the years.

    The weft of the world was untorn
        That is woven of the day on the night,
        The hair of the hours was not white
    Nor the raiment of time overworn,
        When a wonder, a world's delight,
    A perilous goddess was born;
        And the waves of the sea as she came
    Clove, and the foam at her feet,
        Fawning, rejoiced to bring forth
        A fleshly blossom, a flame
    Filling the heavens with heat
        To the cold white ends of the north.

    And in air the clamorous birds,
        And men upon earth that hear
    Sweet articulate words
        Sweetly divided apart,
        And in shallow and channel and mere
    The rapid and footless herds,
        Rejoiced, being foolish of heart.

For all they said upon earth,
　　She is fair, she is white like a dove,
　　　　And the life of the world in her breath
Breathes, and is born at her birth;
　　For they knew thee for mother of love,
　　　　And knew thee not mother of death.

What hadst thou to do being born,
　　Mother, when winds were at ease,
As a flower of the springtime of corn,
　　A flower of the foam of the seas?
For bitter thou wast from thy birth,
　　Aphrodite, a mother of strife;
For before thee some rest was on earth,
　　A little respite from tears,
　　A little pleasure of life;
For life was not then as thou art,
　　　　But as one that waxeth in years
　　Sweet-spoken, a fruitful wife;
　　Earth had no thorn, and desire
No sting, neither death any dart;
　　What hadst thou to do amongst these,
　　　　Thou, clothed with a burning fire,
Thou, girt with sorrow of heart,
　　Thou, sprung of the seed of the seas
As an ear from a seed of corn,
　　As a brand plucked forth of a pyre,
As a ray shed forth of the morn,
　　For division of soul and disease,
For a dart and a sting and a thorn?
What ailed thee then to be born?

Was there not evil enough,
　　Mother, and anguish on earth
　　Born with a man at his birth,

Wastes underfoot, and above
  Storm out of heaven, and dearth
Shaken down from the shining thereof,
    Wrecks from afar overseas
  And peril of shallow and firth,
    And tears that spring and increase
  In the barren places of mirth,
That thou, having wings as a dove,
  Being girt with desire for a girth,
    That thou must come after these,
That thou must lay on him love?

Thou shouldst not so have been born:
  But death should have risen with thee,
    Mother, and visible fear,
      Grief, and the wringing of hands,
And noise of many that mourn;
  The smitten bosom, the knee
    Bowed, and in each man's ear
      A cry as of perishing lands,
A moan as of people in prison,
  A tumult of infinite griefs;
    And thunder of storm on the sands,
    And wailing of wives on the shore;
And under thee newly arisen
  Loud shoals and shipwrecking reefs,
    Fierce air and violent light;
    Sail rent and sundering oar,
      Darkness, and noises of night;
Clashing of streams in the sea,
  Wave against wave as a sword,
    Clamour of currents, and foam;
      Rains making ruin on earth,
    Winds that wax ravenous and roam
  As wolves in a wolfish horde;

Fruits growing faint in the tree,
     And blind things dead in their birth;
   Famine, and blighting of corn,
   When thy time was come to be born.

All these we know of; but thee
   Who shall discern or declare?
In the uttermost ends of the sea
   The light of thine eyelids and hair,
     The light of thy bosom as fire
       Between the wheel of the sun
   And the flying flames of the air?
     Wilt thou turn thee not yet nor have pity,
But abide with despair and desire
   And the crying of armies undone,
     Lamentation of one with another
     And breaking of city by city;
   The dividing of friend against friend,
     The severing of brother and brother;
   Wilt thou utterly bring to an end?
     Have mercy, mother!

For against all men from of old
   Thou hast set thine hand as a curse,
     And cast out gods from their places.
     These things are spoken of thee.
Strong kings and goodly with gold
   Thou hast found out arrows to pierce,
     And made their kingdoms and races
     As dust and surf of the sea.
All these, overburdened with woes
   And with length of their days waxen weak,
     Thou slewest; and sentest moreover
       Upon Tyro an evil thing,
Rent hair and a fetter and blows

Making bloody the flower of the cheek,
   Though she lay by a god as a lover,
      Though fair, and the seed of a king.

For of old, being full of thy fire,
   She endured not longer to wear
      On her bosom a saffron vest,
         On her shoulder an ashwood quiver;
Being mixed and made one through desire
   With Enipeus, and all her hair
      Made moist with his mouth, and her breast
      Filled full of the foam of the river.

ATALANTA

Sun, and clear light among green hills, and day
Late risen and long sought after, and you just gods
Whose hands divide anguish and recompense,
But first the sun's white sister, a maid in heaven,
On earth of all maids worshipped—hail, and hear,
And witness with me if not without sign sent,
Not without rule and reverence, I a maid
Hallowed, and huntress holy as whom I serve,
Here in your sight and eyeshot of these men
Stand, girt as they toward hunting, and my shafts
Drawn; wherefore all ye stand up on my side,
If I be pure and all ye righteous gods,
Lest one revile me, a woman, yet no wife,
That bear a spear for spindle, and this bow strung
For a web woven; and with pure lips salute
Heaven, and the face of all the gods, and dawn
Filling with maiden flames and maiden flowers
The starless fold o' the stars, and making sweet
The warm wan heights of the air, moon-trodden ways
And breathless gates and extreme hills of heaven.
Whom, having offered water and bloodless gifts,

Flowers, and a golden circlet of pure hair,
Next Artemis I bid be favourable
And make this day all golden, hers and ours,
Gracious and good and white to the unblamed end.
But thou, O well-beloved, of all my days
Bid it be fruitful, and a crown for all,
To bring forth leaves and bind round all my hair
With perfect chaplets woven for thine of thee.
For not without the word of thy chaste mouth,
For not without law given and clean command,
Across the white straits of the running sea
From Elis even to the Acheloïan horn,
I with clear winds came hither and gentle gods,
Far off my father's house, and left uncheered
Iasius, and uncheered the Arcadian hills
And all their green-haired waters, and all woods
Disconsolate, to hear no horn of mine
Blown, and behold no flash of swift white feet.

MELEAGER

For thy name's sake and awe toward thy chaste head,
O holiest Atalanta, no man dares
Praise thee, though fairer than whom all men praise,
And godlike for thy grace of hallowed hair
And holy habit of thine eyes, and feet
That make the blown foam neither swift nor white
Though the wind winnow and whirl it; yet we praise
Gods, found because of thee adorable
And for thy sake praiseworthiest from all men:
Thee therefore we praise also, thee as these,
Pure, and a light lit at the hands of gods.

TOXEUS

How long will ye whet spears with eloquence,

Fight, and kill beasts dry-handed with sweet words?
Cease, or talk still and slay thy boars at home.

PLEXIPPUS

Why, if she ride among us for a man,
Sit thou for her and spin; a man grown girl
Is worth a woman weaponed; sit thou here.

MELEAGER

Peace, and be wise; no gods love idle speech.

PLEXIPPUS

Nor any man a man's mouth woman-tongued.

MELEAGER

For my lips bite not sharper than mine hands.

PLEXIPPUS

Nay, both bite soft, but no whit softly mine.

MELEAGER

Keep thine hands clean; they have time enough to stain.

PLEXIPPUS

For thine shall rest and wax not red to-day.

MELEAGER

Have all thy will of words; talk out thine heart.

ALTHAEA

Refrain your lips, O brethren, and my son,
Lest words turn snakes and bite you uttering them.

Except she give her blood before the gods,
What profit shall a maid be among men?

PLEXIPPUS

Let her come crowned and stretch her throat for a knife,
Bleat out her spirit and die, and so shall men
Through her too prosper and through prosperous gods,
But nowise through her living; shall she live
A flower-bud of the flower-bed, or sweet fruit
For kisses and the honey-making mouth,
And play the shield for strong men and the spear?
Then shall the heifer and her mate lock horns,
And the bride overbear the groom, and men
Gods; for no less division sunders these;
Since all things made are seasonable in time,
But if one alter unseasonable are all.
But thou, O Zeus, hear me that I may slay
This beast before thee and no man halve with me
Nor woman, lest these mock thee, though a god,
Who hast made men strong, and thou being wise be held
Foolish; for wise is that thing which endures.

ATALANTA

Men, and the chosen of all this people, and thou,
King, I beseech you a little bear with me.
For if my life be shameful that I live,
Let the gods witness and their wrath; but these
Cast no such word against me. Thou, O mine,
O holy, O happy goddess, if I sin
Changing the words of women and the works
For spears and strange men's faces, hast not thou
One shaft of all thy sudden seven that pierced
Seven through the bosom or shining throat or side,

All couched about one mother's loosening knees,
All holy born, engraffed of Tantalus?
But if toward any of you I am overbold
That take thus much upon me, let him think
How I, for all my forest holiness,
Fame, and this armed and iron maidenhood,
Pay thus much also; I shall have no man's love
For ever, and no face of children born
Or feeding lips upon me or fastening eyes
For ever, nor being dead shall kings my sons
Mourn me and bury, and tears on daughters' cheeks
Burn; but a cold and sacred life, but strange,
But far from dances and the back-blowing torch,
Far off from flowers or any bed of man,
Shall my life be for ever: me the snows
That face the first o' the morning, and cold hills
Full of the land-wind and sea-travelling storms
And many a wandering wing of noisy nights
That know the thunder and hear the thickening wolves—
Me the utmost pine and footless frost of woods
That talk with many winds and gods, the hours
Re-risen, and white divisions of the dawn,
Springs thousand-tongued with the intermitting reed
And streams that murmur of the mother snow—
Me these allure, and know me; but no man
Knows, and my goddess only. Lo now, see
If one of all you these things vex at all.
Would God that any of you had all the praise
And I no manner of memory when I die,
So might I show before her perfect eyes
Pure, whom I follow, a maiden to my death.
But for the rest let all have all they will;
For is it a grief to you that I have part,
Being woman merely, in your male might and deeds
Done by main strength? yet in my body is throned

As great a heart, and in my spirit, O men,
I have not less of godlike.   Evil it were
That one a coward should mix with you, one hand
Fearful, one eye abase itself; and these
Well might ye hate and well revile, not me.
For not the difference of the several flesh
Being vile or noble or beautiful or base
Makes praiseworthy, but purer spirit and heart
Higher than these meaner mouths and limbs, that feed,
Rise, rest, and are and are not; and for me,
What should I say? but by the gods of the world
And this my maiden body, by all oaths
That bind the tongue of men and the evil will,
I am not mighty-minded, nor desire
Crowns, nor the spoil of slain things nor the fame;
Feed ye on these, eat and wax fat; cry out,
Laugh, having eaten, and leap without a lyre,
Sing, mix the wind with clamour, smite and shake
Sonorous timbrels and tumultuous hair,
And fill the dance up with tempestuous feet,
For I will none; but having prayed my prayers
And made thank-offering for prosperities,
I shall go hence and no man see me more.
What thing is this for you to shout me down,
What, for a man to grudge me this my life
As it were envious of all yours, and I
A thief of reputations? nay, for now,
If there be any highest in heaven, a god
Above all thrones and thunders of the gods
Throned, and the wheel of the world roll under him,
Judge he between me and all of you, and see
If I trangress at all: but ye, refrain
Transgressing hands and reinless mouths, and keep
Silence, lest by much foam of violent words
And proper poison of your lips ye die.

OENEUS

O flower of Tegea, maiden, fleetest foot
And holiest head of women, have good cheer
Of thy good words: but ye, depart with her
In peace and reverence, each with blameless eye
Following his fate; exalt your hands and hearts,
Strike, cease not, arrow on arrow and wound on wound,
And go with gods and with the gods return.

CHORUS

Who hath given man speech? or who hath set therein
A thorn for peril and a snare for sin?
For in the word his life is and his breath,
    And in the word his death,
That madness and the infatuate heart may breed
    From the word's womb the deed
And life bring one thing forth ere all pass by,
Even one thing which is ours yet cannot die—
Death. Hast thou seen him ever anywhere,
Time's twin-born brother, imperishable as he
Is perishable and plaintive, clothed with care
    And mutable as sand,
But death is strong and full of blood and fair
And perdurable and like a lord of land?
Nay, time thou seest not, death thou wilt not see
Till life's right hand be loosened from thine hand
    And thy life-days from thee.

For the gods very subtly fashion
    Madness with sadness upon earth:
Not knowing in any wise compassion,
    Nor holding pity of any worth;

And many things they have given and taken,
  And wrought and ruined many things;
The firm land have they loosed and shaken,
  And sealed the sea with all her springs;
They have wearied time with heavy burdens
  And vexed the lips of life with breath:
Set men to labour and given them guerdons,
  Death, and great darkness after death:
Put moans into the bridal measure
  And on the bridal wools a stain;
And circled pain about with pleasure,
  And girdled pleasure about with pain;
And strewed one marriage-bed with tears and fire
For extreme loathing and supreme desire.

What shall be done with all these tears of ours?
  Shall they make watersprings in the fair heaven
To bathe the brows of morning? or like flowers
Be shed and shine before the starriest hours,
  Or made the raiment of the weeping Seven?
Or rather, O our masters, shall they be
Food for the famine of the grievous sea,
  A great well-head of lamentation
Satiating the sad gods? or fall and flow
Among the years and seasons to and fro,
  And wash their feet with tribulation
And fill them full with grieving ere they go?
  Alas, our lords, and yet alas again,
Seeing all your iron heaven is gilt as gold
  But all we smite thereat in vain;
Smite the gates barred with groanings manifold,
  But all the floors are paven with our pain.
Yea, and with weariness of lips and eyes,
  With breaking of the bosom, and with sighs,
    We labour, and are clad and fed with grief

And filled with days we would not fain behold
And nights we would not hear of; we wax old,
  All we wax old and wither like a leaf.
We are outcast, strayed between bright sun and moon;
  Our light and darkness are as leaves of flowers,
Black flowers and white, that perish; and the noon
  As midnight, and the night as daylight hours.
  A little fruit a little while is ours,
    And the worm finds it soon.

But up in heaven the high gods one by one
  Lay hands upon the draught that quickeneth,
Fulfilled with all tears shed and all things done,
  And stir with soft imperishable breath
  The bubbling bitterness of life and death,
And hold it to our lips and laugh; but they
Preserve their lips from tasting night or day,
  Lest they too change and sleep, the fates that spun,
The lips that made us and the hands that slay;
  Lest all these change, and heaven bow down to none,
Change and be subject to the secular sway
  And terrene revolution of the sun.
Therefore they thrust it from them, putting time away.

I would the wine of time, made sharp and sweet
  With multitudinous days and nights and tears
  And many mixing savours of strange years,
Were no more trodden of them under feet,
  Cast out and spilt about their holy places:
That life were given them as a fruit to eat
And death to drink as water; that the light
Might ebb, drawn backward from their eyes, and night
  Hide for one hour the imperishable faces.
That they might rise up sad in heaven, and know

Sorrow and sleep, one paler than young snow,
    One cold as blight of dew and ruinous rain;
Rise up and rest and suffer a little, and be
Awhile as all things born with us and we,
    And grieve as men, and like slain men be slain.

For now we know not of them; but one saith
    The gods are gracious, praising God; and one,
When hast thou seen? or hast thou felt his breath
    Touch, nor consume thine eyelids as the sun,
Nor fill thee to the lips with fiery death?
    None hath beheld him, none
Seen above other gods and shapes of things,
Swift without feet and flying without wings,
Intolerable, not clad with death or life,
    Insatiable, not known of night or day,
The lord of love and loathing and of strife
    Who gives a star and takes a sun away;
Who shapes the soul, and makes her a barren wife
    To the earthly body and grievous growth of clay;
Who turns the large limbs to a little flame
    And binds the great sea with a little sand;
Who makes desire, and slays desire with shame;
    Who shakes the heaven as ashes in his hand;
Who, seeing the light and shadow for the same,
    Bids day waste night as fire devours a brand,
Smites without sword, and scourges without rod;
    The supreme evil, God.
Yea, with thine hate, O God, thou hast covered us,
    One saith, and hidden our eyes away from sight,
And made us transitory and hazardous,
    Light things and slight;
Yet have men praised thee, saying, He hath made man
    thus,
    And he doeth right.

Thou hast kissed us, and hast smitten; thou hast laid
Upon us with thy left hand life, and said,
Live: and again thou hast said, Yield up your breath,
And with thy right hand laid upon us death.
Thou hast sent us sleep, and stricken sleep with dreams,
　　Saying, Joy is not, but love of joy shall be;
Thou hast made sweet springs for all the pleasant streams,
　　In the end thou hast made them bitter with the sea.
Thou hast fed one rose with dust of many men;
　　Thou hast marred one face with fire of many tears;
Thou hast taken love, and given us sorrow again;
　　With pain thou hast filled us full to the eyes and ears.
Therefore because thou art strong, our father, and we
　　Feeble; and thou art against us, and thine hand
Constrains us in the shallows of the sea
　　And breaks us at the limits of the land;
Because thou hast bent thy lightnings as a bow,
　　And loosed the hours like arrows; and let fall
Sins and wild words and many a wingèd woe
　　And wars among us, and one end of all;
Because thou hast made the thunder, and thy feet
　　Are as a rushing water when the skies
Break, but thy face as an exceeding heat
　　And flames of fire the eyelids of thine eyes;
Because thou art over all who are over us;
　　Because thy name is life and our name death;
Because thou art cruel and men are piteous,
　　And our hands labour and thine hand scattereth;
Lo, with hearts rent and knees made tremulous,
　　Lo, with ephemeral lips and casual breath,
　　　At least we witness of thee ere we die
That these things are not otherwise, but thus;
　　That each man in his heart sigheth, and saith,
　　　That all men even as I,
All we are against thee, against thee, O God most high.

But ye, keep ye on earth
    Your lips from over‑speech,
Loud words and longing are so little worth;
    And the end is hard to reach.
For silence after grievous things is good,
    And reverence, and the fear that makes men whole,
And shame, and righteous governance of blood,
    And lordship of the soul.
But from sharp words and wits men pluck no fruit,
And gathering thorns they shake the tree at root;
For words divide and rend;
But silence is most noble till the end.

ALTHAEA

I heard within the house a cry of news
And came forth eastward hither, where the dawn
Cheers first these warder gods that face the sun
And next our eyes unrisen; for unaware
Came clashes of swift hoofs and trampling feet
And through the windy pillared corridor
Light sharper than the frequent flames of day
That daily fill it from the fiery dawn;
Gleams, and a thunder of people that cried out,
And dust and hurrying horsemen; lo their chief,
That rode with Oeneus rein by rein, returned.
What cheer, O herald of my lord the king?

HERALD

Lady, good cheer and great; the boar is slain.

CHORUS

Praised be all gods that look toward Calydon.

ALTHAEA

Good news and brief; but by whose happier hand?

HERALD

A maiden's and a prophet's and thy son's.

ALTHAEA

Well fare the spear that severed him and life.

HERALD

Thine own, and not an alien, hast thou blest.

ALTHAEA

Twice be thou too for my sake blest and his.

HERALD

At the king's word I rode afoam for thine.

ALTHAEA

Thou sayest he tarrieth till they bring the spoil?

HERALD

Hard by the quarry, where they breathe, O queen.

ALTHAEA

Speak thou their chance; but some bring flowers and
    crown
These gods and all the lintel, and shed wine,
Fetch sacrifice and slay; for heaven is good.

HERALD

Some furlongs northward where the brakes begin
West of that narrowing range of warrior hills
Whose brooks have bled with battle when thy son
Smote Acarnania, there all they made halt,
And with keen eye took note of spear and hound,
Royally ranked; Laertes island-born,

The young Gerenian Nestor, Panopeus,
And Cepheus and Ancaeus, mightiest thewed,
Arcadians; next, and evil-eyed of these,
Arcadian Atalanta, with twain hounds
Lengthening the leash, and under nose and brow
Glittering with lipless tooth and fire-swift eye;
But from her white braced shoulder the plumed shafts
Rang, and the bow shone from her side; next her
Meleager, like a sun in spring that strikes
Branch into leaf and bloom into the world,
A glory among men meaner; Iphicles,
And following him that slew the biform bull
Pirithous, and divine Eurytion,
And, bride-bound to the gods, Aeacides.
Then Telamon his brother, and Argive-born
The seer and sayer of visions and of truth,
Amphiaraus; and a four-fold strength,
Thine, even thy mother's and thy sister's sons.
And recent from the roar of foreign foam
Jason, and Dryas twin-begot with war,
A blossom of bright battle, sword and man
Shining; and Idas, and the keenest eye
Of Lynceus, and Admetus twice-espoused,
And Hippasus and Hyleus, great in heart.
These having halted bade blow horns, and rode
Through woods and waste lands cleft by stormy streams,
Past yew-trees and the heavy hair of pines,
And where the dew is thickest under oaks,
This way and that; but questing up and down
They saw no trail nor scented; and one said,
Plexippus, Help, or help not, Artemis,
And we will flay thy boarskin with male hands;
But saying, he ceased and said not that he would,
Seeing where the green ooze of a sun-struck marsh
Shook with a thousand reeds untunable,

And in their moist and multitudinous flower
Slept no soft sleep, with violent visions fed,
The blind bulk of the immeasurable beast.
And seeing, he shuddered with sharp lust of praise
Through all his limbs, and launched a double dart.
And missed; for much desire divided him,
Too hot of spirit and feebler than his will,
That his hand failed, though fervent; and the shaft,
Sundering the rushes, in a tamarisk stem
Shook, and stuck fast; then all abode save one,
The Arcadian Atalanta; from her side
Sprang her hounds, labouring at the leash, and slipped,
And plashed ear-deep with plunging feet; but she
Saying, Speed it as I send it for thy sake,
Goddess, drew bow and loosed; the sudden string
Rang, and sprang inward, and the waterish air
Hissed, and the moist plumes of the songless reeds
Moved as a wave which the wind moves no more.
But the boar heaved half out of ooze and slime
His tense flank trembling round the barbèd wound,
Hateful; and fiery with invasive eyes
And bristling with intolerable hair
Plunged, and the hounds clung, and green flowers and
white
Reddened and broke all round them where they came.
And charging with sheer tusk he drove, and smote
Hyleus; and sharp death caught his sudden soul,
And violent sleep shed night upon his eyes.
Then Peleus, with strong strain of hand and heart,
Shot; but the sidelong arrow slid, and slew
His comrade born and loving countryman,
Under the left arm smitten, as he no less
Poised a like arrow; and bright blood brake afoam,
And falling, and weighed back by clamorous arms,
Sharp rang the dead limbs of Eurytion.

.Then one shot happier, the Cadmean seer,
Amphiaraus; for his sacred shaft
Pierced the red circlet of one ravening eye
Beneath the brute brows of the sanguine boar,
Now bloodier from one slain; but he so galled
Sprang straight, and rearing cried no lesser cry
Than thunder and the roar of wintering streams
That mix their own foam with the yellower sea;
And as a tower that falls by fire in fight
With ruin of walls and all its archery,
And breaks the iron flower of war beneath,
Crushing charred limbs and molten arms of men;
So through crushed branches and the reddening brake
Clamoured and crushed the fervour of his feet,
And trampled, springing sideways from the tusk,
Too tardy a moving mould of heavy strength,
Ancaeus; and as flakes of weak-winged snow
Break, all the hard thews of his heaving limbs
Broke, and rent flesh fell every way, and blood
Flew, and fierce fragments of no more a man.
Then all the heroes drew sharp breath, and gazed,
And smote not; but Meleager, but thy son,
Right in the wild way of the coming curse
Rock-rooted, fair with fierce and fastened lips,
Clear eyes, and springing muscle and shortening limb—
With chin aslant indrawn to a tightening throat,
Grave, and with gathered sinews, like a god,—
Aimed on the left side his well-handled spear
Grasped where the ash was knottiest hewn, and smote,
And with no missile wound, the monstrous boar
Right in the hairiest hollow of his hide
Under the last rib, sheer through bulk and bone,
Deep in; and deeply smitten, and to death,
The heavy horror with his hanging shafts
Leapt, and fell furiously, and from raging lips

Foamed out the latest wrath of all his life.
And all they praised the gods with mightier heart,
Zeus and all gods, but chiefliest Artemis,
Seeing; but Meleager bade whet knives and flay,
Strip and stretch out the splendour of the spoil;
And hot and horrid from the work all these
Sat, and drew breath and drank and made great cheer
And washed the hard sweat off their calmer brows.
For much sweet grass grew higher than grew the reed,
And good for slumber, and every holier herb,
Narcissus, and the low-lying melilote,
And all of goodliest blade and bloom that springs
Where, hid by heavier hyacinth, violet buds
Blossom and burn; and fire of yellower flowers
And light of crescent lilies, and such leaves
As fear the Faun's and know the Dryad's foot;
Olive and ivy and poplar dedicate,
And many a well-spring overwatched of these.
There now they rest; but me the king bade bear
Good tidings to rejoice this town and thee.
Wherefore be glad, and all ye give much thanks,
For fallen is all the trouble of Calydon.

ALTHAEA

Laud ye the gods; for this they have given is good,
And what shall be they hide until their time.
Much good and somewhat grievous hast thou said,
And either well; but let all sad things be,
Till all have made before the prosperous gods
Burnt-offering, and poured out the floral wine.
Look fair, O gods, and favourable; for we
Praise you with no false heart or flattering mouth,
Being merciful, but with pure souls and prayer.

Thou hast prayed well; for whoso fears not these,
But once being prosperous waxes huge of heart,
Him shall some new thing unaware destroy.

O that I now, I too were
By deep wells and water-floods,
Streams of ancient hills, and where
All the wan green places bear
Blossoms cleaving to the sod,
Fruitless fruit, and grasses fair,
Or such darkest ivy-buds
As divide thy yellow hair,
Bacchus, and their leaves that nod
Round thy fawnskin brush the bare
Snow-soft shoulders of a god;
There the year is sweet, and there
Earth is full of secret springs,
And the fervent rose-cheeked hours,
Those that marry dawn and noon,
There are sunless, there look pale
In dim leaves and hidden air,
Pale as grass or latter flowers
Or the wild vine's wan wet rings
Full of dew beneath the moon,
And all day the nightingale
Sleeps, and all night sings;
There in cold remote recesses
That nor alien eyes assail,
Feet, nor imminence of wings,
Nor a wind nor any tune,
Thou, O queen and holiest,
Flower the whitest of all things,
With reluctant lengthening tresses

And with sudden splendid breast
Save of maidens unbeholden,
There art wont to enter, there
Thy divine swift limbs and golden
Maiden growth of unbound hair,
Bathed in waters white,
Shine, and many a maid's by thee
In moist woodland or the hilly
Flowerless brakes where wells abound
Out of all men's sight;
Or in lower pools that see
All their marges clothed all round
With the innumerable lily,
Whence the golden-girdled bee
Flits through flowering rush to fret
White or duskier violet,
Fair as those that in far years
With their buds left luminous
And their little leaves made wet,
From the warmer dew of tears,
Mother's tears in extreme need,
Hid the limbs of Iamus,
Of thy brother's seed;
For his heart was piteous
Toward him, even as thine heart now
Pitiful toward us;
Thine, O goddess, turning hither
A benignant blameless brow;
Seeing enough of evil done
And lives withered as leaves wither
In the blasting of the sun;
Seeing enough of hunters dead,
Ruin enough of all our year,
Herds and harvests slain and shed,
Herdsmen stricken many an one,

Fruits and flocks consumed together,
And great length of deadly days.
Yet with reverent lips and fear
Turn we toward thee, turn and praise
For this lightening of clear weather
And prosperities begun.
For not seldom, when all air
As bright water without breath
Shines, and when men fear not, fate
Without thunder unaware
Breaks, and brings down death.
Joy with grief ye great gods give,
Good with bad, and overbear
All the pride of us that live,
All the high estate,
As ye long since overbore,
As in old time long before,
Many a strong man and a great,
All that were.
But do thou, sweet, otherwise,
Having heed of all our prayer,
Taking note of all our sighs;
We beseech thee by thy light,
By thy bow, and thy sweet eyes,
And the kingdom of the night,
Be thou favourable and fair;
By thine arrows and thy might
And Orion overthrown;
By the maiden thy delight,
By the indissoluble zone
And the sacred hair.

MESSENGER

Maidens, if ye will sing now, shift your song,
Bow down, cry, wail for pity; is this a time

For singing? nay, for strewing of dust and ash,
Rent raiment, and for bruising of the breast.

CHORUS

What new thing wolf-like lurks behind thy words?
What snake's tongue in thy lips? what fire in the eyes?

MESSENGER

Bring me before the queen and I will speak.

CHORUS

Lo, she comes forth as from thank-offering made.

MESSENGER

A barren offering for a bitter gift.

ALTHAEA

What are these borne on branches, and the face
Covered? no mean men living, but now slain
Such honour have they, if any dwell with death.

MESSENGER

Queen, thy twain brethren and thy mother's sons.

ALTHAEA

Lay down your dead till I behold their blood
If it be mine indeed, and I will weep.

MESSENGER

Weep if thou wilt, for these men shall no more.

ALTHAEA

O brethren, O my father's sons, of me
Well loved and well reputed, I should weep

Tears dearer than the dear blood drawn from you
But that I know you not uncomforted,
Sleeping no shameful sleep, however slain,
For my son surely hath avenged you dead.

MESSENGER

Nay, should thine own seed slay himself, O queen?

ALTHAEA

Thy double word brings forth a double death.

MESSENGER

Know this then singly, by one hand they fell.

ALTHAEA

What mutterest thou with thine ambiguous mouth?

MESSENGER

Slain by thy son's hand; is that saying so hard?

ALTHAEA

Our time is come upon us: it is here.

CHORUS

O miserable, and spoiled at thine own hand.

ALTHAEA

Wert thou not called Meleager from this womb?

CHORUS

A grievous huntsman hath it bred to thee.

ALTHAEA

Wert thou born fire, and shalt thou not devour?

CHORUS

The fire thou madest, will it consume even thee?

ALTHAEA

My dreams are fallen upon me; burn thou too.

CHORUS

Not without God are visions born and die.

ALTHAEA

The gods are many about me; I am one.

CHORUS

She groans as men wrestling with heavier gods.

ALTHAEA

They rend me, they divide me, they destroy.

CHORUS

Or one labouring in travail of strange births.

ALTHAEA

They are strong, they are strong; I am broken, and these
    prevail.

CHORUS

The god is great against her; she will die.

ALTHAEA

Yea, but not now; for my heart too is great.
I would I were not here in sight of the sun.
But thou, speak all thou sawest, and I will die.

O queen, for queenlike hast thou borne thyself,
A little word may hold so great mischance.
For in division of the sanguine spoil
These men thy brethren wrangling bade yield up
The boar's head and the horror of the hide
That this might stand a wonder in Calydon,
Hallowed; and some drew toward them; but thy son
With great hands grasping all that weight of hair
Cast down the dead heap clanging and collapsed
At female feet, saying This thy spoil not mine,
Maiden, thine own hand for thyself hath reaped,
And all this praise God gives thee: she thereat
Laughed, as when dawn touches the sacred night
The sky sees laugh and redden and divide
Dim lips and eyelids virgin of the sun,
Hers, and the warm slow breasts of morning heave,
Fruitful, and flushed with flame from lamp-lit hours,
And maiden undulation of clear hair
Colour the clouds; so laughed she from pure heart,
Lit with a low blush to the braided hair,
And rose-coloured and cold like very dawn,
Golden and godlike, chastely with chaste lips,
A faint grave laugh; and all they held their peace,
And she passed by them. Then one cried Lo now,
Shall not the Arcadian shoot out lips at us,
Saying all we were despoiled by this one girl?
And all they rode against her violently
And cast the fresh crown from her hair, and now
They had rent her spoil away, dishonouring her,
Save that Meleager, as a tame lion chafed,
Bore on them, broke them, and as fire cleaves wood
So clove and drove them, smitten in twain; but she
Smote not nor heaved up hand; and this man first,
Plexippus, crying out This for love's sake, sweet,

Drove at Meleager, who with spear straightening
Pierced his cheek through; then Toxeus made for him,
Dumb, but his spear spake; vain and violent words.
Fruitless; for him too stricken through both sides
The earth felt falling, and his horse's foam
Blanched thy son's face, his slayer; and these being slain,
None moved nor spake; but Oeneus bade bear hence
These made of heaven infatuate in their deaths,
Foolish; for these would baffle fate, and fell.
And they passed on, and all men honoured her,
Being honourable, as one revered of heaven.

ALTHAEA

What say you, women? is all this not well done?

CHORUS

No man doth well but God hath part in him.

ALTHAEA

But no part here; for these my brethren born
Ye have no part in, these ye know not of
As I that was their sister, a sacrifice
Slain in their slaying.   I would I had died for these;
For this man dead walked with me, child by child,
And made a weak staff for my feebler feet
With his own tender wrist and hand, and held
And led me softly and showed me gold and steel
And shining shapes of mirror and bright crown
And all things fair; and threw light spears, and brought
Young hounds to huddle at my feet and thrust
Tame heads against my little maiden breasts
And please me with great eyes; and those days went
And these are bitter and I a barren queen
And sister miserable, a grievous thing

147

And mother of many curses; and she too,
My sister Leda, sitting overseas
With fair fruits round her, and her faultless lord,
Shall curse me, saying A sorrow and not a son,
Sister, thou barest, even a burning fire,
A brand consuming thine own soul and me.
But ye now, sons of Thestius, make good cheer,
For ye shall have such wood to funeral fire
As no king hath; and flame that once burnt down
Oil shall not quicken or breath relume or wine
Refresh again; much costlier than fine gold,
And more than many lives of wandering men.

CHORUS

O queen, thou hast yet with thee love-worthy things,
Thine husband, and the great strength of thy son.

ALTHAEA

Who shall get brothers for me while I live?
Who bear them? who bring forth in lieu of these?
Are not our fathers and our brethren one,
And no man like them? are not mine here slain?
Have we not hung together, he and I,
Flowerwise feeding as the feeding bees,
With mother-milk for honey? and this man too,
Dead, with my son's spear thrust between his sides,
Hath he not seen us, later born than he,
Laugh with lips filled, and laughed again for love?
There were no sons then in the world, nor spears,
Nor deadly births of women; but the gods
Allowed us, and our days were clear of these.
I would I had died unwedded, and brought forth
No swords to vex the world; for these that spake
Sweet words long since and loved me will not speak
Nor love nor look upon me; and all my life

I shall not hear nor see them living men.
But I too living, how shall I now live?
What life shall this be with my son, to know
What hath been and desire what will not be,
Look for dead eyes and listen for dead lips,
And kill mine own heart with remembering them,
And with those eyes that see their slayer alive
Weep, and wring hands that clasp him by the hand?
How shall I bear my dreams of them, to hear
False voices, feel the kisses of false mouths
And footless sound of perished feet, and then
Wake and hear only it may be their own hounds
Whine masterless in miserable sleep,
And see their boar-spears and their beds and seats
And all the gear and housings of their lives
And not the men? shall hounds and horses mourn,
Pine with strange eyes, and prick up hungry ears,
Famish and fail at heart for their dear lords,
And I not heed at all? and those blind things
Fall off from life for love's sake, and I live?
Surely some death is better than some life,
Better one death for him and these and me.
For if the gods had slain them it may be
I had endured it; if they had fallen by war
Or by the nets and knives of privy death
And by hired hands while sleeping, this thing too
I had set my soul to suffer; or this hunt,
Had this dispatched them, under tusk or tooth
Torn, sanguine, trodden, broken; for all deaths
Or honourable or with facile feet avenged
And hands of swift gods following, all save this,
Are bearable; but not for their sweet land
Fighting, but not a sacrifice, lo these
Dead; for I had not then shed all mine heart
Out at mine eyes: then either with good speed,

Being just, I had slain their slayer atoningly,
Or strewn with flowers their fire and on their tombs
Hung crowns, and over them a song, and seen
Their praise outflame their ashes: for all men,
All maidens, had come thither, and from pure lips
Shed songs upon them, from heroic eyes
Tears; and their death had been a deathless life;
But now, by no man hired nor alien sword,
By their own kindred are they fallen, in peace,
After much peril, friendless among friends,
By hateful hands they loved: and how shall mine
Touch these returning red and not from war,
These fatal from the vintage of men's veins,
Dead men my brethren? how shall these wash off
No festal stains of undelightful wine,
How mix the blood, my blood on them, with me,
Holding mine hand? or how shall I say, son,
That am no sister? but by night and day
Shall we not sit and hate each other, and think
Things hate-worthy? not live with shamefast eyes,
Brow-beaten, treading soft with fearful feet,
Each unupbraided, each without rebuke
Convicted, and without a word reviled
Each of another? and I shall let thee live
And see thee strong and hear men for thy sake
Praise me, but these thou wouldest not let live
No man shall praise for ever? these shall lie
Dead, unbeloved, unholpen, all through thee?
Sweet were they toward me living, and mine heart
Desired them, but was then well satisfied,
That now is as men hungered; and these dead
I shall want always to the day I die.
For all things else and all men may renew;
Yea, son for son the gods may give and take,
But never a brother or sister any more.

Nay, for the son lies close about thine heart,
Full of thy milk, warm from thy womb, and drains
Life and the blood of life and all thy fruit,
Eats thee and drinks thee as who breaks bread and eats,
Treads wine and drinks, thyself, a sect of thee;
And if he feed not, shall not thy flesh faint?
Or drink not, are not thy lips dead for thirst?
This thing moves more than all things, even thy son,
That thou cleave to him; and he shall honour thee,
Thy womb that bare him and the breasts he knew,
Reverencing most for thy sake all his gods.

ALTHAEA

But these the gods too gave me, and these my son,
Not reverencing his gods nor mine own heart
Nor the old sweet years nor all venerable things,
But cruel, and in his ravin like a beast,
Hath taken away to slay them: yea, and she,
She the strange woman, she the flower, the sword,
Red from spilt blood, a mortal flower to men,
Adorable, detestable—even she
Saw with strange eyes and with strange lips rejoiced,
Seeing these mine own slain of mine own, and me
Made miserable above all miseries made,
A grief among all women in the world,
A name to be washed out with all men's tears.

CHORUS

Strengthen thy spirit; is this not also a god,
Chance, and the wheel of all necessities?
Hard things have fallen upon us from harsh gods,
Whom lest worse hap rebuke we not for these.

My spirit is strong against itself, and I
For these things' sake cry out on mine own soul
That it endures outrage, and dolorous days,
And life, and this inexpiable impotence.
Weak am I, weak and shameful; my breath drawn
Shames me, and monstrous things and violent gods.
What shall atone? what heal me? what bring back
Strength to the foot, light to the face? what herb
Assuage me? what restore me? what release?
What strange thing eaten or drunken, O great gods,
Make me as you or as the beasts that feed,
Slay and divide and cherish their own hearts?
For these ye show us; and we less than these
Have not wherewith to live as all these things
Which all their lives fare after their own kind
As who doth well rejoicing; but we ill,
Weeping or laughing, we whom eyesight fails,
Knowledge and light of face and perfect heart,
And hands we lack, and wit; and all our days
Sin, and have hunger, and die infatuated.
For madness have ye given us and not health,
And sins whereof we know not; and for these
Death, and sudden destruction unaware.
What shall we say now? what thing comes of us?

CHORUS

Alas, for all this all men undergo.

ALTHAEA

Wherefore I will not that these twain, O gods,
Die as a dog dies, eaten of creeping things,
Abominable, a loathing; but though dead
Shall they have honour and such funereal flame

As strews men's ashes in their enemies' face
And blinds their eyes who hate them: lest men say,
'Lo how they lie, and living had great kin,
And none of these hath pity of them, and none
Regards them lying, and none is wrung at heart,
None moved in spirit for them, naked and slain,
Abhorred, abased, and no tears comfort them':
And in the dark this grieve Eurythemis,
Hearing how these her sons come down to her
Unburied, unavenged, as kinless men,
And had a queen their sister. That were shame
Worse than this grief. Yet how to atone at all
I know not; seeing the love of my born son,
A new-made mother's new-born love, that grows
From the soft child to the strong man, now soft
Now strong as either, and still one sole same love,
Strives with me, no light thing to strive withal;
This love is deep, and natural to man's blood,
And ineffaceable with many tears.
Yet shall not these rebuke me though I die,
Nor she in that waste world with all her dead,
My mother, among the pale flocks fallen as leaves,
Folds of dead people, and alien from the sun;
Nor lack some bitter comfort, some poor praise,
Being queen, to have borne her daughter like a queen,
Righteous; and though mine own fire burn me too,
She shall have honour and these her sons, though dead.
But all the gods will, all they do, and we
Not all we would, yet somewhat; and one choice
We have, to live and do just deeds and die.

CHORUS

Terrible words she communes with, and turns
Swift fiery eyes in doubt against herself,
And murmurs as who talks in dreams with death.

For the unjust also dieth, and him all men
Hate, and himself abhors the unrighteousness,
And seeth his own dishonour intolerable.
But I being just, doing right upon myself,
Slay mine own soul, and no man born shames me.
For none constrains nor shall rebuke, being done,
What none compelled me doing; thus these things fare.
Ah, ah, that such things should so fare; ah me,
That I am found to do them and endure,
Chosen and constrained to choose, and bear myself
Mine own wound through mine own flesh to the heart
Violently stricken, a spoiler and a spoil,
A ruin ruinous, fallen on mine own son.
Ah, ah, for me too as for these; alas,
For that is done that shall be, and mine hand
Full of the deed, and full of blood mine eyes,
That shall see never nor touch anything
Save blood unstanched and fire unquenchable.

CHORUS

What wilt thou do? what ails thee? for the house
Shakes ruinously; wilt thou bring fire for it?

ALTHAEA

Fire in the roofs, and on the lintels fire.
Lo ye, who stand and weave, between the doors,
There; and blood drips from hand and thread, and stains
Threshold and raiment and me passing in
Flecked with the sudden sanguine drops of death.

CHORUS

Alas that time is stronger than strong men,
Fate than all gods: and these are fallen on us.

ALTHAEA

A little since and I was glad; and now
I never shall be glad or sad again.

CHORUS

Between two joys a grief grows unaware.

ALTHAEA

A little while and I shall laugh; and then
I shall weep never and laugh not any more.

CHORUS

What shall be said? for words are thorns to grief.
Withhold thyself a little and fear the gods.

ALTHAEA

Fear died when these were slain; and I am as dead,
And fear is of the living; these fear none.

CHORUS

Have pity upon all people for their sake.

ALTHAEA

It is done now; shall I put back my day?

CHORUS

An end is come, an end; this is of God.

ALTHAEA

I am fire, and burn myself; keep clear of fire.

CHORUS

The house is broken, is broken; it shall not stand.

Woe, woe for him that breaketh; and a rod
Smote it of old, and now the axe is here.

CHORUS

Not as with sundering of the earth
    Nor as with cleaving of the sea
Nor fierce foreshadowings of a birth
    Nor flying dreams of death to be
Nor loosening of the large world's girth
And quickening of the body of night,
    And sound of thunder in men's ears
And fire of lightning in men's sight,
    Fate, mother of desires and fears,
    Bore unto men the law of tears;
But sudden, an unfathered flame,
    And broken out of night, she shone,
She, without body, without name,
    In days forgotten and foregone;
And heaven rang round her as she came
Like smitten cymbals, and lay bare;
    Clouds and great stars, thunders and snows,
The blue sad fields and folds of air,
    The life that breathes, the life that grows,
    All wind, all fire, that burns or blows,
Even all these knew her: for she is great;
    The daughter of doom, the mother of death,
The sister of sorrow; a lifelong weight
    That no man's finger lighteneth,
    Nor any god can lighten fate;
A landmark seen across the way
    Where one race treads as the other trod;
An evil sceptre, an evil stay,
    Wrought for a staff, wrought for a rod,
    The bitter jealousy of God.

For death is deep as the sea,
    And fate as the waves thereof.
Shall the waves take pity on thee
    Or the south wind offer thee love?
Wilt thou take the night for thy day
Or the darkness for light on thy way,
    Till thou say in thine heart Enough?
Behold, thou art over fair, thou art over wise;
The sweetness of spring in thine hair, and the light in
    thine eyes.
The light of the spring in thine eyes, and the sound in
    thine ears;
Yet thine heart shall wax heavy with sighs and thine
    eyelids with tears.
Wilt thou cover thine hair with gold, and with silver thy
    feet?
Hast thou taken the purple to fold thee, and made thy
    mouth sweet?
Behold, when thy face is made bare, he that loved thee
    shall hate;
Thy face shall be no more fair at the fall of thy fate.
For thy life shall fall as a leaf and be shed as the rain,
And the veil of thine head shall be grief; and the crown
    shall be pain.

ALTHAEA

Ho, ye that wail, and ye that sing, make way
Till I be come among you.   Hide your tears,
Ye little weepers, and your laughing lips,
Ye laughers for a little; lo mine eyes
That outweep heaven at rainiest, and my mouth
That laughs as gods laugh at us.   Fate's are we,
Yet fate is ours a breathing space; yea, mine,
Fate is made mine for ever; he is my son,
My bedfellow, my brother.   You strong gods,

Give place unto me; I am as any of you,
To give life and to take life.   Thou, old earth,
That hast made man and unmade; thou whose mouth
Looks red from the eaten fruits of thine own womb;
Behold me with what lips upon what food
I feed and fill my body; even with flesh
Made of my body.   Lo, the fire I lit
I burn with fire to quench it; yea, with flame
I burn up even the dust and ash thereof.

CHORUS

Woman, what fire is this thou burnest with?

ALTHAEA

Yea to the bone, yea to the blood and all.

CHORUS

For this thy face and hair are as one fire.

ALTHAEA

A tongue that licks and beats upon the dust.

CHORUS

And in thine eyes are hollow light and heat.

ALTHAEA

Of flame not fed with hand or frankincense.

CHORUS

I fear thee for the trembling of thine eyes.

ALTHAEA

Neither with love they tremble nor for fear.

CHORUS

And thy mouth shuddering like a shot bird.

ALTHAEA

Not as the bride's mouth when man kisses it.

CHORUS

Nay, but what thing is this thing thou hast done?

ALTHAEA

Look, I am silent, speak your eyes for me.

CHORUS

I see a faint fire lightening from the hall.

ALTHAEA

Gaze, stretch your eyes, strain till the lids drop off.

CHORUS

Flushed pillars down the flickering vestibule.

ALTHAEA

Stretch with your necks like birds: cry, chirp as they.

CHORUS

And a long brand that blackens: and white dust.

ALTHAEA

O children, what is this ye see? your eyes
Are blinder than night's face at fall of moon.
That is my son, my flesh, my fruit of life,
My travail, and the year's weight of my womb,
Meleager, a fire enkindled of mine hands
And of mine hands extinguished; this is he.

O gods, what word has flown out at thy mouth?

I did this and I say this and I die.

Death stands upon the doorway of thy lips,
And in thy mouth has death set up his house.

O death, a little, a little while, sweet death,
Until I see the brand burnt down and die.

She reels as any reed under the wind,
And cleaves unto the ground with staggering feet.

Girls, one thing will I say and hold my peace.
I that did this will weep not nor cry out,
Cry ye and weep: I will not call on gods,
Call ye on them; I will not pity man,
Show ye your pity. I know not if I live;
Save that I feel the fire upon my face
And on my cheek the burning of a brand.
Yea the smoke bites me, yea I drink the steam
With nostril and with eyelid and with lip
Insatiate and intolerant; and mine hands
Burn, and fire feeds upon mine eyes; I reel
As one made drunk with living, whence he draws
Drunken delight; yet I, though mad for joy,
Loathe my long living and am waxen red
As with the shadow of shed blood; behold,
I am kindled with the flames that fade in him,

I am swollen with subsiding of his veins,
I am flooded with his ebbing; my lit eyes
Flame with the falling fire that leaves his lids
Bloodless; my cheek is luminous with blood
Because his face is ashen.   Yet, O child,
Son, first-born, fairest—O sweet mouth, sweet eyes,
That drew my life out through my suckling breast,
That shone and clove mine heart through—O soft knees
Clinging, O tender treadings of soft feet,
Cheeks warm with little kissings—O child, child,
What have we made each other?   Lo, I felt
Thy weight cleave to me, a burden of beauty, O son,
Thy cradled brows and loveliest loving lips,
The floral hair, the little lightening eyes,
And all thy goodly glory; with mine hands
Delicately I fed thee, with my tongue
Tenderly spake, saying, Verily in God's time,
For all the little likeness of thy limbs,
Son, I shall make thee a kingly man to fight,
A lordly leader; and hear before I die,
'She bore the goodliest sword of all the world.'
Oh! oh!   For all my life turns round on me;
I am severed from myself, my name is gone,
My name that was a healing, it is changed,
My name is a consuming.   From this time,
Though mine eyes reach to the end of all these things,
My lips shall not unfasten till I die.

SEMI-CHORUS

She has filled with sighing the city,
    And the ways thereof with tears;
She arose, she girdled her sides,
She set her face as a bride's;
She wept, and she had no pity;
    Trembled, and felt no fears.

Her eyes were clear as the sun,
  Her brows were fresh as the day;
She girdled herself with gold,
Her robes were manifold;
But the days of her worship are done,
  Her praise is taken away.

For she set her hand to the fire,
  With her mouth she kindled the same;
As the mouth of a flute-player,
So was the mouth of her;
With the might of her strong desire
  She blew the breath of the flame.

She set her hand to the wood,
  She took the fire in her hand;
As one who is nigh to death,
She panted with strange breath;
She opened her lips unto blood,
  She breathed and kindled the brand.

As a wood-dove newly shot,
  She sobbed and lifted her breast;
She sighed and covered her eyes,
Filling her lips with sighs;
She sighed, she withdrew herself not,
  She refrained not, taking not rest;

But as the wind which is drouth,
  And as the air which is death,

As storm that severeth ships,
Her breath severing her lips,
The breath came forth of her mouth
    And the fire came forth of her breath.

SECOND MESSENGER

Queen, and you maidens, there is come on us
A thing more deadly than the face of death;
Meleager the good lord is as one slain.

SEMI-CHORUS

Without sword, without sword is he stricken;
    Slain, and slain without hand.

SECOND MESSENGER

For as keen ice divided of the sun
His limbs divide, and as thawed snow the flesh
Thaws from off all his body to the hair.

SEMI-CHORUS

He wastes as the embers quicken;
    With the brand he fades as a brand.

SECOND MESSENGER

Even while they sang and all drew hither and he
Lifted both hands to crown the Arcadian's hair
And fix the looser leaves, both hands fell down.

SEMI-CHORUS

With rending of cheek and of hair
    Lament ye, mourn for him, weep.

SECOND MESSENGER

Straightway the crown slid off and smote on earth,
First fallen; and he, grasping his own hair, groaned
And cast his raiment round his face and fell.

Alas for visions that were,
And soothsayings spoken in sleep.

SECOND MESSENGER

But the king twitched his reins in and leapt down
And caught him, crying out twice 'O child' and thrice,
So that men's eyelids thickened with their tears.

SEMI-CHORUS

Lament with a long lamentation,
Cry, for an end is at hand.

SECOND MESSENGER

O son, he said, son, lift thine eyes, draw breath,
Pity me; but Meleager with sharp lips
Gasped, and his face waxed like as sunburnt grass.

SEMI-CHORUS

Cry aloud, O thou kingdom, O nation,
O stricken, a ruinous land.

SECOND MESSENGER

Whereat King Oeneus, straightening feeble knees,
With feeble hands heaved up a lessening weight,
And laid him sadly in strange hands, and wept.

SEMI-CHORUS

Thou art smitten, her lord, her desire,
Thy dear blood wasted as rain.

SECOND MESSENGER

And they with tears and rendings of the beard
Bear hither a breathing body, wept upon
And lightening at each footfall, sick to death.

Thou madest thy sword as a fire,
　　With fire for a sword thou art slain.

SECOND MESSENGER

And lo, the feast turned funeral, and the crowns
Fallen; and the huntress and the hunter trapped;
And weeping and changed faces and veiled hair.

MELEAGER

　　Let your hands meet
　　　Round the weight of my head;
　　Lift ye my feet
　　　As the feet of the dead;
For the flesh of my body is molten, the limbs of it molten
　　as lead.

CHORUS

　　O thy luminous face,
　　　Thine imperious eyes!
　　O the grief, O the grace,
　　　As of day when it dies!
Who is this bending over thee, lord, with tears and sup-
　　pression of sighs?

MELEAGER

　　Is a bride so fair?
　　　Is a maid so meek?
　　With unchapleted hair,
　　　With unfilleted cheek,
Atalanta, the pure among women, whose name is as
　　blessing to speak.

ATALANTA

　　I would that with feet
　　　Unsandalled, unshod,

Overbold, overfleet,
    I had swum not nor trod
From Arcadia to Calydon northward, a blast of the envy
    of God.

Unto each man his fate;
    Unto each as he saith
In whose fingers the weight
    Of the world is as breath;
Yet I would that in clamour of battle mine hands had laid
    hold upon death.

Not with cleaving of shields
    And their clash in thine ear,
When the lord of fought fields
    Breaketh spearshaft from spear,
Thou art broken, our lord, thou art broken, with travail
    and labour and fear.

Would God he had found me
    Beneath fresh boughs!
Would God he had bound me
    Unawares in mine house,
With light in mine eyes, and songs in my lips, and a crown
    on my brows!

Whence art thou sent from us?
    Whither thy goal?
How art thou rent from us,
    Thou that wert whole,
As with severing of eyelids and eyes, as with sundering of
    body and soul!

My heart is within me
    As an ash in the fire;
Whosoever hath seen me,
    Without lute, without lyre,
Shall sing of me grievous things, even things that were ill
    to desire.

CHORUS

Who shall raise thee
    From the house of the dead?
Or what man praise thee
    That thy praise may be said?
Alas thy beauty! alas thy body! alas thine head!

MELEAGER

But thou, O mother,
    The dreamer of dreams,
Wilt thou bring forth another
    To feel the sun's beams
When I move among shadows a shadow, and wail by
    impassable streams?

OENEUS

What thing wilt thou leave me
    Now this thing is done?
A man wilt thou give me,
    A son for my son,
For the light of mine eyes, the desire of my life, the desirable
    one?

CHORUS

Thou wert glad above others,
    Yea, fair beyond word;

167

Thou wert glad among mothers;
For each man that heard
Of thee, praise there was added unto thee, as wings to the
feet of a bird.

OENEUS

Who shall give back
Thy face of old years,
With travail made black,
Grown grey among fears,
Mother of sorrow, mother of cursing, mother of tears?

MELEAGER

Though thou art as fire
Fed with fuel in vain,
My delight, my desire,
Is more chaste than the rain,
More pure than the dewfall, more holy than stars are that
live without stain.

ATALANTA

I would that as water
My life's blood had thawn,
Or as winter's wan daughter
Leaves lowland and lawn
Spring-stricken, or ever mine eyes had beheld thee made
dark in thy dawn.

CHORUS

When thou dravest the men
Of the chosen of Thrace,
None turned him again
Nor endured he thy face
Clothed round with the blush of the battle, with light from
a terrible place.

Thou shouldst die as he dies
   For whom none sheddeth tears;
Filling thine eyes
   And fulfilling thine ears
With the brilliance of battle, the bloom and the beauty, the
   splendour of spears.

CHORUS

In the ears of the world
   It is sung, it is told,
And the light thereof hurled
   And the noise thereof rolled
From the Acroceraunian snow to the ford of the fleece of
   gold.

MELEAGER

Would God ye could carry me
   Forth of all these;
Heap sand and bury me
   By the Chersonese
Where the thundering Bosphorus answers the thunder of
   Pontic seas.

OENEUS

Dost thou mock at our praise
   And the singing begun
And the men of strange days
   Praising my son
In the folds of the hills of home, high places of Calydon?

MELEAGER

For the dead man no home is;
   Ah, better to be

What the flower of the foam is
    In fields of the sea,
That the sea-waves might be as my raiment, the gulf-stream
    a garment for me.

CHORUS

Who shall seek thee and bring
    And restore thee thy day,
When the dove dipt her wing
    And the oars won their way
Where the narrowing Symplegades whitened the straits of
    Propontis with spray?

MELEAGER

Will ye crown me my tomb
    Or exalt me my name,
Now my spirits consume,
    Now my flesh is a flame?
Let the sea slake it once, and men speak of me sleeping to
    praise me or shame.

CHORUS

Turn back now, turn thee,
    As who turns him to wake;
Though the life in thee burn thee,
    Couldst thou bathe it and slake
Where the sea-ridge of Helle hangs heavier, and east upon
    west waters break?

MELEAGER

Would the winds blow me back
    Or the waves hurl me home?
Ah, to touch in the track
    Where the pine learnt to roam
Cold girdles and crowns of the sea-gods, cool blossoms of
    water and foam!

The gods may release
That they made fast;
Thy soul shall have ease
In thy limbs at the last;
But what shall they give thee for life, sweet life that is
overpast?

MELEAGER

Not the life of men's veins,
Not of flesh that conceives;
But the grace that remains,
The fair beauty that cleaves
To the life of the rains in the grasses, the life of the dews on
the leaves.

CHORUS

Thou wert helmsman and chief;
Wilt thou turn in an hour,
Thy limbs to the leaf,
Thy face to the flower,
Thy blood to the water, thy soul to the gods who divide and
devour?

MELEAGER

The years are hungry,
They wail all their days;
The gods wax angry
And weary of praise;
And who shall bridle their lips? and who shall straiten
their ways?

CHORUS

The gods guard over us
With sword and with rod;

Weaving shadow to cover us,
Heaping the sod,
That law may fulfil herself wholly, to darken man's face
before God.

MELEAGER

O holy head of Oeneus, lo thy son
Guiltless, yet red from alien guilt, yet foul
With kinship of contaminated lives,
Lo, for their blood I die; and mine own blood
For bloodshedding of mine is mixed therewith,
That death may not discern me from my kin.
Yet with clean heart I die and faultless hand,
Not shamefully; thou therefore of thy love
Salute me, and bid fare among the dead
Well, as the dead fare; for the best man dead
Fares sadly; nathless I now faring well
Pass without fear where nothing is to fear
Having thy love about me and thy goodwill,
O father, among dark places and men dead.

OENEUS

Child, I salute thee with sad heart and tears,
And bid thee comfort, being a perfect man
In fight, and honourable in the house of peace.
The gods give thee fair wage and dues of death,
And me brief days and ways to come at thee.

MELEAGER

Pray thou thy days be long before thy death,
And full of ease and kingdom; seeing in death
There is no comfort and none aftergrowth,
Nor shall one thence look up and see day's dawn
Nor light upon the land whither I go.

Live thou and take thy fill of days and die
When thy day comes; and make not much of death
Lest ere thy day thou reap an evil thing.
Thou too, the bitter mother and mother-plague
Of this my weary body—thou too, queen,
The source and end, the sower and the scythe,
The rain that ripens and the drought that slays,
The sand that swallows and the spring that feeds,
To make me and unmake me—thou, I say,
Althaea, since my father's ploughshare, drawn
Through fatal seedland of a female field,
Furrowed thy body, whence a wheaten ear
Strong from the sun and fragrant from the rains
I sprang and cleft the closure of thy womb,
Mother, I dying with unforgetful tongue
Hail thee as holy and worship thee as just
Who art unjust and unholy; and with my knees
Would worship, but thy fire and subtlety,
Dissundering them, devour me; for these limbs
Are as light dust and crumblings from mine urn
Before the fire has touched them; and my face
As a dead leaf or dead foot's mark on snow,
And all this body a broken barren tree
That was so strong, and all this flower of life
Disbranched and desecrated miserably,
And minished all that god-like muscle and might
And lesser than a man's: for all my veins
Fail me, and all mine ashen life burns down.
I would thou hadst let me live; but gods averse,
But fortune, and the fiery feet of change,
And time, these would not, these tread out my life,
These and not thou; me too thou hast loved, and I
Thee; but this death was mixed with all my life,
Mine end with my beginning: and this law,
This only, slays me, and not my mother at all.

And let no brother or sister grieve too sore,
Nor melt their hearts out on me with their tears,
Since extreme love and sorrowing overmuch
Vex the great gods, and overloving men
Slay and are slain for love's sake; and this house
Shall bear much better children; why should these
Weep? but in patience let them live their lives
And mine pass by forgotten: thou alone,
Mother, thou sole and only, thou not these,
Keep me in mind a little when I die
Because I was thy first-born; let thy soul
Pity me, pity even me gone hence and dead,
Though thou wert wroth, and though thou bear again
Much happier sons, and all men later born
Exceedingly excel me; yet do thou
Forget not, nor think shame; I was thy son.
Time was I did not shame thee; and time was
I thought to live and make thee honourable
With deeds as great as these men's; but they live,
These, and I die; and what thing should have been
Surely I know not; yet I charge thee, seeing
I am dead already, love me not the less,
Me, O my mother; I charge thee by these gods,
My father's, and that holier breast of thine,
By these that see me dying, and that which nursed,
Love me not less, thy first-born: though grief come,
Grief only, of me, and of all these great joy,
And shall come always to thee; for thou knowest,
O mother, O breasts that bare me, for ye know,
O sweet head of my mother, sacred eyes,
Ye know my soul albeit I sinned, ye know
Albeit I kneel not neither touch thy knees,
But with my lips I kneel, and with my heart
I fall about thy feet and worship thee.
And ye farewell now, all my friends; and ye,

Kinsmen, much younger and glorious more than I,
Sons of my mother's sister; and all farewell
That were in Colchis with me, and bare down
The waves and wars that met us: and though times
Change, and though now I be not anything,
Forget not me among you, what I did
In my good time; for even by all those days,
Those days and this, and your own living souls,
And by the light and luck of you that live,
And by this miserable spoil, and me
Dying, I beseech you, let my name not die.
But thou, dear, touch me with thy rose-like hands.
And fasten up mine eyelids with thy mouth,
A bitter kiss; and grasp me with thine arms,
Printing with heavy lips my light waste flesh,
Made light and thin by heavy-handed fate,
And with thine holy maiden eyes drop dew,
Drop tears for dew upon me who am dead,
Me who have loved thee; seeing without sin done
I am gone down to the empty weary house
Where no flesh is nor beauty nor swift eyes
Nor sound of mouth nor might of hands and feet.
But thou, dear, hide my body with thy veil,
And with thy raiment cover foot and head,
And stretch thyself upon me and touch hands
With hands and lips with lips: be pitiful
As thou art maiden perfect; let no man
Defile me to despise me, saying, This man
Died woman-wise, a woman's offering, slain
Through female fingers in his woof of life,
Dishonourable; for thou hast honoured me.
And now for God's sake kiss me once and twice
And let me go; for the night gathers me,
And in the night shall no man gather fruit

Hail thou: but I with heavy face and feet
Turn homeward and am gone out of thine eyes.

CHORUS

Who shall contend with his lords
    Or cross them or do them wrong?
Who shall bind them as with cords?
    Who shall tame them as with song?
Who shall smite them as with swords?
    For the hands of their kingdom are strong.

Mentana: First Anniversary

AT the time when the stars are grey,
 And the gold of the molten moon
Fades, and the twilight is thinned,
And the sun leaps up, and the wind,
A light rose, not of the day,
 A stronger light than of noon.

As the light of a face much loved
 Was the face of the light that clomb;
As a mother's whitened with woes
Her adorable head that arose;
As the sound of a God that is moved,
 Her voice went forth upon Rome.

At her lips it fluttered and failed
 Twice, and sobbed into song,
And sank as a flame sinks under;
Then spake, and the speech was thunder,
And the cheek as he heard it paled
 Of the wrongdoer grown grey with the wrong.

'Is it time, is it time appointed,
 Angel of time, is it near?
For the spent night aches into day
When the kings shall slay not or pray,
And the high-priest, accursed and anointed,
 Sickens to deathward with fear.

'For the bones of my slain are stirred,
 And the seed of my earth in her womb

Moves as the heart of a bud
Beating with odorous blood
To the tune of the loud first bird
   Burns and yearns into bloom.

'I lay my hand on her bosom,
   My hand on the heart of my earth,
And I feel as with shiver and sob
The triumphant heart in her throb,
The dead petals dilate into blossom,
   The divine blood beat into birth.

'O my earth, are the springs in thee dry?
   O sweet, is thy body a tomb?
Nay, springs out of springs derive,
And summers from summers alive,
And the living from them that die;
   No tomb is here, but a womb.

'O manifold womb and divine,
   Give me fruit of my children, give!
I have given thee my dew for thy root,
Give thou me for my mouth of thy fruit;
Thine are the dead that are mine,
   And mine are thy sons that live.

'O goodly children, O strong
   Italian spirits, that wear
My glories as garments about you,
Could time or the world misdoubt you,
Behold, in disproof of the wrong,
   The field of the grave-pits there.

'And ye that fell upon sleep,
   We have you too with us yet.

Fairer than life or than youth
Is this, to die for the truth:
No death can sink you so deep
    As their graves whom their brethren forget.

'Were not your pains as my pains?
    As my name are your names not divine?
Was not the light in your eyes
Mine, the light of my skies,
And the sweet shed blood of your veins,
    O my beautiful martyrs, mine?

'Of mine earth were your dear limbs made,
    Of mine air was your sweet life's breath;
At the breasts of my love ye were fed,
O my children, my chosen, my dead,
At my breasts where again ye are laid,
    At the old mother's bosom, in death.

'But ye that live, O their brothers,
    Be ye to me as they were;
Give me, my children that live,
What these dead grudged not to give,
Who alive were sons of your mother's,
    Whose lips drew breath of your air.

'Till darkness by dawn be cloven,
    Let youth's self mourn and abstain;
And love's self find not an hour,
And spring's self wear not a flower,
And Lycoris, with hair unenwoven,
    Hail back to the banquet in vain.

'So sooner and surer the glory
    That is not with us shall be,

And stronger the hands that smite
The heads of the sons of night,
And the sound throughout earth of our story
Give all men heart to be free.'

μᾶ Γᾶ, μᾶ Γᾶ, βοὰν
φοβερὸν ἀπότρεπε.

AESCH. *Supp.* 890.

CHORUS

IF with voice of words or prayers thy sons may reach thee,
  We thy latter sons, the men thine after-birth,
  We the children of thy grey-grown age, O Earth,
O our mother everlasting, we beseech thee,
By the sealed and secret ages of thy life;
  By the darkness wherein grew thy sacred forces;
  By the songs of stars thy sisters in their courses;
By thine own song hoarse and hollow and shrill with strife;
By thy voice distuned and marred of modulation;
  By the discord of thy measure's march with theirs;
  By the beauties of thy bosom, and the cares;
By thy glory of growth, and splendour of thy station;
By the shame of men thy children, and the pride;
  By the pale-cheeked hope that sleeps and weeps and passes,
  As the grey dew from the morning mountain-grasses;
By the white-lipped sightless memories that abide;
By the silence and the sound of many sorrows;
  By the joys that leapt up living and fell dead;
  By the veil that hides thy hands and breasts and head,
Wrought of divers-coloured days and nights and morrows;
Isis, thou that knowest of God what worlds are worth,
  Thou the ghost of God, the mother uncreated,
  Soul for whom the floating forceless ages waited
As our forceless fancies wait on thee, O Earth;
Thou the body and soul, the father-God and mother,
  If at all it move thee, knowing of all things done
  Here where evil things and good things are not one,
But their faces are as fire against each other;

181

* G 961

By thy morning and thine evening, night and day;
By the first white light that stirs and strives and hovers
As a bird above the brood her bosom covers,
By the sweet last star that takes the westward way;
By the night whose feet are shod with snow or thunder,
Fledged with plumes of storm, or soundless as the dew;
By the vesture bound of many-folded blue
Round her breathless breasts, and all the woven wonder;
By the golden-growing eastern stream of sea;
By the sounds of sunrise moving in the mountains;
By the forces of the floods and unsealed fountains;
Thou that badest man be born, bid man be free.

GREECE

I am she that made thee lovely with my beauty
From north to south:
Mine, the fairest lips, took first the fire of duty
From thine own mouth.
Mine, the fairest eyes, sought first thy laws and knew them
Truths undefiled;
Mine, the fairest hands, took freedom first into them,
A weanling child.
By my light, now he lies sleeping, seen above him
Where none sees other;
By my dead that loved and living men that love him;
(*Cho.*) Hear us, O mother.

ITALY

I am she that was the light of thee enkindled
When Greece grew dim;
She whose life grew up with man's free life, and dwindled
With wane of him.
She that once by sword and once by word imperial
Struck bright thy gloom;

And a third time, casting off these years funereal,
    Shall burst thy tomb.
By that bond 'twixt thee and me whereat affrighted
    Thy tyrants fear us;
By that hope and this remembrance reunited;
  (*Cho.*) O mother, hear us.

SPAIN

I am she that set my seal upon the nameless
    West worlds of seas;
And my sons as brides took unto them the tameless
    Hesperides.
Till my sins and sons through sinless lands dispersèd,
    With red flame shod,
Made accurst the name of man, and thrice accursèd
    The name of God.
Lest for those past fires the fires of my repentance
    Hell's fume yet smother,
Now my blood would buy remission of my sentence;
  (*Cho.*) Hear us, O mother.

FRANCE

I am she that was thy sign and standard-bearer,
    Thy voice and cry;
She that washed thee with her blood and left thee fairer,
    The same was I.
Were not these the hands that raised thee fallen and fed thee,
    These hands defiled?
Was not I thy tongue that spake, thine eye that led thee,
    Not I thy child?
By the darkness on our dreams, and the dead errors
    Of dead times near us;
By the hopes that hang around thee, and the terrors;
  (*Cho.*) O mother, hear us.

I am she whose hands are strong and her eyes blinded
      And lips athirst
Till upon the night of nations many-minded
      One bright day burst:
Till the myriad stars be molten into one light,
      And that light thine;
Till the soul of man be parcel of the sunlight,
      And thine of mine.
By the snows that blanch not him nor cleanse from slaughter
      Who slays his brother;
By the stains and by the chains on me thy daughter;
  (*Cho.*) Hear us, O mother.

SWITZERLAND

I am she that shows on mighty limbs and maiden
      Nor chain nor stain;
For what blood can touch these hands with gold unladen,
      These feet what chain?
By the surf of spears one shieldless bosom breasted
      And was my shield,
Till the plume-plucked Austrian vulture-heads twin-crested
      Twice drenched the field;
By the snows and souls untrampled and untroubled
      That shine to cheer us,
Light of those to these responsive and redoubled;
  (*Cho.*) O mother, hear us.

GERMANY

I am she beside whose forest-hidden fountains
      Slept freedom armed,
By the magic born to music in my mountains
      Heart-chained and charmed.

By those days the very dream whereof delivers
  My soul from wrong;
By the sounds that make of all my ringing rivers
  None knows what song;
By the many tribes and names of my division
  One from another;
By the single eye of sun-compelling vision;
 (*Cho.*) Hear us, O mother.

ENGLAND

I am she that was and was not of thy chosen,
  Free, and not free;
She that fed thy springs, till now her springs are frozen;
  Yet I am she.
By the sea that clothed and sun that saw me splendid
  And fame that crowned,
By the song-fires and the sword-fires mixed and blended
  That robed me round;
By the star that Milton's soul for Shelley's lighted,
  Whose rays insphere us;
By the beacon-bright Republic far-off sighted;
 (*Cho.*) O mother, hear us.

CHORUS

Turn away from us the cross-blown blasts of error,
  That drown each other;
Turn away the fearful cry, the loud-tongued terror,
  O Earth, O mother.
Turn away their eyes who track, their hearts who follow,
  The pathless past;
Show the soul of man, as summer shows the swallow,
  The way at last.
By the sloth of men that all too long endure men
  On man to tread,

By the cry of men, the bitter cry of poor men
    That faint for bread;
By the blood-sweat of the people in the garden
    Inwalled of kings;
By his passion interceding for their pardon
    Who do these things;
By the sightless souls and fleshless limbs that labour
    For not their fruit;
By the foodless mouth with foodless heart for neighbour,
    That, mad, is mute;
By the child that famine eats as worms the blossom
    —Ah God, the child!
By the milkless lips that strain the bloodless bosom
    Till woe runs wild;
By the pastures that give grass to feed the lamb in,
    Where men lack meat;
By the cities clad with gold and shame and famine;
    By field and street;
By the people, by the poor man, by the master
    That men call slave;
By the cross-winds of defeat and of disaster,
    By wreck, by wave;
By the helm that keeps us still to sunwards driving,
    Still eastward bound,
Till, as night-watch ends, day burn on eyes reviving,
    And land be found:
We thy children, that arraign not nor impeach thee
    Though no star steer us,
By the waves that wash the morning we beseech thee,
    O mother, hear us.

I AM that which began;
    Out of me the years roll;
Out of me God and man;
    I am equal and whole;
God changes, and man, and the form of them bodily; I am
  the soul.

Before ever land was,
    Before ever the sea,
Or soft hair of the grass,
    Or fair limbs of the tree,
Or the flesh-coloured fruit of my branches, I was, and thy
  soul was in me.

First life on my sources
    First drifted and swam;
Out of me are the forces
    That save it or damn;
Out of me man and woman, and wild-beast and bird; before
  God was, I am.

Beside or above me
    Nought is there to go;
Love or unlove me,
    Unknow me or know,
I am that which unloves me and loves; I am stricken, and
  I am the blow.

I the mark that is missed
    And the arrows that miss,
I the mouth that is kissed
    And the breath in the kiss,
The search, and the sought, and the seeker, the soul and the
  body that is.

I am that thing which blesses
      My spirit elate;
That which caresses
      With hands uncreate
My limbs unbegotten that measure the length of the measure
   of fate.

But what thing dost thou now,
      Looking Godward, to cry
'I am I, thou art thou,
      I am low, thou art high'?
I am thou, whom thou seekest to find him; find thou but
   thyself, thou art I.

I the grain and the furrow,
      The plough-cloven clod
And the ploughshare drawn thorough,
      The germ and the sod,
The deed and the doer, the seed and the sower, the dust
   which is God.

Hast thou known how I fashioned thee,
      Child, underground?
Fire that impassioned thee,
      Iron that bound,
Dim changes of water, what thing of all these hast thou
   known of or found?

Canst thou say in thine heart
      Thou hast seen with thine eyes
With what cunning of art
      Thou wast wrought in what wise,
By what force of what stuff thou wast shapen, and shown on
   my breast to the skies?

Who hath given, who hath sold it thee,
    Knowledge of me?
Hath the wilderness told it thee?
    Hast thou learnt of the sea?
Hast thou communed in spirit with night? have the winds
  taken counsel with thee?

    Have I set such a star
      To show light on thy brow
    That thou sawest from afar
      What I show to thee now?
Have ye spoken as brethren together, the sun and the
  mountains and thou?

    What is here, dost thou know it?
      What was, hast thou known?
    Prophet nor poet
      Nor tripod nor throne
Nor spirit nor flesh can make answer, but only thy mother
  alone.

    Mother, not maker,
      Born, and not made;
    Though her children forsake her,
      Allured or afraid,
Praying prayers to the God of their fashion, she stirs not for
  all that have prayed.

    A creed is a rod,
      And a crown is of night;
    But this thing is God,
      To be man with thy might,
To grow straight in the strength of thy spirit, and live out
  thy life as the light.

I am in thee to save thee,
　　As my soul in thee saith;
Give thou as I gave thee,
　　Thy life-blood and breath,
Green leaves of thy labour, white flowers of thy thought, and
　　red fruit of thy death.

Be the ways of thy giving
　　As mine were to thee;
The free life of thy living,
　　Be the gift of it free;
Not as servant to lord, nor as master to slave, shalt thou give
　　thee to me.

O children of banishment,
　　Souls overcast,
Were the lights ye see vanish meant
　　Alway to last,
Ye would know not the sun overshining the shadows and
　　stars overpast.

I that saw where ye trod
　　The dim paths of the night
Set the shadow called God
　　In your skies to give light;
But the morning of manhood is risen, and the shadowless
　　soul is in sight.

The tree many-rooted
　　That swells to the sky
With frondage red-fruited,
　　The life-tree am I;
In the buds of your lives is the sap of my leaves: ye shall
　　live and not die.

But the Gods of your fashion
That take and that give,
In their pity and passion
That scourge and forgive,
They are worms that are bred in the bark that falls off; they
    shall die and not live.

My own blood is what stanches
The wounds in my bark;
Stars caught in my branches
Make day of the dark,
And are worshipped as suns till the sunrise shall tread out
    their fires as a spark.

Where dead ages hide under
The live roots of the tree,
In my darkness the thunder
Makes utterance of me;
In the clash of my boughs with each other ye hear the waves
    sound of the sea.

That noise is of Time,
As his feathers are spread
And his feet set to climb
Through the boughs overhead,
And my foliage rings round him and rustles, and branches
    are bent with his tread.

The storm-winds of ages
Blow through me and cease,
The war-wind that rages,
The spring-wind of peace,
Ere the breath of them roughen my tresses, ere one of my
    blossoms increase.

All sounds of all changes,
              All shadows and lights
         On the world's mountain-ranges
              And stream-riven heights,
Whose tongue is the wind's tongue and language of storm-
    clouds on earth-shaking mights;

         All forms of all faces,
              All works of all hands
         In unsearchable places
              Of time-stricken lands,
All death and all life, and all reigns and all ruins, drop
    through me as sands.

         Though sore be my burden
              And more than ye know,
         And my growth have no guerdon
              But only to grow,
Yet I fail not of growing for lightnings above me or death-
    worms below.

         These too have their part in me,
              As I too in these;
         Such fire is at heart in me,
              Such sap is this tree's,
Which hath in it all sounds and all secrets of infinite lands
    and of seas.

         In the spring-coloured hours
              When my mind was as May's,
         There brake forth of me flowers
              By centuries of days,
Strong blossoms with perfume of manhood, shot out from
    my spirit as rays.

192

And the sound of them springing
And smell of their shoots
Were as warmth and sweet singing
And strength to my roots;
And the lives of my children made perfect with freedom of
soul were my fruits.

I bid you but be;
I have need not of prayer;
I have need of you free
As your mouths of mine air;
That my heart may be greater within me, beholding the
fruits of me fair.

More fair than strange fruit is
Of faiths ye espouse;
In me only the root is
That blooms in your boughs;
Behold now your God that ye made you, to feed him with
faith of your vows.

In the darkening and whitening
Abysses adored,
With dayspring and lightning
For lamp and for sword,
God thunders in heaven, and his angels are red with the
wrath of the Lord.

O my sons, O too dutiful
Toward Gods not of me,
Was not I enough beautiful?
Was it hard to be free?
For behold, I am with you, am in you and of you; look
forth now and see.

Lo, winged with world's wonders,
    With miracles shod,
With the fires of his thunders
    For raiment and rod,
God trembles in heaven, and his angels are white with the
    terror of God.

For his twilight is come on him,
    His anguish is here;
And his spirits gaze dumb on him,
    Grown grey from his fear;
And his hour taketh hold on him stricken, the last of his
    infinite year.

Thought made him and breaks him,
    Truth slays and forgives;
But to you, as time takes him,
    This new thing it gives,
Even love, the beloved Republic, that feeds upon freedom
    and lives.

For truth only is living,
    Truth only is whole,
And the love of his giving
    Man's polestar and pole;
Man, pulse of my centre, and fruit of my body, and seed of
    my soul.

One birth of my bosom;
    One beam of mine eye;
One topmost blossom
    That scales the sky;
Man, equal and one with me, man that is made of me, man
    that is I.

HERE, down between the dusty trees,
  At this lank edge of haggard wood,
Women with labour-loosened knees,
  With gaunt backs bowed by servitude,
Stop, shift their loads, and pray, and fare
Forth with souls easier for the prayer.

The suns have branded black, the rains
  Striped grey this piteous God of theirs;
The face is full of prayers and pains,
  To which they bring their pains and prayers;
Lean limbs that show the labouring bones,
And ghastly mouth that gapes and groans.

God of this grievous people, wrought
  After the likeness of their race,
By faces like thine own besought,
  Thine own blind helpless eyeless face,
I, too, that have nor tongue nor knee
For prayer, I have a word to thee.

It was for this then, that thy speech
  Was blown about the world in flame
And men's souls shot up out of reach
  Of fear or lust or thwarting shame—
That thy faith over souls should pass
As sea-winds burning the grey grass?

It was for this, that prayers like these
  Should spend themselves about thy feet,
And with hard overlaboured knees
  Kneeling, these slaves of men should beat
Bosoms too lean to suckle sons
And fruitless as their orisons?

It was for this, that men should make
　Thy name a fetter on men's necks,
Poor men's made poorer for thy sake,
　And women's withered out of sex?
It was for this, that slaves should be,
Thy word was passed to set men free?

The nineteenth wave of the ages rolls
　Now deathward since thy death and birth.
Hast thou fed full men's starved-out souls?
　Hast thou brought freedom upon earth?
Or are there less oppressions done
In this wild world under the sun?

Nay, if indeed thou be not dead,
　Before thy terrene shrine be shaken,
Look down, turn usward, bow thine head;
　O thou that wast of God forsaken,
Look on thine household here, and see
These that have not forsaken thee.

Thy faith is fire upon their lips,
　Thy kingdom golden in their hands;
They scourge us with thy words for whips,
　They brand us with thy words for brands;
The thirst that made thy dry throat shrink
To their moist mouths commends the drink.

The toothèd thorns that bit thy brows
　Lighten the weight of gold on theirs;
Thy nakedness enrobes thy spouse
　With the soft sanguine stuff she wears
Whose old limbs use for ointment yet
Thine agony and bloody sweat.

The blinding buffets on thine head
　　On their crowned heads confirm the crown;
Thy scourging dyes their raiment red,
　　And with thy bands they fasten down
For burial in the blood-bought field
The nations by thy stripes unhealed.

With iron for thy linen bands
　　And unclean cloths for winding-sheet
They bind the people's nail-pierced hands,
　　They hide the people's nail-pierced feet;
And what man or what angel known
Shall roll back the sepulchral stone?

But these have not the rich man's grave
　　To sleep in when their pain is done.
These were not fit for God to save.
　　As naked hell-fire is the sun
In their eyes living, and when dead
These have not where to lay their head.

They have no tomb to dig, and hide;
　　Earth is not theirs, that they should sleep.
On all these tombless crucified
　　No lovers' eyes have time to weep.
So still, for all man's tears and creeds,
The sacred body hangs and bleeds.

Through the left hand a nail is driven,
　　Faith, and another through the right,
Forged in the fires of hell and heaven,
　　Fear that puts out the eye of light:
And the feet soiled and scarred and pale
Are pierced with falsehood for a nail.

And priests against the mouth divine
　　Push their sponge full of poison yet
And bitter blood for myrrh and wine,
　　And on the same reed is it set
Wherewith before they buffeted
The people's disanointed head.

O sacred head, O desecrate,
　　O labour-wounded feet and hands,
O blood poured forth in pledge to fate
　　Of nameless lives in divers lands,
O slain and spent and sacrificed
People, the grey-grown speechless Christ!

Is there a gospel in the red
　　Old witness of thy wide-mouthed wounds?
From thy blind stricken tongueless head
　　What desolate evangel sounds
A hopeless note of hope deferred?
What word, if there be any word?

O son of man, beneath man's feet
　　Cast down, O common face of man
Whereon all blows and buffets meet,
　　O royal, O republican
Face of the people bruised and dumb
And longing till thy kingdom come!

The soldiers and the high priests part
　　Thy vesture: all thy days are priced,
And all the nights that eat thine heart.
　　And that one seamless coat of Christ,
The freedom of the natural soul,
They cast their lots for to keep whole.

No fragment of it save the name
    They leave thee for a crown of scorns
Wherewith to mock thy naked shame
    And forehead bitten through with thorns
And, marked with sanguine sweat and tears,
The stripes of eighteen hundred years.

And we seek yet if God or man
    Can loosen thee as Lazarus,
Bid thee rise up republican
    And save thyself and all of us;
But no disciple's tongue can say
When thou shalt take our sins away.

And mouldering now and hoar with moss
    Between us and the sunlight swings
The phantom of a Christless cross
    Shadowing the sheltered heads of kings
And making with its moving shade
The souls of harmless men afraid.

It creaks and rocks to left and right
    Consumed of rottenness and rust,
Worm-eaten of the worms of night,
    Dead as their spirits who put trust,
Round its base muttering as they sit,
In the time-cankered name of it.

Thou, in the day that breaks thy prison,
    People, though these men take thy name,
And hail and hymn thee rearisen,
    Who made songs erewhile of thy shame,
Give thou not ear; for these are they
Whose good day was thine evil day.

Set not thine hand unto their cross.
  Give not thy soul up sacrificed.
Change not the gold of faith for dross
  Of Christian creeds that spit on Christ.
Let not thy tree of freedom be
Regrafted from that rotting tree.

This dead God here against my face
  Hath help for no man; who hath seen
The good works of it, or such grace
  As thy grace in it, Nazarene,
As that from thy live lips which ran
For man's sake, O thou son of man?

The tree of faith ingraffed by priests
  Puts its foul foliage out above thee,
And round it feed man-eating beasts
  Because of whom we dare not love thee;
Though hearts reach back and memories ache,
We cannot praise thee for their sake.

O hidden face of man, whereover
  The years have woven a viewless veil,
If thou wast verily man's lover,
  What did thy love or blood avail?
Thy blood the priests make poison of,
And in gold shekels coin thy love.

So when our souls look back to thee
  They sicken, seeing against thy side,
Too foul to speak of or to see,
  The leprous likeness of a bride,
Whose kissing lips through his lips grown
Leave their God rotten to the bone.

When we would see thee man, and know
　　What heart thou hadst toward men indeed,
Lo, thy blood-blackened altars; lo,
　　The lips of priests that pray and feed
While their own hell's worm curls and licks
The poison of the crucifix.

Thou bad'st let children come to thee;
　　What children now but curses come?
What manhood in that God can be
　　Who sees their worship, and is dumb?
No soul that lived, loved, wrought, and died,
Is this their carrion crucified.

Nay, if their God and thou be one,
　　If thou and this thing be the same,
Thou shouldst not look upon the sun;
　　The sun grows haggard at thy name.
Come down, be done with, cease, give o'er;
Hide thyself, strive not, be no more.

During the session in Rome of the Oecumenical Council

IN the grey beginning of years, in the twilight of things
　　that began,
The word of the earth in the ears of the world, was it God?
　　was it man?
The word of the earth to the spheres her sisters, the note of
　　her song,
The sound of her speech in the ears of the starry and sisterly
　　throng,
Was it praise or passion or prayer, was it love or devotion
　　or dread,
When the veils of the shining air first wrapt her jubilant
　　head?
When her eyes new-born of the night saw yet no star out of
　　reach;
When her maiden mouth was alight with the flame of
　　musical speech;
When her virgin feet were set on the terrible heavenly way,
And her virginal lids were wet with the dew of the birth of
　　the day:
Eyes that had looked not on time, and ears that had heard
　　not of death;
Lips that had learnt not the rhyme of change and passionate
　　breath,
The rhythmic anguish of growth, and the motion of mutable
　　things,
Of love that longs and is loth, and plume-plucked hope
　　without wings,
Passions and pains without number, and life that runs and
　　is lame,
From slumber again to slumber, the same race set for the
　　same,

Where the runners outwear each other, but running with
    lampless hands

No man takes light from his brother till blind at the goal
    he stands:

Ah, did they know, did they dream of it, counting the cost
    and the worth?

The ways of her days, did they seem then good to the new-
    souled earth?

Did her heart rejoice, and the might of her spirit exult in
    her then,

Child yet no child of the night, and motherless mother of men?

Was it Love brake forth flower-fashion, a bird with gold
    on his wings,

Lovely, her firstborn passion, and impulse of firstborn
    things?

Was Love that nestling indeed that under the plumes of the
    night

Was hatched and hidden as seed in the furrow, and brought
    forth bright?

Was it Love lay shut in the shell world-shaped, having
    over him there

Black world-wide wings that impel the might of the night
    through air?

And bursting his shell as a bird, night shook through her
    sail-stretched vans,

And her heart as a water was stirred, and its heat was the
    firstborn man's.

For the waste of the dead void air took form of a world at
    birth,

And the waters and firmaments were, and light, and the
    life-giving earth.

The beautiful bird unbegotten that night brought forth
    without pain

In the fathomless years forgotten whereover the dead gods
    reign,

Was it love, life, godhead, or fate? we say the spirit is one

That moved on the dark to create out of darkness the stars and the sun.

Before the growth was the grower, and the seed ere the plant was sown;

But what was seed of the sower? and the grain of him, whence was it grown?

Foot after foot ye go back and travail and make yourselves mad;

Blind feet that feel for the track where highway is none to be had.

Therefore the God that ye make you is grievous, and gives not aid,

Because it is but for your sake that the God of your making is made.

Thou and I and he are not gods made men for a span,

But God, if a God there be, is the substance of men which is man.

Our lives are as pulses or pores of his manifold body and breath;

As waves of his sea on the shores where birth is the beacon of death.

We men, the multiform features of man, whatsoever we be,

Recreate him of whom we are creatures, and all we only are he.

Not each man of all men is God, but God is the fruit of the whole;

Indivisible spirit and blood, indiscernible body from soul.

Not men's but man's is the glory of godhead, the kingdom of time,

The mountainous ages made hoary with snows for the spirit to climb.

A God with the world inwound whose clay to his footsole clings;

A manifold God fast-bound as with iron of adverse things.

A soul that labours and lives, an emotion, a strenuous breath,

From the flame that its own mouth gives reillumed, and refreshed with death.

In the sea whereof centuries are waves the live God plunges and swims;

His bed is in all men's graves, but the worm hath not hold on his limbs.

Night puts out not his eyes, nor time sheds change on his head;

With such fire as the stars of the skies are the roots of his heart are fed.

Men are the thoughts passing through it, the veins that fulfil it with blood,

With spirit of sense to renew it as springs fulfilling a flood.

Men are the heartbeats of man, the plumes that feather his wings,

Storm-worn, since being began, with the wind and thunder of things.

Things are cruel and blind; their strength detains and deforms:

And the wearying wings of the mind still beat up the stream of their storms.

Still, as one swimming up stream, they strike out blind in the blast,

In thunders of vision and dream, and lightnings of future and past.

We are baffled and caught in the current and bruised upon edges of shoals;

As weeds or as reeds in the torrent of things are the wind-shaken souls.

Spirit by spirit goes under, a foam-bell's bubble of breath,

That blows and opens in sunder and blurs not the mirror of death.

For a worm or a thorn in his path is a man's soul quenched
   as a flame;
For his lust of an hour or his wrath shall the worm and the
   man be the same.
O God sore stricken of things! they have wrought him a
   raiment of pain;
Can a God shut eyelids and wings at a touch on the nerves
   of the brain?
O shamed and sorrowful God, whose force goes out at a
   blow!
What world shall shake at his nod? at his coming what
   wilderness glow?
What help in the work of his hands? what light in the track
   of his feet?
His days are snowflakes or sands, with cold to consume him
   and heat.
He is servant with Change for lord, and for wages he hath
   to his hire
Folly and force, and a sword that devours, and a ravening fire.
From the bed of his birth to his grave he is driven as a wind
   at their will;
Lest Change bow down as his slave, and the storm and the
   sword be still;
Lest earth spread open her wings to the sunward, and sing
   with the spheres;
Lest man be master of things, to prevail on their forces and
   fears.
By the spirit are things overcome; they are stark, and the
   spirit hath breath;
It hath speech, and their forces are dumb; it is living, and
   things are of death.
But they know not the spirit for master, they feel not force
   from above,
While man makes love to disaster, and woos desolation
   with love.

206

Yea, himself too hath made himself chains, and his own hands plucked out his eyes;

For his own soul only constrains him, his own mouth only denies.

The herds of kings and their hosts and the flocks of the high priests bow

To a master whose face is a ghost's; O thou that wast God, is it thou?

Thou madest man in the garden; thou temptedst man, and he fell;

Thou gavest him poison and pardon for blood and burnt offering to sell.

Thou hast sealed thine elect to salvation, fast locked with faith for the key;

Make now for thyself expiation, and be thine atonement for thee.

Ah, thou that darkenest heaven—ah, thou that bringest a sword—

By the crimes of thine hands unforgiven they beseech thee to hear them, O Lord.

By the balefires of ages that burn for thine incense, by creed and by rood,

By the famine and passion that yearn and that hunger to find of thee food,

By the children that asked at thy throne of the priests that were fat with thine hire

For bread, and thou gavest a stone; for light, and thou madest them fire;

By the kiss of thy peace like a snake's kiss, that leaves the soul rotten at root;

By the savours of gibbets and stakes thou hast planted to bear to thee fruit;

By torture and terror and treason, that make to thee weapons and wings;

By thy power upon men for a season, made out of the malice
    of things;
O thou that hast built thee a shrine of the madness of man
    and his shame,
And hast hung in the midst for a sign of his worship the
    lamp of thy name;
That hast shown him for heaven in a vision a void world's
    shadow and shell,
And hast fed thy delight and derision with fire of belief as
    of hell;
That hast fleshed on the souls that believe thee the fang of
    the death-worm fear,
With anguish of dreams to deceive them whose faith cries
    out in thine ear;
By the face of the spirit confounded before thee and humbled
    in dust,
By the dread wherewith life was astounded and shamed out
    of sense of its trust,
By the scourges of doubt and repentance that fell on the
    soul at thy nod,
Thou art judged, O judge, and the sentence is gone forth
    against thee, O God.
Thy slave that slept is awake; thy slave but slept for a
    span;
Yea, man thy slave shall unmake thee, who made thee lord
    over man.
For his face is set to the east, his feet on the past and its dead;
The sun rearisen is his priest, and the heat thereof hallows
    his head.
His eyes take part in the morning; his spirit outsounding
    the sea
Asks no more witness or warning from temple or tripod or
    tree.
He hath set the centuries at union; the night is afraid at his
    name;

Equal with life, in communion with death, he hath found
them the same.

Past the wall unsurmounted that bars out our vision with
iron and fire

He hath sent forth his soul for the stars to comply with and
suns to conspire.

His thought takes flight for the centre wherethrough it hath
part in the whole;

The abysses forbid it not enter: the stars make room for the
soul.

Space is the soul's to inherit; the night is hers as the day;

Lo, saith man, this is my spirit; how shall not the worlds
make way?

Space is thought's, and the wonders thereof, and the secret
of space;

Is thought not more than the thunders and lightnings? shall
thought give place?

Is the body not more than the vesture, the life not more than
the meat?

The will than the word or the gesture, the heart than the
hands or the feet?

Is the tongue not more than the speech is? the head not more
than the crown?

And if higher than is heaven be the reach of the soul, shall
not heaven bow down?

Time, father of life, and more great than the life it begat and
began,

Earth's keeper and heaven's and their fate, lives, thinks, and
hath substance in man.

Time's motion that throbs in his blood is the thought that
gives heart to the skies,

And the springs of the fire that is food to the sunbeams are
light to his eyes.

The minutes that beat with his heart are the words to which
worlds keep chime,

And the thought in his pulses is part of the blood and the
  spirit of time.
He saith to the ages, Give; and his soul foregoes not her
  share;
Who are ye that forbid him to live, and would feed him
  with heavenlier air?
Will he feed him with poisonous dust, and restore him with
  hemlock for drink,
Till he yield you his soul up in trust, and have heart not to
  know or to think?
He hath stirred him, and found out the flaw in his fetters,
  and cast them behind;
His soul to his soul is a law, and his mind is a light to his
  mind.
The seal of his knowledge is sure, the truth and his spirit
  are wed;
Men perish, but man shall endure; lives die, but the life is
  not dead.
His soul is at one with the reason of things that is sap to the
  roots.
He can hear in their changes a sound as the conscience of
  consonant spheres;
He can see through the years flowing round him the law
  lying under the years.
Who are ye that would bind him with curses and blind him
  with vapour of prayer?
Your might is as night that disperses when light is alive in
  the air.
The bow of your godhead is broken, the arm of your con-
  quest is stayed;
Though ye call down God to bear token, for fear of you
  none is afraid.
Will ye turn back times, and the courses of stars, and the
  season of souls?

Shall God's breath dry up the sources that feed time full as it rolls?

Nay, cry on him then till he show you a sign, till he lift up a rod;

Hath he made not the nations to know him of old if indeed he be God?

Is no heat of him left in the ashes of thousands burnt up for his sake?

Can prayer not rekindle the flashes that shone in his face from the stake?

Cry aloud; for your God is a God and a Saviour; cry, make yourselves lean;

Is he drunk or asleep, that the rod of his wrath is unfelt and unseen?

Is the fire of his old loving-kindness gone out, that his pyres are acold?

Hath he gazed on himself unto blindness, who made men blind to behold?

Cry out, for his kingdom is shaken; cry out, for the people blaspheme;

Cry aloud till his godhead awaken; what doth he to sleep and to dream?

Cry, cut yourselves, gash you with knives and with scourges, heap on to you dust;

Is his life but as other gods' lives? is not this the Lord God of your trust?

Is not this the great God of your sires, that with souls and with bodies was fed,

And the world was on flame with his fires? O fools, he was God, and is dead.

He will hear not again the strong crying of earth in his ears as before,

And the fume of his multitudes dying shall flatter his nostrils no more.

By the spirit he ruled as his slave is he slain who was mighty
    to slay,
And the stone that is sealed on his grave he shall rise not
    and roll not away.
Yea, weep to him, lift up your hands; be your eyes as a
    fountain of tears;
Where he stood there is nothing that stands; if he call, there
    is no man that hears.
He hath doffed his king's raiment of lies now the wane of
    his kingdom is come;
Ears hath he, and hears not; and eyes, and he sees not; and
    mouth, and is dumb.
His red king's raiment is ripped from him naked, his staff
    broken down;
And the signs of his empire are stripped from him shudder-
    ing; and where is his crown?
And in vain by the wellsprings refrozen ye cry for the
    warmth of his sun—
O God, the Lord God of thy chosen, thy will in thy king-
    dom be done.
Kingdom and will hath he none in him left him, nor
    warmth in his breath;
Till his corpse be cast out of the sun will ye know not the
    truth of his death?
Surely, ye say, he is strong, though the times be against him
    and men;
Yet a little, ye say, and how long, till he come to show
    judgment again?
Shall God then die as the beasts die? who is it hath broken
    his rod?
O God, Lord God of thy priests, rise up now and show
    thyself God.
They cry out, thine elect, thine aspirants to heavenward,
    whose faith is as flame;

O thou the Lord God of our tyrants, they call thee, their God, by thy name.
By thy name that in hell-fire was written, and burned at the point of thy sword,
Thou art smitten, thou God, thou art smitten; thy death is upon thee, O Lord.
And the love-song of earth as thou diest resounds through the wind of her wings—
Glory to Man in the highest! for Man is the master of things.

Cor Cordium

O HEART of hearts, the chalice of love's fire,
    Hid round with flowers and all the bounty of bloom;
  O wonderful and perfect heart, for whom
The lyrist liberty made life a lyre;
O heavenly heart, at whose most dear desire
    Dead love, living and singing, cleft his tomb,
    And with him risen and regent in death's room
All day thy choral pulses rang full choir;
O heart whose beating blood was running song,
  O sole thing sweeter than thine own songs were,
    Help us for thy free love's sake to be free,
True for thy truth's sake, for thy strength's sake strong,
  Till very liberty make clean and fair
    The nursing earth as the sepulchral sea.

On the Downs

A FAINT sea without wind or sun;
  A sky like flameless vapour dun;
A valley like an unsealed grave
That no man cares to weep upon,
  Bare, without boon to crave,
    Or flower to save.

And on the lip's edge of the down,
Here where the bent-grass burns to brown
  In the dry sea-wind, and the heath
Crawls to the cliff-side and looks down,
  I watch, and hear beneath
    The low tide breathe.

Along the long lines of the cliff,
Down the flat sea-line without skiff
  Or sail or back-blown fume for mark,
Through wind-worn heads of heath and stiff
  Stems blossomless and stark
    With dry sprays dark,

I send mine eyes out as for news
Of comfort that all these refuse,
  Tidings of light or living air
From windward where the low clouds muse
  And the sea blind and bare
    Seems full of care.

So is it now as it was then,
And as men have been such are men.
  There as I stood I seem to stand,
Here sitting chambered, and again
  Feel spread on either hand
    Sky, sea, and land.

As a queen taken and stripped and bound
Sat earth, discoloured and discrowned;
  As a king's palace empty and dead
The sky was, without light or sound;
    And on the summer's head
      Were ashes shed.

Scarce wind enough was on the sea,
Scarce hope enough there moved in me,
  To sow with live blown flowers of white
The green plain's sad serenity,
    Or with stray thoughts of light
      Touch my soul's sight.

By footless ways and sterile went
My thought unsatisfied, and bent
  With blank unspeculative eyes
On the untracked sands or discontent
    Where, watched of helpless skies,
      Life hopeless lies.

East and west went my soul to find
Light, and the world was bare and blind
  And the soil herbless where she trod
And saw men laughing scourge mankind,
    Unsmitten by the rod
      Of any God.

Out of time's blind old eyes were shed
Tears that were mortal, and left dead
  The heart and spirit of the years,
And on man's fallen and helmless head
    Time's disanointing tears
      Fell cold as fears.

Hope flowering had but strength to bear
The fruitless fruitage of despair;
  Grief trod the grapes of joy for wine,
Whereof love drinking unaware
    Died as one undivine
      And made no sign.

And soul and body dwelt apart;
And weary wisdom without heart
  Stared on the dead round heaven and sighed,
'Is death too hollow as thou art,
    Or as man's living pride?'
      And saying so died.

And my soul heard the songs and groans
That are about and under thrones,
  And felt through all time's murmur thrill
Fate's old imperious semitones
    That made of good and ill
      One same tune still.

Then 'Where is God? and where is aid?
Or what good end of these?' she said;
  'Is there no God or end at all,
Nor reason with unreason weighed,
    Nor force to disenthral
      Weak feet that fall?

'No light to lighten and no rod
To chasten men? Is there no God?'
  So girt with anguish, iron-zoned,
Went my soul weeping as she trod
    Between the men enthroned
      And men that groaned.

O fool, that for brute cries of wrong
Heard not the grey glad mother's song
  Ring response from the hills and waves,
But heard harsh noises all day long
   Of spirits that were slaves
     And dwelt in graves.

The wise word of the secret earth
Who knows what life and death are worth,
  And how no help and no control
Can speed or stay things come to birth,
   Nor all worlds' wheels that roll
     Crush one born soul.

With all her tongues of life and death,
With all her bloom and blood and breath,
  From all years dead and all things done,
In the ear of man the mother saith,
   'There is no God, O son,
     If thou be none.'

So my soul sick with watching heard
That day the wonder of that word,
  And as one springs out of a dream
Sprang, and the stagnant wells were stirred
   Whence flows through gloom and gleam
     Thought's soundless stream.

Out of pale cliff and sunburnt heath,
Out of the low sea curled beneath
  In the land's bending arm embayed,
Out of all lives that thought hears breathe
   Life within life inlaid,
     Was answer made.

A multitudinous monotone
Of dust and flower and seed and stone,
  In the deep sea-rock's mid-sea sloth,
In the live water's trembling zone,
  In all men love and loathe,
    One God at growth.

One forceful nature uncreate
That feeds itself with death and fate,
  Evil and good, and change and time,
That within all men lies at wait
  Till the hour shall bid them climb
    And live sublime.

For all things come by fate to flower
At their unconquerable hour,
  And time brings truth, and truth makes free,
And freedom fills time's veins with power,
  As, brooding on that sea,
    My thought filled me.

And the sun smote the clouds and slew,
And from the sun the sea's breath blew,
  And white waves laughed and turned and fled
The long green heaving sea-field through,
  And on them overhead
    The sky burnt red.

Like a furled flag that wind sets free,
On the swift summer-coloured sea
  Shook out the red lines of the light,
The live sun's standard, blown to lee
  Across the live sea's white
    And green delight.

And with divine triumphant awe
My spirit moved within me saw,
   With burning passion of stretched eyes,
Clear as the light's own firstborn law,
   In windless wastes of skies
      Time's deep dawn rise.

The Oblation

ASK nothing more of me, sweet;
   All I can give you I give.
      Heart of my heart, were it more,
More would be laid at your feet:
   Love that should help you to live,
      Song that should spur you to soar.

All things were nothing to give
   Once to have sense of you more,
      Touch you and taste of you sweet,
Think you and breathe you and live,
   Swept of your wings as they soar,
      Trodden by chance of your feet.

I that have love and no more
   Give you but love of you, sweet:
      He that hath more, let him give;
He that hath wings, let him soar;
   Mine is the heart at your feet
      Here, that must love you to live.

POEMS AND BALLADS

Second and Third Series

A Forsaken Garden

IN a coign of the cliff between lowland and highland,
   At the sea-down's edge between windward and lee,
Walled round with rocks as an inland island,
   The ghost of a garden fronts the sea.
A girdle of brushwood and thorn encloses
   The steep square slope of the blossomless bed
Where the weeds that grew green from the graves of its
     roses
       Now lie dead.

The fields fall southward, abrupt and broken,
   To the low last edge of the long lone land.
If a steep should sound or a word be spoken,
   Would a ghost not rise at the strange guest's hand?
So long have the grey bare walks lain guestless,
   Through branches and briars if a man make way,
He shall find no life but the sea-wind's, restless
     Night and day.

The dense hard passage is blind and stifled
   That crawls by a track none turn to climb
To the strait waste place that the years have rifled
   Of all but the thorns that are touched not of time.
The thorns he spares when the rose is taken;
   The rocks are left when he wastes the plain.
The wind that wanders, the weeds wind-shaken,
     These remain.

Not a flower to be pressed of the foot that falls not;
   As the heart of a dead man the seed-plots are dry;

From the thicket of thorns whence the nightingale calls not,
  Could she call, there were never a rose to reply.
Over the meadows that blossom and wither
  Rings but the note of a sea-bird's song;
Only the sun and the rain come hither
    All year long.

The sun burns sere and the rain dishevels
  One gaunt bleak blossom of scentless breath.
Only the wind here hovers and revels
  In a round where life seems barren as death.
Here there was laughing of old, there was weeping,
  Haply, of lovers none ever will know,
Whose eyes went seaward a hundred sleeping
    Years ago.

Heart handfast in heart as they stood, 'Look thither,'
  Did he whisper? 'look forth from the flowers to the sea;
For the foam-flowers endure when the rose-blossoms
    wither,
  And men that love lightly may die—but we?'
And the same wind sang and the same waves whitened,
  And or ever the garden's last petals were shed,
In the lips that had whispered, the eyes that had lightened,
    Love was dead.

Or they loved their life through, and then went whither?
  And were one to the end—but what end who knows?
Love deep as the sea as a rose must wither,
  As the rose-red seaweed that mocks the rose.
Shall the dead take thought for the dead to love them?
  What love was ever as deep as a grave?
They are loveless now as the grass above them
    Or the wave.

All are at one now, roses and lovers,
  Not known of the cliffs and the fields and the sea.
Not a breath of the time that has been hovers
  In the air now soft with a summer to be.
Not a breath shall there sweeten the seasons hereafter
  Of the flowers or the lovers that laugh now or weep,
When as they that are free now of weeping and laughter
      We shall sleep.

Here death may deal not again for ever;
  Here change may come not till all change end.
From the graves they have made they shall rise up never,
  Who have left nought living to ravage and rend.
Earth, stones, and thorns of the wild ground growing,
  While the sun and the rain live, these shall be;
Till a last wind's breath upon all these blowing
      Roll the sea.

Till the slow sea rise and the sheer cliff crumble,
  Till terrace and meadow the deep gulfs drink,
Till the strength of the waves of the high tides humble
  The fields that lessen, the rocks that shrink,
Here now in his triumph where all things falter,
  Stretched out on the spoils that his own hand spread,
As a god self-slain on his own strange altar,
      Death lies dead.

I SAW my soul at rest upon a day
  As a bird sleeping in the nest of night,
Among soft leaves that give the starlight way
  To touch its wings but not its eyes with light
So that it knew as one in visions may,
  And knew not as men waking, of delight.

This was the measure of my soul's delight;
  It had no power of joy to fly by day,
Nor part in the large lordship of the light;
  But in a secret moon-beholden way
Had all its will of dreams and pleasant night,
  And all the love and life that sleepers may.

But such life's triumph as men waking may
  It might not have to feed its faint delight
Between the stars by night and sun by day,
  Shut up with green leaves and a little light;
Because its way was as a lost star's way,
  A world's not wholly known of day or night.

All loves and dreams and sounds and gleams of night
  Made it all music that such minstrels may,
And all they had they gave it of delight;
  But in the full face of the fire of day
What place shall be for any starry light,
  What part of heaven in all the wide sun's way?

Yet the soul woke not, sleeping by the way,
  Watched as a nursling of the large-eyed night,
And sought no strength nor knowledge of the day,
  Nor closer touch conclusive of delight,
Nor mightier joy nor truer than dreamers may,
  Nor more of song than they, nor more of light.

For who sleeps once and sees the secret light
    Whereby sleep shows the soul a fairer way
Between the rise and rest of day and night,
    Shall care no more to fare as all men may,
But be his place of pain or of delight,
    There shall he dwell, beholding night as day.

Song, have thy day and take thy fill of light
    Before the night be fallen across thy way;
Sing while he may, man hath no long delight.

In Memory of Charles Baudelaire

Nous devrions pourtant lui porter quelques fleurs;
Les morts, les pauvres morts, ont de grandes douleurs,
Et quand Octobre souffle, émondeur des vieux arbres,
Son vent mélancolique à l'entour de leurs marbres,
Certe, ils doivent trouver les vivants bien ingrats.

Les Fleurs du Mal.

I

SHALL I strew on thee rose or rue or laurel,
    Brother, on this that was the veil of thee?
      Or quiet sea-flower moulded by the sea,
Or simplest growth of meadow-sweet or sorrel,
    Such as the summer-sleepy Dryads weave,
      Waked up by snow-soft sudden rains at eve?
Or wilt thou rather, as on earth before,
    Half-faded fiery blossoms, pale with heat
    And full of bitter summer, but more sweet
To thee than gleanings of a northern shore
    Trod by no tropic feet?

II

For always thee the fervid languid glories
    Allured of heavier suns in mightier skies;
      Thine ears knew all the wandering watery sighs
Where the sea sobs round Lesbian promontories,
    The barren kiss of piteous wave to wave
      That knows not where is that Leucadian grave
Which hides too deep the supreme head of song.
    Ah, salt and sterile as her kisses were,
    The wild sea winds her and the green gulfs bear
Hither and thither, and vex and work her wrong,
    Blind gods that cannot spare.

III

Thou sawest, in thine old singing season, brother,
    Secrets and sorrows unbeheld of us:
    Fierce loves, and lovely leaf-buds poisonous,
Bare to thy subtler eye, but for none other
    Blowing by night in some unbreathed-in clime;
    The hidden harvest of luxurious time,
Sin without shape, and pleasure without speech;
    And where strange dreams in a tumultuous sleep
    Make the shut eyes of stricken spirits weep;
And with each face thou sawest the shadow on each,
    Seeing as men sow men reap.

IV

O sleepless heart and sombre soul unsleeping,
    That were athirst for sleep and no more life
    And no more love, for peace and no more strife!
Now the dim gods of death have in their keeping
    Spirit and body and all the springs of song,
    Is it well now where love can do no wrong,
Where stingless pleasure has no foam or fang
    Behind the unopening closure of her lips?
    Is it not well where soul from body slips
And flesh from bone divides without a pang
    As dew from flower-bell drips?

V

It is enough; the end and the beginning
    Are one thing to thee, who art past the end.
    O hand unclasped of unbeholden friend,
For thee no fruits to pluck, no palms for winning,
    No triumph and no labour and no lust,
    Only dead yew-leaves and a little dust.

O quiet eyes wherein the light saith nought,
    Whereto the day is dumb, nor any night
    With obscure finger silences your sight,
Nor in your speech the sudden soul speaks thought,
    Sleep, and have sleep for light.

VI

Now all strange hours and all strange loves are over,
    Dreams and desires and sombre songs and sweet,
    Hast thou found place at the great knees and feet
Of some pale Titan-woman like a lover,
    Such as thy vision here solicited,
    Under the shadow of her fair vast head,
The deep division of prodigious breasts,
    The solemn slope of mighty limbs asleep,
    The weight of awful tresses that still keep
The savour and shade of old-world pine-forests
    Where the wet hill-winds weep?

VII

Hast thou found any likeness for thy vision?
    O gardener of strange flowers, what bud, what bloom,
    Hast thou found sown, what gathered in the gloom?
What of despair, of rapture, of derision,
    What of life is there, what of ill or good?
    Are the fruits grey like dust or bright like blood?
Does the dim ground grow any seed of ours,
    The faint fields quicken any terrene root,
    In low lands where the sun and moon are mute
And all the stars keep silence? Are there flowers
    At all, or any fruit?

VIII

Alas, but though my flying song flies after,
    O sweet strange elder singer, thy more fleet
    Singing, and footprints of thy fleeter feet,

Some dim derision of mysterious laughter
  From the blind tongueless warders of the dead,
  Some gainless glimpse of Proserpine's veiled head,
Some little sound of unregarded tears
  Wept by effaced unprofitable eyes,
  And from pale mouths some cadence of dead sighs—
These only, these the hearkening spirit hears,
  Sees only such things rise.

IX

Thou art far too far for wings of words to follow,
  Far too far off for thought or any prayer.
  What ails us with thee, who art wind and air?
What ails us gazing where all seen is hollow?
  Yet with some fancy, yet with some desire,
  Dreams pursue death as winds a flying fire,
Our dreams pursue our dead and do not find.
  Still, and more swift than they, the thin flame flies,
  The low light fails us in elusive skies,
Still the foiled earnest ear is deaf, and blind
  Are still the eluded eyes.

X

Not thee, O never thee, in all time's changes,
  Not thee, but this the sound of thy sad soul,
  The shadow of thy swift spirit, this shut scroll
I lay my hand on, and not death estranges
  My spirit from communion of thy song—
  These memories and these melodies that throng
Veiled porches of a Muse funereal—
  These I salute, these touch, these clasp and fold
  As though a hand were in my hand to hold,
Or through mine ears a mourning musical
  Of many mourners rolled.

XI

I among these, I also, in such station
  As when the pyre was charred, and piled the sods,
  And offering to the dead made, and their gods,
The old mourners had, standing to make libation,
  I stand, and to the gods and to the dead
  Do reverence without prayer or praise, and shed
Offering to these unknown, the gods of gloom,
  And what of honey and spice my seedlands bear,
  And what I may of fruits in this chilled air,
And lay, Orestes-like, across the tomb
  A curl of severed hair.

XII

But by no hand nor any treason stricken,
  Not like the low-lying head of Him, the King,
  The flame that made of Troy a ruinous thing,
Thou liest, and on this dust no tears could quicken
  There fall no tears like theirs that all men hear
  Fall tear by sweet imperishable tear
Down the opening leaves of holy poets' pages.
  Thee not Orestes, not Electra mourns;
  But bending us-ward with memorial urns
The most high Muses that fulfil all ages
  Weep, and our God's heart yearns.

XIII

For, sparing of his sacred strength, not often
  Among us darkling here the lord of light
  Makes manifest his music and his might
In hearts that open and in lips that soften
  With the soft flame and heat of songs that shine.
  Thy lips indeed he touched with bitter wine,

And nourished them indeed with bitter bread;
  Yet surely from his hand thy soul's food came,
  The fire that scarred thy spirit at his flame
Was lighted, and thine hungering heart he fed
  Who feeds our hearts with fame.

XIV

Therefore he too now at thy soul's sunsetting,
  God of all suns and songs, he too bends down
  To mix his laurel with thy cypress crown,
And save thy dust from blame and from forgetting.
  Therefore he too, seeing all thou wert and art,
  Compassionate, with sad and sacred heart,
Mourns thee of many his children the last dead,
  And hallows with strange tears and alien sighs
  Thine unmelodious mouth and sunless eyes,
And over thine irrevocable head
  Sheds light from the under skies.

XV

And one weeps with him in the ways Lethean,
  And stains with tears her changing bosom chill
  That obscure Venus of the hollow hill,
That thing transformed which was the Cytherean,
  With lips that lost their Grecian laugh divine
  Long since, and face no more called Erycine;
A ghost, a bitter and luxurious god.
  Thee also with fair flesh and singing spell
  Did she, a sad and second prey, compel
Into the footless places once more trod,
  And shadows hot from hell.

XVI

And now no sacred staff shall break in blossom,
  No choral salutation lure to light
  A spirit sick with perfume and sweet night

And love's tired eyes and hands and barren bosom.
  There is no help for these things; none to mend
  And none to mar; not all our songs, O friend,
Will make death clear or make life durable.
  Howbeit with rose and ivy and wild vine
  And with wild notes about this dust of thine
At least I fill the place where white dreams dwell
  And wreathe an unseen shrine.

XVII

Sleep; and if life was bitter to thee, pardon,
  If sweet, give thanks; thou hast no more to live;
  And to give thanks is good, and to forgive.
Out of the mystic and the mournful garden
  Where all day through thine hands in barren braid
  Wove the sick flowers of secrecy and shade,
Green buds of sorrow and sin, and remnants grey,
  Sweet-smelling, pale with poison, sanguine-hearted,
  Passions that sprang from sleep and thoughts that
    started,
Shall death not bring us all as thee one day
  Among the days departed?

XVIII

For thee, O now a silent soul, my brother,
  Take at my hands this garland, and farewell.
  Thin is the leaf, and chill the wintry smell,
And chill the solemn earth, a fatal mother,
  With sadder than the Niobean womb,
  And in the hollow of her breasts a tomb.
Content thee, howsoe'er, whose days are done;
  There lies not any troublous thing before,
  Nor sight nor sound to war against thee more.
For whom all winds are quiet as the sun,
  All waters as the shore.

Sonnet

With a copy of MADEMOISELLE DE MAUPIN

THIS is the golden book of spirit and sense,
   The holy writ of beauty; he that wrought
  Made it with dreams and faultless words and thought
That seeks and finds and loses in the dense
Dim air of life that beauty's excellence
   Wherewith love makes one hour of life distraught
   And all hours after follow and find not aught.
Here is that height of all love's eminence
Where man may breathe but for a breathing-space
   And feel his soul burn as an altar-fire
   To the unknown God of unachieved desire,
And from the middle mystery of the place
   Watch lights that break, hear sounds as of a quire,
But see not twice unveiled the veiled God's face.

A Ballad of François Villon

Prince of all Ballad-makers

BIRD of the bitter bright grey golden morn
    Scarce risen upon the dusk of dolorous years,
First of us all and sweetest singer born
    Whose far shrill note the world of new men hears
    Cleave the cold shuddering shade as twilight clears;
When song new-born put off the old world's attire
And felt its tune on her changed lips expire,
    Writ foremost on the roll of them that came
Fresh girt for service of the latter lyre,
    Villon, our sad bad glad mad brother's name!

Alas the joy, the sorrow, and the scorn,
    That clothed thy life with hopes and sins and fears,
And gave thee stones for bread and tares for corn
    And plume-plucked gaol-birds for thy starveling peers
    Till death clipt close their flight with shameful shears;
Till shifts came short and loves were hard to hire,
When lilt of song nor twitch of twangling wire
    Could buy thee bread or kisses; when light fame
Spurned like a ball and haled through brake and briar,
    Villon, our sad bad glad mad brother's name!

Poor splendid wings so frayed and soiled and torn!
    Poor kind wild eyes so dashed with light quick tears!
Poor perfect voice, most blithe when most forlorn,
    That rings athwart the sea whence no man steers
    Like joy-bells crossed with death-bells in our ears!
What far delight has cooled the fierce desire
That like some ravenous bird was strong to tire
    On that frail flesh and soul consumed with flame,
But left more sweet than roses to respire,
    Villon, our sad bad glad mad brother's name?

Prince of sweet songs made out of tears and fire,
A harlot was thy nurse, a God thy sire;
   Shame soiled thy song, and song assoiled thy shame.
But from thy feet now death has washed the mire,
Love reads out first at head of all our quire,
   Villon, our sad bad glad mad brother's name.

Before Sunset

IN the lower lands of day
  On the hither side of night,
There is nothing that will stay,
   There are all things soft to sight;
   Lighted shade and shadowy light
In the wayside and the way,
   Hours the sun has spared to smite,
Flowers the rain has left to play.

Shall these hours run down and say
  No good thing of thee and me?
Time that made us and will slay
   Laughs at love in me and thee;
   But if here the flowers may see
One whole hour of amorous breath,
   Time shall die, and love shall be
Lord as time was over death.

I

O TENDER time that love thinks long to see,
    Sweet foot of spring that with her footfall sows
  Late snowlike flowery leavings of the snows,
Be not too long irresolute to be;
O mother-month, where have they hidden thee?
    Out of the pale time of the flowerless rose
I reach my heart out toward the springtime lands,
    I stretch my spirit forth to the fair hours,
        The purplest of the prime;
I lean my soul down over them, with hands
    Made wide to take the ghostly growths of flowers;
        I send my love back to the lovely time.

II

Where has the green wood hid thy gracious head?
    Veiled with what visions while the grey world grieves,
    Or muffled with what shadows of green leaves,
What warm intangible green shadows spread
To sweeten the sweet twilight for thy bed?
    What sleep enchants thee? what delight deceives?
Where the deep dreamlike dew before the dawn
    Feels not the fingers of the sunlight yet
        Its silver web unweave,
Thy footless ghost on some unfooted lawn
    Whose air the unrisen sunbeams fear to fret
        Lives a ghost's life of daylong dawn and eve.

III

Sunrise it sees not, neither set of star,
    Large nightfall, nor imperial plenilune,
    Nor strong sweet shape of the full-breasted noon;
But where the silver-sandalled shadows are,

235

Too soft for arrows of the sun to mar,
　　Moves with the mild gait of an ungrown moon:
Hard overhead the half-lit crescent swims,
　　The tender-coloured night draws hardly breath,
　　　　The light is listening;
They watch the dawn of slender-shapen limbs,
　　Virginal born again of doubtful death,
　　　　Chill foster-father of the weanling spring.

IV

As sweet desire of day before the day,
　　As dreams of love before the true love born,
　　From the outer edge of winter overworn
The ghost arisen of May before the May
Takes through dim air her unawakened way,
　　The gracious ghost of morning risen ere morn.
With little unblown breasts and child-eyed looks
　　Following, the very maid, the girl-child spring,
　　　　Lifts windward her bright brows,
Dips her light feet in warm and moving brooks,
　　And kindles with her own mouth's colouring
　　　　The fearful firstlings of the plumeless boughs.

V

I seek thee sleeping, and awhile I see,
　　Fair face that art not, how thy maiden breath
　　Shall put at last the deadly days to death
And fill the fields and fire the woods with thee
And seaward hollows where my feet would be
　　When heaven shall hear the word that April saith
To change the cold heart of the weary time,
　　To stir and soften all the time to tears,
　　　　Tears joyfuller than mirth;

As even to May's clear height the young days climb
    With feet not swifter than those fair first years
        Whose flowers revive not with thy flowers on earth.

VI

I would not bid thee, though I might, give back
    One good thing youth has given and borne away;
    I crave not any comfort of the day
That is not, nor on time's retrodden track
Would turn to meet the white-robed hours or black
    That long since left me on their mortal way;
Nor light nor love that has been, nor the breath
    That comes with morning from the sun to be
        And sets light hope on fire;
No fruit, no flower thought once too fair for death,
    No flower nor hour once fallen from life's green tree,
        No leaf once plucked or once fulfilled desire.

VII

The morning song beneath the stars that fled
    With twilight through the moonless mountain air,
    While youth with burning lips and wreathless hair
Sang toward the sun that was to crown his head,
Rising; the hopes that triumphed and fell dead,
    The sweet swift eyes and songs of hours that were;
These may'st thou not give back for ever; these,
    As at the sea's heart all her wrecks lie waste,
        Lie deeper than the sea;
But flowers thou may'st, and winds, and hours of ease,
    And all its April to the world thou may'st
        Give back, and half my April back to me.

At Parting

FOR a day and a night Love sang to us, played with us,
    Folded us round from the dark and the light;
And our hearts were fulfilled of the music he made with us,
Made with our hearts and our lips while he stayed with us,
    Stayed in mid passage his pinions from flight
        For a day and a night.

From his foes that kept watch with his wings had he hidden
    us,
    Covered us close from the eyes that would smite,
From the feet that had tracked and the tongues that had
    chidden us
Sheltering in shade of the myrtles forbidden us
    Spirit and flesh growing one with delight
        For a day and a night.

But his wings will not rest and his feet will not stay for us:
    Morning is here in the joy of its might;
With his breath has he sweetened a night and a day for us;
Now let him pass, and the myrtles make way for us;
    Love can but last in us here at his height
        For a day and a night.

Triads

I

THE word of the sun to the sky,
The word of the wind to the sea,
The word of the moon to the night,
What may it be?

II

The sense to the flower of the fly,
The sense of the bird to the tree,
The sense to the cloud of the light,
Who can tell me?

III

The song of the fields to the kye,
The song of the lime to the bee,
The song of the depth to the height,
Who knows all three?

THE year lies fallen and faded
  On cliffs by clouds invaded,
With tongues of storms upbraided,
  With wrath of waves bedinned;
And inland, wild with warning,
As in deaf ears or scorning,
The clarion even and morning
  Rings of the south-west wind.

The wild bents wane and wither
In blasts whose breath bows hither
Their grey-grown heads and thither,
  Unblest of rain or sun;
The pale fierce heavens are crowded
With shapes like dreams beclouded,
As though the old year enshrouded
  Lay, long ere life were done.

Full-charged with oldworld wonders,
From dusk Tintagel thunders
A note that smites and sunders
  The hard frore fields of air;
A trumpet stormier-sounded
Than once from lists rebounded
When strong men sense-confounded
  Fell thick in tourney there.

From scarce a duskier dwelling
Such notes of wail rose welling
Through the outer darkness, telling
  In the awful singer's ears
What souls the darkness covers,

What love-lost souls of lovers,
Whose cry still hangs and hovers
    In each man's born that hears.

For there by Hector's brother
And yet some thousand other
He that had grief to mother
    Passed pale from Dante's sight;
With one fast linked as fearless,
Perchance, there only tearless;
Iseult and Tristram, peerless
    And perfect queen and knight.

A shrill-winged sound comes flying
North, as of wild souls crying
The cry of things undying,
    That know what life must be;
Or as the old year's heart, stricken
Too sore for hope to quicken
By thoughts like thorns that thicken,
    Broke, breaking with the sea.

Ballad of the Women of Paris

ALBEIT the Venice girls get praise
　　For their sweet speech and tender air,
And though the old women have wise ways
　　Of chaffering for amorous ware,
　　Yet at my peril dare I swear,
Search Rome, where God's grace mainly tarries,
　　Florence and Savoy, everywhere,
There's no good girl's lip out of Paris.

The Naples women, as folk prattle,
　　Are sweetly spoken and subtle enough:
German girls are good at tattle,
　　And Prussians make their boast thereof;
　　Take Egypt for the next remove,
Or that waste land the Tartar harries,
　　Spain or Greece, for the matter of love,
There's no good girl's lip out of Paris.

Breton and Swiss know nought of the matter,
　　Gascony girls or girls of Toulouse;
Two fishwives here with a half-hour's chatter
　　Would shut them up by threes and twos;
　　Calais, Lorraine, and all their crews,
(Names enow the mad song marries)
　　England and Picardy, search them and choose,
There's no good girl's lip out of Paris.

Prince, give praise to our French ladies
　　For the sweet sound their speaking carries;
'Twixt Rome and Cadiz many a maid is,
　　But no good girl's lip out of Paris.

MEN, brother men, that after us yet live,
    Let not your hearts too hard against us be;
For if some pity of us poor men ye give,
    The sooner God shall take of you pity.
    Here are we five or six strung up, you see,
And here the flesh that all too well we fed
Bit by bit eaten and rotten, rent and shred,
    And we the bones grow dust and ash withal;
Let no man laugh at us discomforted,
    But pray to God that he forgive us all.

If we call on you, brothers, to forgive,
    Ye should not hold our prayer in scorn, though we
Were slain by law; ye know that all alive
    Have not wit alway to walk righteously;
    Make therefore intercession heartily
With him that of a virgin's womb was bred,
That his grace be not as a dry well-head
    For us, not let hell's thunder on us fall;
We are dead, let no man harry or vex us dead,
    But pray to God that he forgive us all.

The rain has washed and laundered us all five,
    And the sun dried and blackened; yea, perdie,
Ravens and pies with beaks that rend and rive
    Have dug our eyes out, and plucked off for fee
    Our beards and eyebrows; never are we free,
Not once, to rest; but here and there still sped,
Drive at its wild will by the wind's change led,
    More pecked of birds than fruits on garden-wall;
Men, for God's love, let no gibe here be said,
    But pray to God that he forgive us all.

Prince Jesus, that of all art lord and head,
Keep us, that hell be not our bitter bed;
    We have nought to do in such a master's hall
Be not ye therefore of our fellowhead,
    But pray to God that he forgive us all.

A Baby's Epitaph

APRIL made me: winter laid me here away asleep.
    Bright as Maytime was my daytime; night is soft and
    deep:
Though the morrow bring forth sorrow, well are ye that
    weep.

Ye that held me dear beheld me not a twelvemonth long:
All the while ye saw me smile, ye knew not whence the song
Came that made me smile, and laid me here, and wrought
    you wrong.

Angels, calling from your brawling world one undefiled,
Homeward bade me, and forbade me here to rest beguiled:
Here I sleep not: pass, and weep not here upon your child.

ERECHTHEUS

A TRAGEDY

PERSONS

Erechtheus	Herald of Eumolpus
Chorus of Athenian Elders	Messenger
Praxithea	Athenian Herald
Chthonia	Athena

ὦ ταὶ λιπαραὶ καὶ ἰοστέφανοι καὶ ἀοίδιμοι,
Ἑλλάδος ἔρεισμα, κλεινaὶ Ἀθᾶναι, δαιμόνιον πτολίεθρον.

PIND. *Fr.* 47.

AT.   λίς δὲ ποιμάνωρ ἔπεστι κἀπιδεσπόζει στρατοῦ;
XO.   οὔτινος δοῦλοι κέκληνται φωτὸς οὐδ' ὑπηκόοι.

ÆSCH. *Pers.* 241-2.

ERECHTHEUS

MOTHER of life and death and all men's days,
Earth, whom I chief of all men born would bless,
And call thee with more loving lips than theirs
Mother, for of this very body of thine
And living blood I have my breath and live,
Behold me, even thy son, me crowned of men,
Me made thy child by that strong cunning God
Who fashions fire and iron, who begat
Me for a sword and beacon-fire on thee,
Me fosterling of Pallas, in her shade
Reared, that I first might pay the nursing debt,
Hallowing her fame with flower of third-year feasts,
And first bow down the bridled strength of steeds
To lose the wild wont of their birth, and bear
Clasp of man's knees and steerage of his hand,
Or fourfold service of his fire-swift wheels
That whirl the four-yoked chariot; me the king
Who stand before thee naked now, and cry,
O holy and general mother of all men born,
But mother most and motherliest of mine,
Earth, for I ask thee rather of all the Gods,
What have we done? what word mistimed or work
Hath winged the wild feet of this timeless curse
To fall as fire upon us? Lo, I stand
Here on this brow's crown of the city's head
That crowns its lovely body, till death's hour
Waste it; but now the dew of dawn and birth
Is fresh upon it from thy womb, and we
Behold it born how beauteous; one day more
I see the world's wheel of the circling sun
Roll up rejoicing to regard on earth
This one thing goodliest, fair as heaven or he,

Worth a God's gaze or strife of Gods; but now
Would this day's ebb of their spent wave of strife
Sweep it to sea, wash it on wreck, and leave
A costless thing contemned; and in our stead,
Where these walls were and sounding streets of men,
Make wide a waste for tongueless water-herds
And spoil of ravening fishes; that no more
Should men say, Here was Athens. This shalt thou
Sustain not, nor thy son endure to see,
Nor thou to live and look on; for the womb
Bare me not base that bare me miserable,
To hear this loud brood of the Thracian foam
Break its broad strength of billowy-beating war
Here, and upon it as a blast of death
Blowing, the keen wrath of a fire-souled king,
A strange growth grafted on our natural soil,
A root of Thrace in Eleusinian earth
Set for no comfort to the kindly land,
Son of the sea's lord and our first-born foe,
Eumolpus; nothing sweet in ears of thine
The music of his making, nor a song
Toward hopes of ours auspicious; for the note
Rings as for death oracular to thy sons
That goes before him on the sea-wind blown
Full of this charge laid on me, to put out
The brief light kindled of mine own child's life,
Or with this helmsman hand that steers the state
Run right on the under shoal and ridge of death
The populous ship with all its fraughtage gone
And sails that were to take the wind of time
Rent, and the tackling that should hold out fast
In confluent surge of loud calamities
Broken, with spars of rudders and lost oars
That were to row toward harbour and find rest
In some most glorious haven of all the world

And else may never near it; such a song
The Gods have set his lips on fire withal
Who threatens now in all their names to bring
Ruin; but none of these, thou knowest, have I
Chid with my tongue or cursed at heart for grief,
Knowing how the soul runs reinless on sheer death
Whose grief or joy takes part against the Gods.
And what they will is more than our desire,
And their desire is more than what we will.
For no man's will and no desire of man's
Shall stand as doth a God's will.   Yet, O fair
Mother, that seest me how I cast no word
Against them, plead no reason, crave no cause,
Boast me not blameless, nor beweep me wronged,
By this fair wreath of towers we have decked thee with,
This chaplet that we give thee woven of walls,
This girdle of gate and temple and citadel
Drawn round beneath thy bosom, and fast linked
As to thine heart's root—this dear crown of thine.
This present light, this city—be not thou
Slow to take heed nor slack to strengthen her,
Fare we so short-lived howsoe'er, and pay
What price we may to ransom thee thy town,
Not me my life; but thou that diest not, thou,
Though all our house die for this people's sake,
Keep thou for ours thy crown our city, guard
And give it life the lovelier that we died.

CHORUS

Sun, thou hast lightened and loosed by thy might
Ocean and Earth from the lordship of night,
Quickening with vision his eye that was veiled,
Freshening the force in her heart that had failed,
That sister fettered and blinded brother

248

Should have sight by thy grace and delight of each other,
    Behold now and see
    What profit is given them of thee;
What wrath has enkindled with madness of mind
Her limbs that were bounden, his face that was blind,
To be locked as in wrestle together, and lighten
With fire that shall darken thy fire in the sky,
Body to body and eye against eye
    In a war against kind,
Till the bloom of her fields and her high hills whiten
    With the foam of his waves more high.
For the sea-marks set to divide of old
The kingdoms to Ocean and Earth assigned,
The hoar sea-fields from the cornfields' gold,
His wine-bright waves from her vineyards' fold,
    Frail forces we find
To bridle the spirit of Gods or bind
    Till the heat of their hearts wax cold.
But the peace that was stablished between them to stand
Is rent now in twain by the strength of his hand
Who stirs up the storm of his sons overbold
To pluck from fight when he lost of right,
By council and judgment of Gods that spake
And gave great Pallas the strife's fair stake,
The lordship and love of the lovely land,
The grace of the town that hath on it for crown
    But a headband to wear
    Of violets one-hued with her hair:
For the vales and the green high places of earth
    Hold nothing so fair,
And the depths of the sea bear no such birth
    Of the manifold births they bear.
Too well, too well was the great stake worth
A strife divine for the Gods to judge,
A crowned God's triumph, a foiled God's grudge,

Though the loser be strong and the victress wise
Who played long since for so large a prize,
The fruitful immortal anointed adored
Dear city of men without master or lord,
Fair fortress and fostress of sons born free,
Who stand in her sight and in thine, O sun,
Slaves of no man, subjects of none;
A wonder enthroned on the hills and sea,
A maiden crowned with a fourfold glory
That none from the pride of her head may rend,
Violet and olive-leaf purple and hoary,
Song-wreath and story the fairest of fame,
Flowers that the winter can blast not or bend;
A light upon earth as the sun's own flame,
 A name as his name,
 Athens, a praise without end.

A noise is arisen against us of waters,   [*Str.* 1.
 A sound as of battle come up from the sea.
Strange hunters are hard on us, hearts without pity;
They have staked their nets round the fair young city,
 That the sons of her strength and her virgin daughters
  Should find not whither alive to flee.
And we know not yet of the word unwritten, [*Ant.* 1
 The doom of the Pythian we have not heard;
From the navel of earth and the veiled mid altar
We wait for a token with hopes that falter,
With fears that hang on our hearts thought-smitten
 Lest her tongue be kindled with no good word.
O thou not born of the womb, nor bred   [*Str.* 2.
In the bride-night's warmth of a changed God's bed,
But thy life as a lightning was flashed from the light of
 thy father's head,
 O chief God's child by a motherless birth,
 If aught in thy sight we indeed be worth,

250

Keep death from us thou, that art none of the Gods of the
   dead under earth.

   Thou that hast power on us, save, if thou wilt;   [*Ant.* 2.
   Let the blind wave breach not thy wall scarce built;
But bless us not so as by bloodshed, impute not for grace
   to us guilt,
   Nor by price of pollution of blood set us free;
   Let the hands be taintless that clasp thy knee,
Nor a maiden be slain to redeem for a maiden her shrine
   from the sea.

   O earth, O sun, turn back   [*Str.* 3.
   Full on his deadly track
Death, that would smite you black and mar your creatures,
   And with one hand disroot
   All tender flower and fruit,
With one strike blind and mute the heaven's fair features,
   Pluck out the eyes of morn, and make
Silence in the east and blackness whence the bright songs
   break.

   Help, earth, help, heaven, that hear   [*Ant.* 3.
   The song-notes of our fear,
Shrewd notes and shrill, not clear or joyful-sounding;
   Hear, highest of Gods, and stay
   Death on his hunter's way,
Full on his forceless prey his beagles hounding;
   Break thou his bow, make short his hand,
Maim his fleet foot whose passage kills the living land.

   Let a third wave smite not us, father,   [*Str.* 4.
   Long since sore smitten of twain,
      Lest the house of thy son's son perish
      And his name be barren on earth.
   Whose race wilt thou comfort rather
   If none to thy son remain?
      Whose seed wilt thou choose to cherish
      If his be cut off in the birth?

For the first fair graft of his graffing   *[Ant. 4.*
  Was rent from its maiden root
    By the strong swift hand of a lover
      Who fills the night with his breath;
On the lip of the stream low-laughing
  Her green soft virginal shoot
    Was plucked from the stream-side cover
      By the grasp of a love like death.
For a God's was the mouth that kissed her   *[Str. 5.*
  Who speaks, and the leaves lie dead,
    When winter awakes as at warning
      To the sound of his foot from Thrace.
Nor happier the bed of her sister
  Though Love's self laid her abed
    By a bridegroom beloved of the morning
      And fair as the dawn's own face.
For Procris, ensnared and ensnaring   *[Ant. 5.*
  By the fraud of a twofold wile,
    With the point of her own spear stricken
      By the gift of her own hand fell.
Oversubtle in doubts, overdaring
  In deeds and devices of guile,
    And strong to quench as to quicken,
      O Love, have we named thee well?
By thee was the spear's edge whetted   *[Str. 6.*
  That laid her dead in the dew,
    In the moist green glens of the midland
      By her dear lord slain and thee.
And him at the cliff's end fretted
  By the grey keen waves, him too,
    Thine hand from the white-browed headland
      Flung down for a spoil to the sea.
But enough now of grief's grey-growing   *[Ant. 6.*
  Have darkened the house divine,
    Have flowered on its boughs and faded,

And green is the brave stock yet.
O father all seeing and all knowing,
Let the last fruit fall not of thine
From the tree with whose boughs we are shaded,
From the stock that thy son's hand set.

ERECHTHEUS

O daughter of Cephisus, from all time
Wise have I found thee, wife and queen, of heart
Perfect; nor in the days that knew not wind
Nor days when storm blew death upon our peace
Was thine heart swoln with seed of pride, or bowed
With blasts of bitter fear that break men's souls
Who lift too high their minds toward heaven, in thought
Too godlike grown for worship; but of mood
Equal, in good time reverent of time bad,
And glad in ill days of the good that were.
Nor now too would I fear thee, now misdoubt
Lest fate should find thee lesser than thy doom,
Chosen if thou be to bear and to be great
Haply beyond all women; and the word
Speaks thee divine, dear queen, that speaks thee dead,
Dead being alive, or quick and dead in one
Shall not men call thee living? yet I fear
To slay thee timeless with my proper tongue,
With lips, thou knowest, that love thee; and such work
Was never laid of Gods on men, such word
No mouth of man learnt ever, as from mine
Most loth to speak thine ear most loth shall take
And hold it hateful as the grave to hear.

PRAXITHEA

That word there is not in all speech of man,
King, that being spoken of the Gods and thee
I have not heart to honour, or dare hold

More than I hold thee or the Gods in hate
Hearing; but if my heart abhor it heard
Being insubmissive, hold me not thy wife
But use me like a stranger, whom thine hand
Hath fed by chance and finding thence no thanks
Flung off for shame's sake to forgetfulness.

ERECHTHEUS

O, of what breath shall such a word be made,
Or from what heart find utterance?   Would my tongue
Were rent forth rather from the quivering root
Than made as fire or poison thus for thee.

PRAXITHEA

But if thou speak of blood, and I that hear
Be chosen of all for this land's love to die
And save to thee thy city, know this well,
Happiest I hold me of her seed alive.

ERECHTHEUS

O sun that seest, what saying was this of thine,
God, that thy power has breathed into my lips?
For from no sunlit shrine darkling it came.

PRAXITHEA

What portent from the mid oracular place
Hath smitten thee so like a curse that flies
Wingless, to waste men with its plagues? yet speak.

ERECHTHEUS

Thy blood the Gods require not; take this first.

PRAXITHEA

To me than thee more grievous this should sound.

ERECHTHEUS

That word rang truer and bitterer than it knew.

PRAXITHEA

This is not then thy grief, to see me die?

ERECHTHEUS

Die shalt thou not, yet give thy blood to death.

PRAXITHEA

If this ring worse I know not; strange it rang.

ERECHTHEUS

Alas, thou knowest not; woe is me that know.

PRAXITHEA

And woe shall mine be, knowing; yet halt not here.

ERECHTHEUS

Guiltless of blood this state may stand no more.

PRAXITHEA

Firm let it stand whatever bleed or fall.

ERECHTHEUS

O Gods, that I should say it shall and weep.

PRAXITHEA

Weep, and say this? no tears should bathe such words.

ERECHTHEUS

Woe' s me that I must weep upon them, woe.

255

PRAXITHEA

What stain is on them for thy tears to cleanse?

ERECHTHEUS

A stain of blood unpurgeable with tears.

PRAXITHEA

Whence? for thou sayest it is and is not mine.

ERECHTHEUS

Hear then and know why only of all men I
That bring such news as mine is, I alone
Must wash good words with weeping; I and thou,
Woman, must wail to hear men sing, must groan
To see their joy who love us; all our friends
Save only we, and all save we that love
This holiness of Athens, in our sight
Shall lift their hearts up, in our hearing praise
Gods whom we may not; for to these they give
Life of their children, flower of all their seed,
For all their travail fruit, for all their hopes
Harvest; but we for all our good things, we
Have at their hands which fill all these folk full
Death, barrenness, child-slaughter, curses, cares,
Sea-leaguer and land-shipwreck; which of these,
Which wilt thou first give thanks for? all are thine.

PRAXITHEA

What first they give who give this city good,
For that first given to save it I give thanks
First, and thanks heartier from a happier tongue,
More than for any my peculiar grace
Shown me and not my country; next for this,
That none of all these but for all these I

Must bear my burden, and no eye but mine
Weep of all women's in this broad land born
Who see their land's deliverance; but much more,
But most for this I thank them most of all,
That this their edge of doom is chosen to pierce
My heart and not my country's; for the sword
Drawn to smite there and sharpened for such stroke
Should wound more deep than any turned on me.

CHORUS

Well fares the land that bears such fruit, and well
The spirit that breeds such thought and speech in man.

ERECHTHEUS

O woman, thou hast shamed my heart with thine,
To show so strong a patience; take then all;
For all shall break not nor bring down thy soul.
The word that journeying to the bright God's shrine
Who speaks askance and darkling, but his name
Hath in it slaying and ruin broad writ out,
I heard, hear thou: thus saith he; There shall die
One soul for all this people; from thy womb
Came forth the seed that here on dry bare ground
Death's hand must sow untimely, to bring forth
Nor blade nor shoot in season, being by name
To the under Gods made holy, who require
For this land's life her death and maiden blood
To save a maiden city.   Thus I heard,
And thus with all said leave thee; for save this
No word is left us, and no hope alive.

CHORUS

He hath uttered too surely his wrath not obscurely, nor
     wrapt as in mists of his breath,   [*Str.*
257

The master that lightens not hearts he enlightens, but gives
     them foreknowledge of death.
As a bolt from the cloud hath he sent it aloud and pro-
     claimed it afar,
From the darkness and height of the horror of night hath
     he shown us a star.
    Star may I name it and err not, or flame shall I say,
    Born of the womb that was born for the tomb of the
       day?
O Night, whom other but thee for mother, and Death for
     the father, Night,   [*Ant.*
Shall we dream to discover, save thee and thy lover, to bring
     such a sorrow to sight?
From the slumberless bed for thy bedfellow spread and his
     bride under earth
Hast thou brought forth a wild and insatiable child, an
     unbearable birth.
    Fierce are the fangs of his wrath, and the pangs that
     they give;
    None is there, none that may bear them, not one that
     would live.

CHTHONIA

Forth of the fine-spun folds of veils that hide
My virgin chamber toward the full-faced sun
I set my foot not moved of mine own will,
Unmaidenlike, nor with unprompted speed
Turn eyes too broad or doglike unabashed
On reverend heads of men and thence on thine,
Mother, now covered from the light and bowed
As hers who mourns her brethren; but what grief
Bends thy blind head thus earthward, holds thus mute,
I know not till thy will be to lift up
Toward mine thy sorrow-muffled eyes and speak;
And till thy will be would I know this not.

Old men and childless, or if sons ye have seen
And daughters, elder-born were these than mine,
Look on this child, how young of years, how sweet,
How scant of time and green of age her life
Puts forth its flower of girlhood; and her gait
How virginal, how soft her speech, her eyes
How seemly smiling; wise should all ye be,
All honourable and kindly men of age;
Now give me counsel and one word to say
That I may bear to speak, and hold my peace
Henceforth for all time even as all ye now.
Dumb are ye all, bowed eyes and tongueless mouths,
Unprofitable; if this were wind that speaks,
As much its breath might move you.   Thou then, child,
Set thy sweet eyes on mine; look through them well;
Take note of all the writing of my face
As of a tablet or a tomb inscribed
That bears me record; lifeless now, my life
Thereon that was think written; brief to read,
Yet shall the scripture sear thine eyes as fire
And leave them dark as dead men's.   Nay, dear child,
Thou hast no skill, my maiden, and no sense
To take such knowledge; sweet is all thy lore,
And all this bitter; yet I charge thee learn
And love and lay this up within thine heart,
Even this my word; less ill it were to die
Than live and look upon thy mother dead,
Thy mother-land that bare thee; no man slain
But him who hath seen it shall men count unblest,
None blest as him who hath died and seen it not.

CHTHONIA

That sight some God keep from me though I die.

PRAXITHEA

A God from thee shall keep it; fear not this.

CHTHONIA

Thanks all my life long shall he gain of mine.

PRAXITHEA

Short gain of all yet shall he get of thee.

CHTHONIA

Brief be my life, yet so long live my thanks.

PRAXITHEA

So long? so little; how long shall they live?

CHTHONIA

Even while I see the sunlight and thine eyes.

PRAXITHEA

Would mine might shut ere thine upon the sun.

CHTHONIA

For me thou prayest unkindly; change that prayer.

PRAXITHEA

Not well for me thou sayest, and ill for thee.

CHTHONIA

Nay, for me well, if thou shalt live, not I.

PRAXITHEA

How live, and lose these loving looks of thine?

CHTHONIA

It seems I too, thus praying, then, love thee not.

PRAXITHEA

Lov'st thou not life? what wouldst thou do to die?

CHTHONIA

Well, but not more than all things, love I life.

PRAXITHEA

And fain wouldst keep it as thine age allows?

CHTHONIA

Fain would I live, and fain not fear to die.

PRAXITHEA

That I might bid thee die not! Peace; no more.

CHORUS

A godlike race of grief the Gods have set
For these to run matched equal, heart with heart.

PRAXITHEA

Child of the chief of Gods, and maiden crowned,
Queen of these towers and fostress of their king,
Pallas, and thou my father's holiest head,
A living well of life nor stanched nor stained,
O God Cephisus, thee too charge I next,
Be to me judge and witness; nor thine ear
Shall now my tongue invoke not, thou to me
Most hateful of things holy, mournfullest
Of all old sacred streams that wash the world,
Ilissus, on whose marge at flowery play

A whirlwind-footed bridegroom found my child
And rapt her northward where mine elder-born
Keeps now the Thracian bride-bed of a God
Intolerable to seamen, but this land
Finds him in hope for her sake favourable,
A gracious son by wedlock; hear me then
Thou likewise, if with no faint heart or false
The word I say be said, the gift be given,
Which might I choose I had rather die than give
Or speak and die not. Ere thy limbs were made
Or thine eyes lightened, strife, thou knowest, my child,
'Twixt God and God had risen, which heavenlier name
Should here stand hallowed, whose more liberal grace
Should win this city's worship, and our land
To which of these do reverence; first the lord
Whose wheels make lightnings of the foam-flowered sea
Here on this rock, whose height brow-bound with dawn
Is head and heart of Athens, one sheer blow
Struck, and beneath the triple wound that shook
The stony sinews and stark roots of the earth
Sprang toward the sun a sharp salt fount, and sank
Where lying it lights the heart up of the hill,
A well of bright strange brine; but she that reared
Thy father with her same chaste fostering hand
Set for a sign against it in our guard
The holy bloom of the olive, whose hoar leaf
High in the shadowy shrine of Pandrosus
Hath honour of us all; and of this strife
The twelve most high Gods judging with one mouth
Acclaimed her victress; wroth whereat, as wronged
That she should hold from him such prize and place,
The strong king of the tempest-rifted sea
Loosed reinless on the low Thriasian plain
The thunders of his chariots, swallowing stunned
Earth, beasts, and men, the whole blind foundering world

That was the sun's at morning, and ere noon
Death's; nor this only prey fulfilled his mind;
For with strange crook-toothed prows of Carian folk
Who snatch a sanguine life out of the sea,
Thieves keen to pluck their bloody fruit of spoil
From the grey fruitless waters, has their God
Furrowed our shores to waste them, as the fields
Were landward harried from the north with swords
Aonian, sickles of man-slaughtering edge
Ground for no hopeful harvest of live grain
Against us in Bœotia; these being spent,
Now this third time his wind of wrath has blown
Right on this people a mightier wave of war,
Three times more huge a ruin; such its ridge
Foam-rimmed and hollow like the womb of heaven,
But black for shining, and with death for life
Big now to birth and ripe with child, full-blown
With fear and fruit of havoc, takes the sun
Out of our eyes, darkening the day, and blinds
The fair sky's face unseasonably with change,
A cloud in one and billow of battle, a surge
High reared as heaven with monstrous surf of spears
That shake on us their shadow, till men's heads
Bend, and their hearts even with its forward wind
Wither, so blasts all seed in them of hope
Its breath and blight of presage; yea, even now
The winter of this wind out of the deeps
Makes cold our trust in comfort of the Gods
And blind our eye toward outlook; yet not here,
Here never shall the Thracian plant on high
For ours his father's symbol, nor with wreaths
A strange folk wreathe it upright set and crowned
Here where our natural people born behold
The golden Gorgon of the shield's defence
That screens their flowering olive, nor strange Gods

Be graced, and Pallas here have praise no more.
And if this be not I must give my child,
Thee, mine own very blood and spirit of mine,
Thee to be slain. Turn from me, turn thine eyes
A little from me; I can bear not yet
To see if still they smile on mine or no,
If fear make faint the light in them, or faith
Fix them as stars of safety. Need have we,
Sore need of stars that set not in mid storm,
Lights that outlast the lightnings; yet my heart
Endures not to make proof of thine or these,
Not yet to know these whom I made, and bare
What manner of woman; had I borne thee man,
I had made no question of thine eyes or heart,
Nor spared to read the scriptures in them writ,
Wert thou my son; yet couldst thou then but die
Fallen in sheer fight by chance and charge of spears
And have no more of memory, fill no tomb
More famous than thy fellows in fair field,
Where many share the grave, many the praise;
But one crown shall one only girl my child
Wear, dead for this dear city, and give back life
To him that gave her and to me that bare,
And save two sisters living; and all this,
Is this not all good? I shall give thee, child,
Thee but by fleshly nature mine, to bleed
For dear land's love; but if the city fall
What part is left me in my children then?
But if it stand and thou for it lie dead,
Then hast thou in it a better part than we,
A holier portion than we all; for each
Hath but the length of his own life to live,
And this most glorious mother-land on earth
To worship till that life have end; but thine
Hath end no more than hers; thou, dead, shalt live

Till Athens live not; for the days and nights
Given of thy bare brief dark dividual life.
Shall she give thee half all her agelong own
And all its glory; for thou givest her these;
But with one hand she takes and gives again
More than I gave or she requires of thee.
Come therefore, I will make thee fit for death,
I that could give thee, dear, no gift at birth
Save of light life that breathes and bleeds, even I
Will help thee to this better gift than mine
And lead thee by this little living hand
That death shall make so strong, to that great end
Whence it shall lighten like a God's, and strike
Dead the strong heart of battle that would break
Athens; but ye, pray for this land, old men,
That it may bring forth never child on earth
To love it less, for none may more, than we.

CHORUS

Out of the north wind grief came forth, [Str. 1.
     And the shining of a sword out of the sea.
Yea, of old the first-blown blast blew the prelude of this
          last,
     The blast of his trumpet upon Rhodope.
Out of the north skies full of his cloud,
With the clamour of his storms as of a crowd
At the wheels of a great king crying aloud,
At the axle of a strong king's car
That has girded on the girdle of war—
With hands that lightened the skies in sunder
And feet whose fall was followed of thunder,
     A God, a great God strange of name,
     With horse-yoke fleeter-hoofed than flame,
To the mountain bed of a maiden came,
Oreithyia, the bride mismated,

265

Wofully wed in a snow-strewn bed
With a bridegroom that kisses the bride's mouth dead;
Without garland, without glory, without song,
As a fawn by night on the hills belated,
Given over for a spoil unto the strong.
From lips how pale so keen a wail   [*Ant.* 1.
   At the grasp of a God's hand on her she gave,
When his breath that darkens air made a havoc of her
      hair,
   It rang from the mountain even to the wave;
Rang with a cry, *Woe's me, woe is me*!
From the darkness upon Haemus to the sea:
And with hands that clung to her new lord's knee,
As a virgin overborne with shame,
She besought him by her spouseless fame,
By the blameless breasts of a maid unmarried,
And locks unmaidenly rent and harried,
      And all her flower of body, born
      To match the maidenhood of morn,
With the might of the wind's wrath wrenched and torn.
Vain, all vain as a dead man's vision
Falling by night in his old friends' sight,
To be scattered with slumber and slain ere light;
Such a breath of such a bridegroom in that hour
Of her prayers made mock, of her fears derision,
And a ravage of her youth as of a flower.
With a leap of his limbs as a lion's, a cry from his lips as of
         thunder,   [*Str.* 2.
   In a storm of amorous godhead filled with fire,
From the height of the heaven that was rent with the roar
         of his coming in sunder,
   Sprang the strong God on the spoil of his desire.
   And the pines of the hills were as green reeds shattered,
   And their branches as buds of the soft spring scattered,
   And the west wind and east, and the sound of the south,

266

Fell dumb at the blast of the north wind's mouth,
　　At the cry of his coming out of heaven.
And the wild beasts quailed in the rifts and hollows
Where hound nor clarion of huntsman follows,
And the depths of the sea were aghast, and whitened,
And the crowns of their waves were as flame that
　　　lightened,
　　And the heart of the floods thereof was riven.
But she knew not him coming for terror, she felt not her
　　　wrong that he wrought her,　　　　　　　[*Ant. 2.*
When her locks as leaves were shed before his breath,
And she heard not for terror his prayer, though the cry was
　　　a God's that besought her,
　　Blown from lips that strew the world-wide seas with
　　　death.
For the heart was molten within her to hear,
And her knees beneath her were loosened for fear,
And her blood fast bound as a frost-bound water,
And the soft new bloom of the green earth's daughter
　　Wind-wasted as blossom of a tree;
As the wild God rapt her from earth's breast lifted,
On the strength of the stream of his dark breath drifted,
From the bosom of earth as a bride from the mother,
With storm for bridesman and wreck for brother.
　　As a cloud that he sheds upon the sea.

　　Of this hoary-headed woe　　　　　　　[*Epode*
　　Song made memory long ago;
　　Now a younger grief to mourn
　　Needs a new song younger born.
　　Who shall teach our tongues to reach
　　What strange height of saddest speech,
　　For the new bride's sake that is given to be
　　A stay to fetter the foot of the sea,
　　Lest it quite spurn down and trample the town,

Ere the violets be dead that were plucked for its crown,
   Or its olive-leaf whiten and wither?
Who shall say of the wind's way
That he journeyed yesterday,
Or the track of the storm that shall sound to-morrow,
If the new be more than the grey-grown sorrow?
For the wind of the green first season was keen,
And the blast shall be sharper than blew between
   That the breath of the sea blows hither.

HERALD OF EUMOLPUS

Old men, grey borderers on the march of death,
Tongue-fighters, tough of talk and sinewy speech,
Else nerveless, from no crew of such faint folk
Whose tongues are stouter than their hands come I
To bid not you to battle; let them strike
Whose swords are sharper than your keen-tongued wail,
And ye, sit fast and sorrow; but what man
Of all this land-folk and earth-labouring herd
For heart or hand seems foremost, him I call
If heart be his to hearken, him bid forth
To try if one be in the sun's sight born
Of all that grope and grovel on dry ground
That may join hands in battle grip for death
With them whose seed and strength is of the sea.

CHORUS

Know thou this much for all thy loud blast blown,
We lack not hands to speak with, swords to plead.
For proof of peril, not of boisterous breath,
Sea-wind and storm of barren mouths that foam
And rough rock's edge of menace; and short space
May lesson thy large ignorance and inform
This insolence with knowledge if there live

Men earth-begotten of no tenderer thews
Than knit the great joints of the grim sea's brood
With hasps of steel together; heaven to help,
One man shall break, even on their own flood's verge,
That iron bulk of battle; but thine eye
That sees it now swell higher than sand or shore
Haply shall see not when thine host shall shrink.

HERALD OF EUMOLPUS

Not haply, nay, but surely, shall not thine.

CHORUS

That lot shall no God give who fights for thee.

HERALD OF EUMOLPUS

Shall Gods bear bit and bridle, fool, of men?

CHORUS

Nor them forbid we nor shalt thou constrain.

HERALD OF EUMOLPUS

Yet say'st thou none shall make the good lot mine?

CHORUS

Of thy side none, nor moved for fear of thee.

HERALD OF EUMOLPUS

Gods hast thou then to baffle Gods of ours?

CHORUS

Nor thine nor mine, but equal-souled are they.

HERALD OF EUMOLPUS

Toward good and ill, then, equal-eyed of soul?

Nay, but swift-eyed to note where ill thoughts breed.

HERALD OF EUMOLPUS

Thy shaft word-feathered flies yet far of me.

CHORUS

Pride knows not, wounded, till the heart be cleft.

HERALD OF EUMOLPUS

No shaft wounds deep whose wing is plumed with
    words.

CHORUS

Lay that to heart, and bid thy tongue learn grace.

HERALD OF EUMOLPUS

Grace shall thine own crave soon too late of mine.

CHORUS

Boast thou till then, but I wage words no more.

ERECHTHEUS

Man, what shrill wind of speech and wrangling air
Blows in our ears a summons from thy lips
Winged with what message, or what gift or grace
Requiring? none but what his hand may take
Here may the foe think hence to reap, nor this
Except some doom from Godward yield it him.

HERALD OF EUMOLPUS

King of this land-folk, by my mouth to thee

Thus saith the son of him that shakes thine earth,
Eumolpus; now the stakes of war are set,
For land or sea to win by throw and wear;
Choose therefore or to quit thy side and give
The palm unfought for to his bloodless hand,
Or by that father's sceptre, and the foot
Whose tramp far off makes tremble for pure fear
Thy soul-struck mother, piercing like a sword
The immortal womb that bare thee; by the waves
That no man bridles and that bound thy world,
And by the winds and storms of all the sea,
He swears to raze from eyeshot of the sun
This city named not of his father's name,
And wash to deathward down one flood of doom
This whole fresh brood of earth yeaned naturally,
Green yet and faint in its first blade, unblown
With yellow hope of harvest; so do thou,
Seeing whom thy time is come to meet, for fear
Yield, or gird up thy force to fight and die.

ERECHTHEUS

To fight then be it; for if to die or live,
No man but only a God knows this much yet
Seeing us fare forth, who bear but in our hands
The weapons not the fortunes of our fight;
For these now rest as lots that yet undrawn
Lie in the lap of the unknown hour; but this
I know, not thou, whose hollow mouth of storm
Is but a warlike wind, a sharp salt breath
That bites and wounds not; death nor life of mine
Shall give to death or lordship of strange kings
The soul of this live city, nor their heel
Bruise her dear brow discrowned, nor snaffle or goad
Wound her free mouth or stain her sanguine side

Yet masterless of man; so bid thy lord
Learn ere he weep to learn it, and too late
Gnash teeth that could not fasten on her flesh,
And foam his life out in dark froth of blood
Vain as a wind's waif of the loud-mouthed sea
Torn from the wave's edge whitening.   Tell him this;
Though thrice his might were mustered for our scathe
And thicker set with fence of thorn-edged spears
Than sands are whirled about the wintering beach
When storms have swoln the rivers, and their blasts
Have breached the broad sea-banks with stress of sea,
That waves of inland and the main make war
As men that mix and grapple; though his ranks
Were more to number than all wildwood leaves
The wind waves on the hills of all the world,
Yet should the heart not faint, the head not fall,
The breath not fail of Athens.   Say, the Gods
From lips that have no more on earth to say
Have told thee this the last good news or ill
That I shall speak in sight of earth and sun
Or he shall hear and see them: for the next
That ear of his from tongue of mine may take
Must be the first word spoken underground
From dead to dead in darkness.   Hence; make haste,
Lest war's fleet foot be swifter than thy tongue
And I that part not to return again
On him that comes not to depart away
Be fallen before thee; for the time is full,
And with such mortal hope as knows not fear
I go this high last way to the end of all.

CHORUS

Who shall put a bridle in the mourner's lips to chasten
          them,   [*Str.* 1.
     Or seal up the fountains of his tears for shame?

272

Song nor prayer nor prophecy shall slacken tears nor hasten
    them,
  Till grief be within him as a burnt-out flame;
      Till the passion be broken in his breast
      And the might thereof molten into rest,
    And the rain of eyes that weep be dry,
    And the breath be stilled of lips that sigh.
Death at last for all men is a harbour; yet they flee from it,
                                                    [Ant. 1.
  Set sails to the storm-wind and again to sea;
Yet for all their labour no whit further shall they be from it,
  Nor longer but wearier shall their life's work be.
      And with anguish of travail until night
      Shall they steer into shipwreck out of sight,
      And with oars that break and shrouds that strain
      Shall they drive whence no ship steers again.
Bitter and strange is the word of the God most high. [Str. 2.
      And steep the strait of his way.
Through a pass rock-rimmed and narrow the light that
    gleams
On the faces of men falls faint as the dawn of dreams,
The dayspring of death as a star in an under sky
      Where night is the dead men's day.
As darkness and storm is his will that on earth is done, [Ant.2.
      As a cloud is the face of his strength.
King of kings, holiest of holies, and mightiest of might,
Lord of the lords of thine heaven that are humble in thy
    sight,
Hast thou set not an end for the path of the fires of the sun,
    To appoint him a rest at length?
Hast thou told not by measure the waves of the waste wide
    sea,   [Str. 3.
And the ways of the wind their master and thrall to thee?
    Hast thou filled not the furrows with fruit for the
      world's increase?

Has thine ear not heard from of old or thine eye not read
The thought and the deed of us living, the doom of us dead?
      Hast thou made not war upon earth, and again made
        peace?
Therefore, O father, that seest us whose lives are a breath,
                                          [*Ant.* 3.
Take off us thy burden, and give us not wholly to death.
      For lovely is life, and the law wherein all things live,
And gracious the season of each, and the hour of its kind,
And precious the seed of his life in a wise man's mind;
      But all save life for his life will a base man give.
But a life that is given for the life of the whole live land,
                                          [*Str.* 4.
From a heart unspotted a gift of a spotless hand,
Of pure will perfect and free, for the land's life's sake,
What man shall fear not to put forth his hand and take?
For the fruit of a sweet life plucked in its pure green prime
                                        [*Ant.* 4.
On his hand who plucks is as blood, on his soul as crime.
With cursing ye buy not blessing, nor peace with strife,
And the hand is hateful that chaffers with death for life.
      Hast thou heard, O my heart, and endurest   [*Str.* 5.
        The word that is said,
    What a garland by sentence found surest
        Is wrought for what head?
With what blossomless flowerage of sea-foam and blood-
      coloured foliage inwound
It shall crown as a heifer's for slaughter the forehead for
      marriage uncrowned?
      How the veils and the wreaths that should cover [*Ant.* 5.
        The brows of the bride
    Shall be shed by the breath of what lover
        And scattered aside?
With a blast of the mouth of what bridegroom the crowns
      shall be cast from her hair,

And her head by what altar made humble be left of them
  naked and bare?
At a shrine unbeloved of a God unbeholden a gift shall be
  given for the land,   [*Str. 6.*
That its ramparts though shaken with clamour and horror
  of manifold waters may stand:
That the crests of its citadels crowned and its turrets that
  thrust up their heads to the sun
May behold him unblinded with darkness of waves over-
  mastering their bulwarks begun.
As a bride shall they bring her, a prey for the bridegroom, a
  flower for the couch of her lord;   [*Ant. 6.*
They shall muffle her mouth that she cry not or curse them,
  and cover her eyes from the sword.
They shall fasten her lips as with bit and with bridle, and
  darken the light of her face,
That the soul of the slayer may not falter, his heart be not
  molten, his hand give not grace.
  If she weep then, yet may none that hear take pity; [*Str. 7.*
    If she cry not, none should hearken though she cried.
  Shall a virgin shield thine head for love, O city,
    With a virgin's blood anointed as for pride?
  Yet we held thee dear and hallowed of her favour, [*Ant. 7.*
    Dear of all men held thy people to her heart;
Nought she loves the breath of blood, the sanguine savour,
    Who hath built with us her throne and chosen her part.
          Bloodless are her works, and sweet   [*Epode.*
          All the ways that feel her feet;
          From the empire of her eyes
          Light takes life and darkness flies;
          From the harvest of her hands
          Wealth strikes root in prosperous lands;
          Wisdom of her word is made;
          At her strength is strength afraid;
          From the beam of her bright spear

War's fleet foot goes back for fear;
In her shrine she reared the birth
Fire-begotten on live earth;
Glory from her helm was shed
On his olive-shadowed head;
By no hand but his shall she
Scourge the storms back of the sea,
To no fame but his shall give
Grace, being dead, with hers to live,
And in double name divine
Half the godhead of their shrine.
But now with what word, with what woe may we meet
The timeless passage of piteous feet,
Hither that bend to the last way's end
    They shall walk upon earth?
What song be rolled for a bride black-stoled
And the mother whose hand of her hand hath hold?
For anguish of heart is my soul's strength broken
And the tongue sealed fast that would fain have spoken,
To behold thee, O child of so bitter a birth
    That we counted so sweet,
What way thy steps to what bride-feast tend,
What gift he must give that shall wed thee for token
  If the bridegroom be goodly to greet.

CHTHONIA

People, old men of my city, lordly wise and hoar of head,
I a spouseless bride and crownless but with garlands of the
    dead
From the fruitful light turn silent to my dark unchilded bed.

CHORUS

Wise of word was he too surely, but with deadlier wisdom
    wise,

First who gave thee name from under earth, no breath from
upper skies,
When, foredoomed to this day's darkness, their first daylight
filled thine eyes.

PRAXITHEA

Child, my child that wast and art but death's and now no
more of mine,
Half my heart is cloven with anguish by the sword made
sharp for thine,
Half exalts its wing for triumph, that I bare thee thus divine.

CHTHONIA

Though for me the sword's edge thirst that sets no point
against thy breast,
Mother, O my mother, where I drank of life and fell on rest.
Thine, not mine, is all the grief that marks this hour accurst
and blest.

CHORUS

Sweet thy sleep and sweet the bosom was that gave thee
sleep and birth;
Harder now the breast, and girded with no marriage-band
for girth,
Where thine head shall sleep, the namechild of the lords of
under earth.

PRAXITHEA

Dark the name and dark the gifts they gave thee, child, in
childbirth were,
Sprung from him that rent the womb of earth, a bitter seed
to bear,
Born with groanings of the ground that gave him way
toward heaven's dear air.

Day to day makes answer, first to last, and life to death;
  but I,
Born for death's sake, die for life's sake, if indeed this be to
  die,
This my doom that seals me deathless till the springs of
  time run dry.

CHORUS

Children shalt thou bear to memory, that to man shalt
  bring forth none;
Yea, the lordliest that lift eyes and hearts and songs to meet
  the sun,
Names to fire men's ears like music till the round world's
  race be run.

PRAXITHEA

I thy mother, named of Gods that wreak revenge and brand
  with blame,
Now for thy love shall be loved as thou, and famous with
  thy fame,
While this city's name on earth shall be for earth her
  mightiest name.

CHTHONIA

That I may give this poor girl's blood of mine
Scarce yet sun-warmed with summer, this thin life
Still green with flowerless growth of seedling days,
To build again my city; that no drop
Fallen of these innocent veins on the cold ground
But shall help knit the joints of her firm walls
To knead the stones together, and make sure
The band about her maiden girdlestead
Once fastened, and of all men's violent hands

Inviolable for ever; these to me
Were no such gifts as crave no thanksgiving,
If with one blow dividing the sheer life
I might make end, and one pang wind up all
And seal mine eyes from sorrow; for such end
The Gods give none they love not; but my heart,
That leaps up lightened of all sloth or fear
To take the sword's point, yet with one thought's load
Flags, and falls back, broken of wing, that halts
Maimed in mid flight for thy sake and borne down,
Mother, that in the places where I played
An arm's length from thy bosom and no more
Shalt find me never, nor thine eye wax glad
To mix with mine its eyesight and for love
Laugh without word, filled with sweet light, and speak
Divine dumb things of the inward spirit and heart,
Moved silently; nor hand or lip again
Touch hand or lip of either, but for mine
Shall thine meet only shadows of swift night,
Dreams and dead thoughts of dead things; and the bed
Thou strewedst, a sterile place for all time, strewn
For my sleep only, with its void sad sheets
Shall vex thee, and the unfruitful coverlid
For empty days reproach me dead, that leave
No profit of my body, but am gone
As one not worth being born to bear no seed,
A sapless stock and branchless; yet thy womb
Shall want not honour of me, that brought forth
For all this people freedom, and for earth
From the unborn city born out of my blood
To light the face of all men evermore
Glory; but lay thou this to thy great heart
Whereunder in the dark of birth conceived
Mine unlit life lay girdled with the zone
That bound thy bridal bosom; set this thought

Against all edge of evil as a sword
To beat back sorrow, that for all the world
Thou brought'st me forth a saviour, who shall save
Athens; for none but I from none but thee
Shall take this death for garland; and the men
Mine unknown children of unsounded years,
My sons unrisen shall rise up at thine hand,
Sown of thy seed to bring forth seed to thee,
And call thee most of all most fruitful found
Blessed; but me too for my barren womb
More than my sisters for their children born
Shall these give honour, yea in scorn's own place
Shall men set love and bring for mockery praise
And thanks for curses; for the dry wild vine
Scoffed at and cursed of all men that was I
Shall shed them wine to make the world's heart warm,
That all eyes seeing may lighten, and all ears
Hear and be kindled; such a draught to drink
Shall be the blood that bids this dust bring forth,
The chaliced life here spilt on this mine earth,
Mine, my great father's mother; whom I pray
Take me now gently, tenderly take home,
And softly lay in his my cold chaste hand
Who is called of men by my name, being of Gods
Charged only and chosen to bring men under earth,
And now must lead and stay me with his staff
A silent soul led of a silent God,
Toward sightless things led sightless; and on earth
I see now but the shadow of mine end,
And this last light of all for me in heaven.

PRAXITHEA

Farewell I bid thee; so bid thou not me,
Lest the Gods hear and mock us; yet on these

I lay the weight not of this grief, nor cast
Ill words for ill deeds back; for if one say
They have done men wrong, what hurt have they to
   hear,
Or he what help to have said it? surely, child,
If one among men born might say it and live
Blameless, none more than I may, who being vexed
Hold yet my peace; for now through tears enough
Mine eyes have seen the sun that from this day
Thine shall see never more; and in the night
Enough has blown of evil, and mine ears
With wail enough the winds have filled, and brought
Too much of cloud from over the sharp sea
To mar for me the morning; such a blast
Rent from these wide void arms and helpless breast
Long since one graft of me disbranched, and bore
Beyond the wild ways of the unwandered world
And loud wastes of the thunder-throated sea,
Springs of the night and openings of the heaven,
The old garden of the Sun; whence never more
From west or east shall winds bring back that blow
From folds of opening heaven or founts of night
The flower of mine once ravished, born my child
To bear strange children; nor on wings of theirs
Shall comfort come back to me, nor their sire
Breathe help upon my peril, nor his strength
Raise up my weakness; but of Gods and men
I drift unsteered on ruin, and the wave
Darkens my head with imminent height, and hangs
Dumb, filled too full with thunder that shall leave
These ears death-deafened when the tide finds tongue
And all its wrath bears on them; thee, O child,
I help not, nor am holpen; fain, ah fain,
More than was ever mother born of man,
Were I to help thee; fain beyond all prayer,

Beyond all thought fain to redeem thee, torn
More timeless from me sorrowing than the dream
That was thy sister; so shalt thou be too,
Thou but a vision, shadow-shaped of sleep,
By grief made out of nothing; now but once
I touch, but once more hold thee, one more kiss
This last time and none other ever more
Leave on thy lips and leave them.   Go; thou wast
My heart, my heart's blood, life-blood of my life,
My child, my nursling: now this breast once thine
Shall rear again no children; never now
Shall any mortal blossom born like thee
Lie there, nor ever with small silent mouth
Draw the sweet springs dry for an hour that feed
The blind blithe life that knows not; never head
Rest here to make these cold veins warm, nor eye
Laugh itself open with the lips that reach
Lovingly toward a fount more loving; these
Death makes as all good lesser things now dead,
And all the latter hopes that flowered from these
And fall as these fell fruitless; no joy more
Shall man take of thy maidenhood, no tongue
Praise it; no good shall eyes get more of thee
That lightened for thy love's sake.   Now, take note,
Give ear, O all ye people, that my word
May pierce your hearts through, and the stroke that
     cleaves
Be fruitful to them; so shall all that hear
Grow great at heart with child of thought most high
And bring forth seed in season; this my child,
This flower of this my body, this sweet life,
This fair live youth I give you, to be slain,
Spent, shed, poured out, and perish; take my gift
And give it death and the under Gods who crave
So much for that they give; for this is more,

Much more is this than all we; for they give
Freedom, and for a blast, an air of breath,
A little soul that is not, they give back
Light for all eyes, cheer for all hearts, and life
That fills the world's width full of fame and praise
And mightier love than children's. This they give,
The grace to make thy country great, and wrest
From time and death power to take hold on her
And strength to scathe for ever; and this gift,
Is this no more than man's love is or mine,
Mine and all mothers'? nay, where that seems more,
Where one loves life of child, wife, father, friend,
Son, husband, mother, more than this, even there
Are all these lives worth nothing, all loves else
With this love slain and buried, and their tomb
A thing for shame to spit on; for what love
Hath a slave left to love with? or the heart
Base-born and bound in bondage fast to fear.
What should it do to love thee? what hath he,
The man that hath no country? Gods nor men
Have such to friend, yoked beast-like to base life,
Vile, fruitless, grovelling at the foot of death,
Landless and kinless thralls of no man's blood,
Unchilded and unmothered, abject limbs
That breed things abject; but who loves on earth
Not friend, wife, husband, father, mother, child,
Nor loves his own life for his own land's sake,
But only this thing most, more this than all,
He loves all well and well of all is loved,
And this love lives for ever. See now, friends,
My countrymen, my brothers, with what heart
I give you this that of your hands again
The Gods require for Athens; as I give
So give ye to them what their hearts would have
Who shall give back things better; yea, and these

I take for me to witness, all these Gods,
Were their great will more grievous than it is,
Not one but three, for this one thin-spun thread
A threefold band of children would I give
For this land's love's sake; for whose love to-day
I bid thee, child, fare deathward and farewell.

CHORUS

O wofullest of women, yet of all
Happiest, thy word be hallowed; in all time
Thy name shall blossom, and from strange new tongues
High things be spoken of thee; for such grace
The Gods have dealt to no man, that on none
Have laid so heavy sorrow. From this day
Live thou assured of godhead in thy blood,
And in thy fate no lowlier than a God
In all good things and evil; such a name
Shall be thy child this city's, and thine own
Next hers that called it Athens. Go now forth
Blest, and grace with thee to the doors of death.

CHTHONIA

O city, O glory of Athens, O crown of my father's land, farewell.

CHORUS

For welfare is given her of thee.

CHTHONIA

O Goddess, be good to thy people, that in them dominion and freedom may dwell.

CHORUS

Turn from us the strengths of the sea.

284

CHTHONIA

Let glory's and theirs be one name in the mouths of all
nations made glad with the sun.

CHORUS

For the cloud is blown back with thy breath.

CHTHONIA

With the long last love of mine eyes I salute thee, O land
where my days now are done.

CHORUS

But her life shall be born of thy death.

CHTHONIA

I put on me the darkness thy shadow, my mother, and
symbol, O Earth, of my name.

CHORUS

For thine was her witness from birth.

CHTHONIA

In thy likeness I come to thee darkling, a daughter whose
dawn and her even are the same.

CHORUS

Be thine heart to her gracious, O Earth.

CHTHONIA

To thine own kind be kindly, for thy son's name's sake.

CHORUS

That sons unborn may praise thee and thy first-born son.

CHTHONIA

Give me thy sleep, who give thee all my life awake.

CHORUS

Too swift a sleep, ere half the web of day be spun.

CHTHONIA

Death brings the shears or ever life wind up the weft.

CHORUS

Their edge is ground and sharpened; who shall stay his
hand?

CHTHONIA

The woof is thin, a small short life, with no thread left.

CHORUS

Yet hath it strength, stretched out, to shelter all the land.

CHTHONIA

Too frail a tent for covering, and a screen too strait.

CHORUS

Yet broad enough for buckler shall thy sweet life be.

CHTHONIA

A little bolt to bar off battle from the gate.

CHORUS

A wide sea-wall, that shatters the besieging sea.

CHTHONIA

I lift up mine eyes from the skirts of the shadow,   [*Str.*
    From the border of death to the limits of light;

O streams and rivers of mountain and meadow
    That hallow the last of my sight,
    O father that wast of my mother
    Cephisus, O thou too his brother
    From the bloom of whose banks as a prey
    Winds harried my sister away,
    O crown on the world's head lying
      Too high for its waters to drown,
    Take yet this one word of me dying,
        O city, O crown.
Though land-wind and sea wind with mouths that blow
      slaughter   [*Ant.*
  Should gird them to battle against thee again,
New-born of the blood of a maiden thy daughter,
    The rage of their breath shall be vain.
    For their strength shall be quenched and made idle,
    And the foam of their mouths find a bridle,
    And the height of their heads bow down
    At the foot of the towers of the town.
    Be blest and beloved as I love thee
      Of all that shall draw from thee breath;
    Be thy life as the sun's is above thee;
        I go to my death.

CHORUS

  Many loves of many a mood and many a kind   [*Str.* 1.
  Fill the life of man, and mould the secret mind;
  Many days bring many dooms, to loose and bind;
  Sweet is each in season, good the gift it brings,
  Sweet as change of night and day with altering wings,
Night that lulls world-weary day, day that comforts night,
Night that fills our eyes with sleep, day that fills with light.
  None of all is lovelier, loftier love is none,   [*Ant.* 1.
  Less is bride 's for bridegroom, mother 's less for son,

Child, than this that crowns and binds up all in one;
 Love of thy sweet light, thy fostering breast and hand,
 Mother Earth, and city chosen, and natural land;
Hills that bring the strong streams forth, heights of heavenlier
 air,
Fields aflower with winds and suns, woods with shadowing
 hair.
But none of the nations of men shall they liken to thee,

[Str. 2.

Whose children true-born and the fruit of thy body are we.
The rest are thy sons but in figure, in word are thy seed;
We only the flower of thy travail, thy children indeed.
Of thy soil hast thou fashioned our limbs, of thy waters
 their blood,
And the life of thy springs everlasting is fount of our flood.
No wind oversea blew us hither adrift on thy shore,
None sowed us by land in thy womb that conceived us and
 bore.
But the stroke of the shaft of the sunlight that brought us
 to birth
Pierced only and quickened thy furrows to bear us, O Earth,
With the beams of his love wast thou cloven as with iron or
 fire,
And the life in thee yearned for his life, and grew great with
 desire.
And the hunger and thirst to be wounded and healed with
 his dart
Made fruitful the love in thy veins and the depth of thine
 heart.
And the showers out of heaven overflowing and liquid with
 love
Fulfilled thee with child of his godhead as rain from above.
Such desire had ye twain of each other, till molten in one

[Ant. 2.

Ye might bear and beget of your bodies the fruits of the sun.
288

And trees in their season brought forth and were kindled
  anew
By the warmth of the moisture of marriage, the childbearing
  dew.
And the firstlings were fair of the wedlock of heaven and of
  earth;
All countries were bounteous with blossom and burgeon of
  birth.
Green pastures of grass for all cattle, and life-giving corn;
But here of thy bosom, here only, the man-child was born.
All races but one are as aliens engrafted or sown,
Strange children and changelings; but we, O our mother,
  thine own.
Thy nurslings are others, and seedlings they know not of
  whom;
For these hast thou fostered, but us thou hast borne in thy
  womb.
Who is he of us all, O beloved, that owe thee for birth,
Who would give not his blood for his birth's sake, O
  mother, O Earth?
What landsman is he that was fostered and reared of thine
  hand
Who may vaunt him as we may in death though he died
  for the land?

Well doth she therefore who gives thee in guerdon
  The bloom of the life of thy giving;   [*Epode.*
And thy body was bowed by no fruitless burden,
  That bore such fruit of thee living.
    For her face was not darkened for fear,
    For her eyelids conceived not a tear,
      Nor a cry from her lips craved pity;
    But her mouth was a fountain of song,
    And her heart as a citadel strong
      That guards the heart of the city.

289

High things of strong-souled men that loved their land
On brass and stone are written, and their deeds
On high days chanted; but none graven or sung
That ever set men's eyes or spirits on fire,
Athenians, has the sun's height seen, or earth
Heard in her depth reverberate as from heaven,
More worth men's praise and good report of Gods
Than here I bring for record in your ears.
For now being come to the altar, where as priest
Death ministering should meet her, and his hand
Seal her sweet eyes asleep, the maiden stood,
With light in all her face as of a bride
Smiling, or shine of festal flame by night
Far flung from towers of triumph; and her lips
Trembled with pride in pleasure, that no fear
Blanched them nor death before his time drank dry
The blood whose bloom fulfilled them; for her cheeks
Lightened, and brighter than a bridal veil
Her hair enrobed her bosom and enrolled
From face to feet the body's whole soft length
As with a cloud sun-saturate; then she spake
With maiden tongue words manlike, but her eyes
Lit mildly like a maiden's: *Countrymen,*
With more goodwill and height of happier heart
I give me to you than my mother bare,
And go more gladly this great way to death
Than young men bound to battle. Then with face
Turned to the shadowiest part of all the shrine
And eyes fast set upon the further shade,
Take me, dear Gods; and as some form had shone
From the deep hollow shadow, some God's tongue
Answered, *I bless you that your guardian grace*
Gives me to guard this country, takes my blood,
Your child's by name, to heal it. Then the priest

Set to the flower-sweet snow of her soft throat
The sheer knife's edge that severed it, and loosed
From the fair bondage of so spotless flesh
So strong a spirit; and all that girt them round
Gazing, with souls that hung on that sad stroke,
Groaned, and kept silence after while a man
Might count how far the fresh blood crept, and bathed
How deep the dark robe and the bright shrine's base
Red-rounded with a running ring that grew
More large and duskier as the wells that fed
Were drained of that pure effluence: but the queen
Groaned not nor spake nor wept, but as a dream
Floats out of eyes awakening so past forth
Ghost-like, a shadow of sorrow, from all sight
To the inner court and chamber where she sits
Dumb, till word reach her of this whole day's end.

CHORUS

More hapless born by far   [*Str.*
  Beneath some wintrier star,
One sits in stone among high Lydian snows,
  The tomb of her own woes:
Yet happiest was once of the daughters of Gods, and divine
    by her sire and her lord,
Ere her tongue was a shaft for the hearts of her sons, for the
    heart of her husband a sword.

  For she, too great of mind,   [*Ant.*
    Grown through her good things blind,
With godless lips and fire of her own breath
  Spake all her house to death;
But thou, no mother unmothered, nor kindled in spirit
    with pride of thy seed,
Thou hast hallowed thy child for a blameless blood-offering,
    and ransomed thy race by thy deed.

As flower is graffed on flower, so grief on grief
Engraffed brings forth new blossoms of strange tears,
Fresh buds and green fruits of an alien pain;
For now flies rumour on a dark wide wing,
Murmuring of woes more than ye knew, most like
Hers whom ye hailed most wretched; for the twain
Last left of all this house that wore last night
A threefold crown of maidens, and to-day
Should let but one fall dead out of the wreath,
If mad with grief we know not and sore love
For this their sister, or with shame soul-stung
To outlive her dead or doubt lest their lives too
The Gods require to seal their country safe
And bring the oracular doom to perfect end,
Have slain themselves, and fallen at the altar-foot
Lie by their own hands done to death; and fear
Shakes all the city as winds a wintering tree,
And as dead leaves are men's hearts blown about
And shrunken with ill thoughts, and flowerless hopes
Parched up with presage, lest the piteous blood
Shed of these maidens guiltless fall and fix
On this land's forehead like a curse that cleaves
To the unclean soul's inexpiate hunted head
Whom his own crime tracks hotlier than a hound
To life's veiled end unsleeping; and this hour
Now blackens toward the battle that must close
All gates of hope and fear on all their hearts
Who tremble toward its issue, knowing not yet
If blood may buy them surety, cleanse or soil
The helpless hands men raise and reach no stay.

CHORUS

Ill thoughts breed fear, and fear ill words; but these
The Gods turn from us that have kept their law.

Let us lift up the strength of our hearts in song, [*Str.* 1.
　And our souls to the height of the darkling day.
　If the wind in our eyes blow blood for spray,
Be the spirit that breathes in us life more strong,
Though the prow reel round and the helm point wrong,
　And sharp reefs whiten the shoreward way.
For the steersman time sits hidden astern, [*Ant.* 1.
　With dark hand plying the rudder of doom,
　And the surf-smoke under it flies like fume
As the blast shears off and the oar-blades churn
The foam of our lives that to death return,
　Blown back as they break to the gulfing gloom.
What cloud upon heaven is arisen, what shadow, what
　　sound, [*Str.* 2.
　From the world beyond earth, from the night under-
　　ground,
That scatters from wings unbeholden the weight of its dark-
　　ness around?
For the sense of my spirit is broken, and blinded its eye,
　　　　　　　　　　　　[*Ant.* 2.
　As the soul of a sick man ready to die,
With fear of the hour that is on me, with dread if an end be
　　not nigh.
　O Earth, O Gods of the land, have ye heart now to see
　　and to hear [*Str.* 3.
　What slays with terror mine eyesight and seals mine
　　ear?
O fountains of streams everlasting, are all ye not shrunk up
　　and withered for fear?
　Lo, night is arisen on the noon, and her hounds are in
　　quest by day, [*Ant.* 3.
　And the world is fulfilled of the noise of them crying
　　for their prey,
And the sun's self stricken in heaven, and cast out of his
　　course as a blind man astray.

From east to west of the south sea-line   [*Str.* 4.
　Glitters the lightning of spears that shine;
As a storm-cloud swoln that comes up from the skirts of
　　the sea
　By the wind for helmsman to shoreward ferried,
　So black behind them the live storm serried
Shakes earth with the tramp of its foot, and the terror to be.
　Shall the sea give death whom the land gave birth?
　　　　　　　　　　　　　　　　　　[*Ant.* 4.
　O Earth, fair mother, O sweet live Earth,
Hide us again in thy womb from the waves of it, help us
　　or hide,
　As a sword is the heart of the God thy brother,
　But thine as the heart of a new-made mother,
To deliver thy sons from his ravin, and rage of his tide.
　O strong north wind, the pilot of cloud and rain, [*Str.* 5.
　For the gift we gave thee what gift hast thou given us
　　again?　　　•
O God dark-winged, deep-throated, a terror to forthfaring
　　ships by night,
　What bride-song is this that is blown on the blast of thy
　　breath?
　A gift but of grief to thy kinsmen, a song but of death,
For the bride's folk weeping, and woe for her father, who
　　finds thee against him in fight.
　Turn back from us, turn thy battle, take heed of our cry;
　　　　　　　　　　　　　　　　　　[*Ant.* 5.
　Let thy dread breath sound, and the waters of war be dry;
Let thy strong wrath shatter the strength of our foemen, the
　　sword of their strength and the shield;
　As vapours in heaven, or as waves or the wrecks of ships,
　So break thou the ranks of their spears with the breath of
　　thy lips,
Till their corpses have covered and clothed as with raiment
　　the face of the sword-ploughed field.

O son of the rose-red morning, O God twin-born with
    the day,   [*Str. 6.*

O wind with the young sun waking, and winged for
    the same wide way,

Give up not the house of thy kin to the host thou hast
    marshalled from northward for prey.

From the cold of thy cradle in Thrace, from the mists of
    the fountains of night,   [*Ant. 6.*

From the bride-bed of dawn whence day leaps laughing,
    on fire for his flight,

Come down with their doom in thine hand on the ships
    thou hast brought up against us to fight.

For now not in word but in deed is the harvest of spears
    begun,   [*Str. 7.*

And its clamour outbellows the thunder, its lightning out-
    lightens the sun.

From the springs of the morning it thunders and lightens
    across and afar

To the wave where the moonset ends and the fall of the last
    low star.

With a trampling of drenched red hoofs and an earth quake
    of men that meet,

Strong war sets hand to the scythe, and the furrows take fire
    from his feet.

Earth groans from her great rent heart, and the hollows of
    rocks are afraid,

And the mountains are moved, and the valleys as waves in
    a storm-wind swayed.

From the roots of the hills to the plain's dim verge and the
    dark loud shore,

Air shudders with shrill spears crossing, and hurtling of
    wheels that roar.

As the grinding of teeth in the jaws of a lion that foam as
    they gnash

Is the shriek of the axles that loosen, the shock of the poles
that crash,
The dense manes darken and glitter, the mouths of the mad
steeds champ,
Their heads flash blind through the battle, and death's foot
rings in their tramp.
For a fourfold host upon earth and in heaven is arrayed for
the fight,
Clouds ruining in thunder and armies encountering as
clouds in the night.
Mine ears are amazed with the terror of trumpets, with darkness mine eyes,
At the sound of the sea's host charging that deafens the roar
of the sky's.
White frontlet is dashed upon frontlet, and horse against
horse reels hurled,
And the gorge of the gulfs of the battle is wide for the spoil
of the world.
And the meadows are cumbered with shipwreck of chariots
that founder on land,   [*Ant.* 7.
And the horsemen are broken with breach as of breakers,
and scattered as sand.
Through the roar and recoil of the charges that mingle their
cries and confound,
Like fire are the notes of the trumpets that flash through the
darkness of sound.
As the swing of the sea churned yellow that sways with the
wind as it swells
Is the lift and relapse of the wave of the chargers that clash
with their bells;
And the clang of the sharp shrill brass through the burst
of the wave as it shocks
Rings clean as the clear wind's cry through the roar of the
surge on the rocks:

And the heads of the steeds in their headgear of war, and
their corsleted breasts,
Gleam broad as the brows of the billows that brighten the
storm with their crests,
Gleam dread as their bosoms that heave to the shipwrecking
wind as they rise,
Filled full of the terror and thunder of water, that slays as
it dies.
So dire is the glare of their foreheads, so fearful the fire of
their breath,
And the light of their eyeballs enkindled so bright with the
lightnings of death;
And the foam of their mouths as the sea's when the jaws of
its gulf are as graves,
And the ridge of their necks as the wind-shaken mane on
the ridges of waves:
And their fetlocks afire as they rear drip thick with a dewfall
of blood
As the lips of the rearing breaker with froth of the man-
slaying flood.
And the whole plain reels and resounds as the fields of the
sea by night
When the stroke of the wind falls darkling, and death is the
seafarer's light.

But thou, fair beauty of heaven, dear face of the day nigh
dead,   [*Epode.*
What horror hath hidden thy glory, what hand hath muffled
thine head?
  O sun, with what song shall we call thee, or ward off thy
  wrath by what name,
With what prayer shall we seek to thee, soothe with what
incense, assuage with what gift,
If thy light be such only as lightens to deathward the sea-
man adrift

With the fire of his house for a beacon, that foemen have
    wasted with flame?
Arise now, lift up thy light; give ear to us, put forth thine
    hand,
Reach toward us thy torch of deliverance, a lamp for the
    night of the land.
Thine eye is the light of the living, no lamp for the dead;
O, lift up the light of thine eye on the dark of our dread.
Who hath blinded thee? who hath prevailed on thee? who
    hath ensnared?
Who hath broken thy bow, and the shafts for thy battle
    prepared?
Have they found out a fetter to bind thee, a chain for thine
    arm that was bared?
Be the name of thy conqueror set forth, and the might of
    thy master declared.
O God, fair God of the morning, O glory of day,
What ails thee to cast from thy forehead its garland away?
To pluck from thy temples their chaplet enwreathed of
    the light,
And bind on the brows of thy godhead a frontlet of night?
Thou hast loosened the necks of thine horses, and goaded
    their flanks with affright,
To the race of a course that we know not on ways that are
    hid from our sight.
As a wind through the darkness the wheels of their chariot
    are whirled,
And the light of its passage is night on the face of the
    world.
And there falls from the wings of thy glory no help from
    on high,
But a shadow that smites us with fear and desire of thine
    eye.
For our hearts are as reeds that a wind on the water bows
    down and goes by,

To behold not thy comfort in heaven that hath left us un-
    timely to die.
  But what light is it now leaps forth on the land
  Enkindling the waters and ways of the air
      From thy forehead made bare,
    From the gleam of thy bow-bearing hand?
  Hast thou set not thy right hand again to the string,
  With the back-bowed horns bent sharp for a spring
      And the barbed shaft drawn,
  Till the shrill steel sing and the tense nerve ring
  That pierces the heart of the dark with dawn,
      O huntsman, O king,
  When the flame of thy face hath twilight in chase
    As a hound hath a blood-mottled fawn?
  He has glanced into golden the grey sea-strands,
  And the clouds are shot through with the fires of his
      hands,
  And the height of the hollow of heaven that he fills
  As the heart of a strong man is quickened and thrills;
  High over the folds of the low-lying lands,
      On the shadowless hills
    As a guard on his watchtower he stands.
  All earth and all ocean, all depth and all height,
  At the flash of an eyebeam are filled with his might:
  The sea roars backward, the storm drops dumb,
  And silence as dew on the fire of the fight
  Falls kind in our ears as his face in our sight
      With presage of peace to come.
  Fresh hope in my heart from the ashes of dread
  Leaps clear as a flame from the pyres of the dead,
      That joy out of woe
  May arise as the spring out of tempest and snow,
  With the flower-feasted month in her hands rose-red
  Borne soft as a babe from the bearing-bed.
  Yet it knows not indeed if a God be friend,

If rescue may be from the rage of the sea,
    Or the wrath of its lord have end.
For the season is full now of death or of birth,
To bring forth life, or an end of all;
And we know not if anything stand or fall
That is girdled about with the round sea's girth
    As a town with its wall;
But thou that art highest of the Gods most high,
That art lord if we live, that art lord though we die,
Have heed of the tongues of our terror that cry
    For a grace to the children of Earth.

ATHENIAN HERALD

Sons of Athens, heavy-laden with the holy weight of years,
Be your hearts as young men's lightened of their loathlier
    load of fears;
For the wave is sunk whose thunder shoreward shook the
    shuddering lands,
And unbreached of warring waters Athens like a sea-rock
    stands.

CHORUS

Well thy word has cheered us, well thy face and glittering
    eyes, that spake
Ere thy tongue spake words of comfort: yet no pause
    behoves it make
Till the whole good hap find utterance that the Gods have
    given at length.

ATHENIAN HERALD

All is this, that yet the city stands unforced by stranger
    strength.

CHORUS

Sweeter sound might no mouth utter in man's ear than this
    thy word.

300

ATHENIAN HERALD

Feed thy soul then full of sweetness till some bitterer note
be heard.

CHORUS

None, if this ring sure, can mar the music fallen from
heaven as rain.

ATHENIAN HERALD

If no fire of sun or star untimely sear the tender grain.

CHORUS

Fresh the dewfall of thy tidings on our hopes reflowering
lies.

ATHENIAN HERALD

Till a joyless shower and fruitless blight them, raining from
thine eyes.

CHORUS

Bitter springs have barren issues; these bedew grief's arid
sands.

ATHENIAN HERALD

Such thank-offerings ask such altars as expect thy suppliant
hands.

CHORUS

Tears for triumph, wail for welfare, what strange godhead's
shrine requires?

ATHENIAN HERALD

Death's or victory's be it, a funeral torch feeds all its festal
fires.

CHORUS

Like a star should burn the beacon flaming from our city's head.

ATHENIAN HERALD

Like a balefire should the flame go up that says the king is dead.

CHORUS

Out of heaven, a wild-haired meteor, shoots this new sign, scattering fear.

ATHENIAN HERALD

Yea, the word has wings of fire that hovered, loth to burn thine ear.

CHORUS

From thy lips it leapt forth loosened on a shrill and shadowy wing.

ATHENIAN HERALD

Long they faltered, fain to hide it deep as death that hides the king.

CHORUS

Dead with him blind hope lies blasted by the lightning of one sword.

ATHENIAN HERALD

On thy tongue truth wars with error; no man's edge hath touched thy lord.

CHORUS

False was thine then, jangling menace like a war-steed's brow-bound bell?

False it rang not joy nor sorrow; but by no man's hand he
fell.

Vainly then good news and evil through so faint a trumpet
spake.

All too long thy soul yet labours, as who sleeping fain would
wake,
Waking, fain would fall on sleep again; the woe thou
knowest not yet,
When thou knowest, shall make thy memory thirst and
hunger to forget.

Long my heart has hearkened, hanging on thy clamorous
ominous cry,
Fain yet fearful of the knowledge whence it looks to live or
die;
Now to take the perfect presage of thy dark and sidelong
flight
Comes a surer soothsayer sorrowing, sable-stoled as birds
of night.

Man, what thy mother bare thee born to say
Speak; for no word yet wavering on thy lip
Can wound me worse than thought forestalls or fear.

I have no will to weave too fine or far,
O queen, the weft of sweet with bitter speech,
Bright words with darkling; but the brief truth shown
Shall plead my pardon for a lingering tongue,

Loth yet to strike hope through the heart and slay.
The sun's light still was lordly housed in heaven
When the twain fronts of war encountering smote
First fire out of the battle; but not long
Had the fresh wave of windy fight begun
Heaving, and all the surge of swords to sway,
When timeless night laid hold of heaven, and took
With its great gorge the noon as in a gulf,
Strangled; and thicker than the shrill-winged shafts
Flew the fleet lightnings, held in chase through heaven
By headlong heat of thunders on their trail
Loosed as on quest of quarry; that our host
Smit with sick presage of some wrathful God
Quailed, but the foe as from one iron throat
With one great sheer sole thousand-throated cry
Shook earth, heart-staggered from their shout, and clove
The eyeless hollow of heaven; and breached therewith
As with an onset of strength-shattering sound
The rent vault of the roaring noon of night
From her throned seat of usurpation rang
Reverberate answer; such response there pealed
As though the tide's charge of a storming sea
Had burst the sky's wall, and made broad a breach
In the ambient girth and bastion flanked with stars
Guarding the fortress of the Gods, and all
Crashed now together on ruin; and through that cry
And higher above it ceasing one man's note
Tore its way like a trumpet: *Charge, make end,*
Charge, halt not, strike, rend up their strength by the roots,
Strike, break them, make your birthright's promise sure,
Show your hearts hardier than the fenced land breeds
And souls breathed in you from no spirit of earth,
Sons of the sea's waves; and all ears that heard
Rang with that fiery cry, that the fine air
Thereat was fired, and kindling filled the plain

Full of that fierce and trumpet-quenching breath
That spake the clarions silent; no glad song
For folk to hear that wist how dire a God
Begat this peril to them, what strong race
Fathered the sea-born tongue that sang them death,
Threatening; so raged through the red foam of fight
Poseidon's son Eumolpus; and the war
Quailed round him coming, and our side bore back,
As a stream thwarted by the wind and sea
That meet it midway mouth to mouth, and beat
The flood back of its issue; but the king
Shouted against them, crying, *O Father-God,*
Source of the God my father, from thine hand
Send me what end seems good now in thy sight,
But death from mine to this man; and the word
Quick on his lips yet like a blast of fire
Blew them together; and round its lords that met
Paused all the reeling battle; two main waves
Meeting, one hurled sheer from the sea-wall back
That shocks it sideways, one right in from sea
Charging, that full in face takes at one blow
That whole recoil and ruin, with less fear
Startle men's eyes late shipwrecked; for a breath,
Crest fronting crest hung, wave to wave rose poised,
Then clashed, breaker to breaker; cloud with cloud
In heaven, chariot with chariot closed on earth,
One fourfold flash and thunder; yet a breath,
And with the king's spear through his red heart's root
Driven, like a rock split from its hill-side, fell
Hurled under his own horsehoofs dead on earth
The sea-beast that made war on earth from sea,
Dumb, with no shrill note left of storming song,
Eumolpus; and his whole host with one stroke
Spear-stricken through its dense deep iron heart
Fell hurtling from us, and in fierce recoil

Drew seaward as with one wide wail of waves,
Resorbed with reluctation; such a groan
Rose from the fluctuant refluence of its ranks,
Sucked sullen back and strengthless; but scarce yet
The steeds had sprung and wheels had bruised their lord
Fallen, when from highest height of the sundering heaven
The Father for his brother's son's sake slain
Sent a sheer shaft of lightning writhen and smote
Right on his son's son's forehead, that unhelmed
Shone like the star that shines down storm, and gave
Light to men's eyes that saw thy lord their king
Stand and take breath from battle; then too soon
Saw sink down as a sunset in sea-mist
The high bright head that here in van of the earth
Rose like a headland, and through storm and night
Took all the sea's wrath on it; and now dead
They bring thee back by war-forsaken ways
The strength called once thy husband, the great guard
That was of all men, stay of all men's lives,
They bear him slain of no man but a God,
Godlike; and toward him dead the city's gates
Fling their arms open mother-like, through him
Saved; and the whole clear land is purged of war
What wilt thou say now of this weal and woe?

PRAXITHEA

I praise the Gods for Athens. O sweet Earth,
Mother, what joy thy soul has of thy son,
Thy life of my dead lord, mine own soul knows
That knows thee godlike; and what grief should mine,
What sorrow should my heart have, who behold
Thee made so heavenlike happy? This alone
I only of all these blessed, all thy kind,
Crave this for blessing to me, that in theirs
Have but a part thus bitter; give me too

Death, and the sight of eyes that meet not mine.
And thee too from no godless heart or tongue
Reproachful, thee too by thy living name,
Father divine, merciful God, I call,
Spring of my life-springs, fountain of my stream,
Pure and poured forth to one great end with thine,
Sweet head sublime of triumph and these tears,
Cephisus, if thou seest as gladly shed
Thy blood in mine as thine own waves are given
To do this great land good, to give for love
The same lips drink and comfort the same hearts,
Do thou then, O my father, white-souled God,
To thy most pure earth-hallowing heart eterne
Take what thou gavest to be given for these,
Take thy child to thee; for her time is full,
For all she hath borne she hath given, seen all she had
Flow from her, from her eyes and breasts and hands
Flow forth to feed this people; but be thou,
Dear God and gracious to all souls alive,
Good to thine own seed also; let me sleep,
Father; my sleepless darkling day is done,
My day of life like night, but slumberless:
For all my fresh fair springs, and his that ran
In one stream's bed with mine, are all run out
Into the deep of death.   The Gods have saved
Athens; my blood has bought her at their hand,
And ye sit safe; be glorious and be glad
As now for all time always, countrymen,
And love my dead for ever; but me, me,
What shall man give for these so good as death?

CHORUS

From the cup of my heart I pour through my lips along

[Str. 1.

The mingled wine of a joyful and sorrowful song;

Wine sweeter than honey and bitterer than blood that is
    poured
From the chalice of gold, from the point of the two-edged
    sword.
For the city redeemed should joy flow forth as a flood,
And a dirge make moan for the city polluted with blood.
Great praise should the Gods have surely, my country, of
    thee,   [*Ant.* 1.
Were thy brow but as white as of old for thy sons to see,
Were thy hands as bloodless, as blameless thy cheek divine;
But a stain on it stands of the life-blood offered for thine.
What thanks shall we give that are mixed not and marred
    with dread
For the price that has ransomed thine own with thine own
    child's head?
    For a taint there cleaves to the people redeemed with
        blood,   [*Str.* 2.
    And a plague to the blood-red hand.
The rain shall not cleanse it, the dew nor the sacred flood
    That blesses the glad live land.
In the darkness of earth beneath, in the world without
    sun,   [*Ant.* 2.
    The shadows of past things reign;
And a cry goes up from the ghost of an ill deed done,
    And a curse for a virgin slain.

ATHENA

Hear, men that mourn, and woman without mate,
Hearken; ye sick of soul with fear, and thou
Dumb-stricken for thy children; hear ye too,
Earth, and the glory of heaven, and winds of the air,
And the most holy heart of the deep sea,
Late wrath, now full of quiet; hear thou, sun,
Rolled round with the upper fire of rolling heaven
And all the stars returning; hills and streams,

Springs and fresh fountains, day that seest these deeds,
Night that shalt hide not; and thou child of mine,
Child of a maiden, by a maid redeemed,
Blood-guiltless, though bought back with innocent
   blood,
City mine own; I Pallas bring thee word,
I virgin daughter of the most high God
Give all you charge and lay command on all
The word I bring be wasted not; for this
The Gods have stablished and his soul hath sworn,
That time nor earth nor changing sons of man
Nor waves of generations, nor the winds
Of ages risen and fallen that steer their tides
Through light and dark of birth and lovelier death
From storm toward haven inviolable, shall see
So great a light alive beneath the sun
As the awless eye of Athens; all fame else
Shall be to her fame as a shadow in sleep
To this wide noon at waking; men most praised
In lands most happy for their children found
Shall hold as highest of honours given of God
To be but likened to the least of thine,
Thy least of all, my city; thine shall be
The crown of all songs sung, of all deeds done
Thine the full flower for all time; in thine hand
Shall time be like a sceptre, and thine head
Wear worship for a garland; nor one leaf
Shall change or winter cast out of thy crown
Till all flowers wither in the world; thine eyes
Shall first in man's flash lightning liberty,
Thy tongue shall first say freedom; thy first hand
Shall loose the thunder terror as a hound
To hunt from sunset to the springs of the sun
Kings that rose up out of the populous east
To make their quarry of thee, and shall strew

With multitudinous limbs of myriad herds
The foodless pastures of the sea, and make
With wrecks immeasurable and unsummed defeat
One ruin of all their many-folded flocks
Ill shepherded from Asia; by thy side
Shall fight thy son the north wind, and the sea
That was thine enemy shall be sworn thy friend
And hand be struck in hand of his and thine
To hold faith fast for aye; with thee, though each
Make war on other, wind and sea shall keep
Peace, and take truce as brethren for thy sake
Leagued with one spirit and single-hearted strength
To break thy foes in pieces, who shall meet
The wind's whole soul and might of the main sea
Full in their face of battle, and become
A laughter to thee; like a shower of leaves
Shall their long galleys rank by staggering rank
Be dashed adrift on ruin, and in thy sight
The sea deride them, and that lord of the air
Who took by violent hand thy child to wife
With his loud lips bemock them, by his breath
Swept out of sight of being; so great a grace
Shall this day give thee, that makes one in heart
With mine the deep sea's godhead, and his son
With him that was thine helmsman, king with king,
Dead man with dead; such only names as these
Shalt thou call royal, take none else or less
To hold of men in honour; but with me
Shall these be worshipped as one God, and mix
With mine the might of their mysterious names
In one same shrine served singly, thence to keep
Perpetual guards on Athens; time and change,
Masters and lords of all men, shall be made
To thee that knowest no master and no lord
Servants; the days that lighten heaven and nights

That darken shall be ministers of thine
To attend upon thy glory, the great years
As light-engraven letters of thy name
Writ by the sun's hand on the front of the earth
For world-beholden witness; such a gift
For one fair chaplet of three lives enwreathed
To hang for ever from thy storied shrine,
And this thy steersman fallen with tiller in hand
To stand for ever at thy ship's helm seen,
Shall he that bade their threefold flower be shorn
And laid him low that planted, give thee back
In sign of sweet land reconciled with sea
And heavenlike earth with heaven; such promise pledge
I daughter without mother born of God
To the most woful mother born of man
Plight for continual comfort.   Hail, and live
Beyond all human hap of mortal doom
Happy; for so my sire hath sworn and I.

PRAXITHEA

O queen Athena, from a heart made whole
Take as thou givest us blessing; never tear
Shall stain for shame nor groan untune the song
That as a bird shall spread and fold its wings
Here in thy praise for ever, and fulfil
The whole world's crowning city crowned with thee
As the sun's eye fulfils and crowns with sight
The circling crown of heaven.   There is no grief
Great as the joy to be made one in will
With him that is the heart and rule of life
And thee, God born of God; thy name is ours,
And thy large grace more great than our desire.

From the depth of the springs of my spirit a fountain is
 poured of thanksgiving,
 My country, my mother, for thee,
That thy dead for their death shall have life in thy sight and
 a name everliving
 At heart of thy people to be
In the darkness of change on the waters of time they shall
 turn from afar
To the beam of this dawn for a beacon, the light of these
 pyres for a star.
They shall see thee who love and take comfort, who hate
 thee shall see and take warning,
 Our mother that makest us free;
And the sons of thine earth shall have help of the Waves
 that made war on their morning,
 And friendship and fame of the sea.

PROSE

From WILLIAM BLAKE: A CRITICAL ESSAY

A PICTURE OF WILLIAM BLAKE

IN the year 1827 there died, after a long dim life of labour, a man as worthy of remark and regret as any then famous. In his time he had little enough of recognition or regard from the world; and now that here and there one man and another begin to observe that after all this one was perhaps better worth notice and honour than most, the justice comes as usual somewhat late.

Between 1757 and 1827 the world, one might have thought, had time to grow aware whether or not a man were worth something. For so long there lived and laboured in more ways than one the single Englishman of supreme and simple poetic genius born before the closing years of the eighteenth century; the one man of that date fit on all accounts to rank with the old great names. A man perfect in his way, and beautifully unfit for walking in the way of any other man. We have now the means of seeing what he was like as to face in the late years of his life: for his biography has at the head of it a clearly faithful and valuable likeness. The face is singular, one that strikes at a first sight and grows upon the observer; a brilliant eager old face, keen and gentle, with a preponderance of brow and head; clear bird-like eyes, eloquent excitable mouth, with a look of nervous and fluent power; the whole lighted through as it were from behind with a strange and pure kind of smile, touched too with something of an impatient prospective rapture. The words clear and sweet seem the best made for it; it has something of fire in its composition, and something of music. If there is a want of balance, there is abundance of melody in the features; melody rather than harmony; for the mould of some is weaker and the look of them vaguer than that of others. Thought and time have played with it, and have nowhere pressed hard; it has the old devotion and desire with which men set to their work at starting. It is not the face of a man who could ever be cured of illusions; here all the medicines of reason and experience must have been spent in pure waste. We know also what sort of man he was at this time by the evidence of living friends. No one, artist or poet, of whatever school, who had any insight or any love of things noble and lovable, ever passed by this man without taking away some pleasant and exalted memory of him. Those with whom he had nothing in common but a clear kind nature and sense of what was sympathetic in men and acceptable in things—those men whose work lay quite apart from his—speak of him still with as ready affection and as full remembrance of his sweet or great qualities as those nearest and likest him. There was a noble attraction in him which came home to all people with any fervour or candour of nature in themselves. One can see, by the roughest draught or slightest glimpse of his face, the look and manner it must have put on towards children. He was about the hardest worker of his time; must have done in his day some horseloads of work. One might almost pity the poor age and the poor men he came among for having such a fiery energy cast unawares into the midst of their small customs and competitions. Unluckily for them, their new prophet had not one point they could lay hold of, not one organ or channel of expression by which to make himself comprehensible to such as they were. Shelley in his time gave enough of perplexity and offence; but even he, mysterious and rebellious as he seemed to most men, was less made up of mist and fire than Blake.

He was born and baptized into the church of rebels; we can hardly imagine a time or scheme of things in which he could have lived and worked without some interval of revolt. All that was accepted for art, all that was taken for poetry, all rejected as barren symbols, and would fain have broken up as mendacious idols. What was best to other men, and

316

in effect excellent of its kind, was to him worst. Reynolds and Rubens were daubers and devils. The complement or corollary of this habit of mind was that he would accept and admire even small and imperfect men whose line of life and action seemed to run on the same tramway as his own. Barry, Fuseli, even such as Mortimer—these were men he would allow and approve of. The devils had not entered into them; they worked, each to himself, on the same ground as Michael Angelo. To such effect he would at times prophesy, standing revealed for a brief glimpse on the cloudy and tottering height of his theories, before the incurious eyes of a public which had no mind to inhale such oracular vapour. It is hard to conjecture how his opinions, as given forth in his 'Catalogue' or other notes on art, would have been received—if indeed they had ever got hearing at all. This they naturally never did; by no means to Blake's discouragement. He spoke with authority; not in the least like the Scribes of his day.

So far one may at least see what he meant; although at sight of it many would cover their eyes and turn away. But the main part of him was, and is yet, simply inexplicable; much like some among his own designs, a maze of cloudy colour and perverse form, without a clue for the hand or a feature for the eye to lay hold of. What he meant, what he wanted, why he did this thing or not that other, no man then alive could make out. Nevertheless it was worth the trying. In a time of critical reason and definite division, he was possessed by a fervour and fury of belief; among sane men who had disproved most things and proved the rest, here was an evident madman who believed a thing, one may say, only insomuch as it was incapable of proof. He lived and worked out of all rule, and yet by law. He had a devil, and its name was Faith. No materialist has such belief in bread and meat as Blake had in the substance underlying appearance which he christened god or spectre, devil or angel, as the fit took him; or rather as he saw it from one or the other side. His faith was absolute and hard, like a pure fanatic's; there was no speculation in him. What could be made of such a man in a country fed and clothed with the teapot pieties of Cowper and the tape-yard infidelities of Paine? Neither set would have to do with him; was he not a believer? and was he not a blasphemer? His licence of thought and talk was always of the maddest, or seemed so in the ears of his generation. People remember at this day with horror and pity the impression of his daring ways of speech, but excuse him still on the old plea of madness. Now on his own ground no man was ever more sane or more reverent. His outcries on various matters of art or morals were in effect the mere expression, not of reasonable dissent, but of violent belief. No artist of equal power had ever a keener and deeper regard for the meaning and teaching—what one may call the moral—of art. He sang and painted as men write or preach. Indifference was impossible to him. Thus every shred of his work has some life, some blood, infused or woven into it. In such a vast tumbling chaos of relics as he left behind to get in time disentangled and cast into shape, there are naturally inequalities enough; rough sides and loose sides, weak points and helpless knots, before which all mere human patience or comprehension recoils and reels back. But in all, at all times, there is the one invaluable quality of actual life.

BLAKE'S LYRICS

Two things here put on record are worthy of recollection: that he began seeing visions at 'eight or ten'; and that he took objections to Ryland (a better known engraver than Basire), when taken to be apprenticed to him, on a singular ground: 'the man's face looks as if he will live to be hanged':
318

which the man was, ten years later. But the first real point in Blake's life worth marking as of especial interest is the publication of his *Poetical Sketches*; which come in date before any of his paintings or illustrative work, and are quite as much matters of art as these. Though never printed till 1783, the latest written appears to belong to 1777, or thereabouts.

Here, at a time when the very notion of poetry, as we now understand it, and as it was understood in older times, had totally died and decayed out of the minds of men; when we not only had no poetry, a thing which was bearable, but had verse in plenty, a thing which was not in the least bearable; a man, hardly twenty years old yet, turns up suddenly with work in that line already done, not simply better than any man could do then; better than all except the greatest have done since: better too than some still ranked among the greatest ever managed to do. With such a poet to bring forward it was needless to fall back upon Wordsworth for excuse or Southey for patronage. The one man of genius alive during any part of Blake's own life who has ever spoken of this poet with anything like a rational admiration is Charles Lamb, the most supremely competent judge and exquisite critic of lyrical and dramatic art that we have ever had. All other extant notices down to our own day, even when well-meaning and not offensive, are to the best of our knowledge and belief utterly futile, incapable, and valueless: burdened more or less with chatter about 'madness' and such-like, obscured in some degree by mere dullness and pitiable assumption.

There is something too rough and hard, too faint and formless, in any critical language yet devised, to pay tribute with the proper grace and sufficiency to the best works of the lyrical art. One can say, indeed, that some of these earliest songs of Blake's have the scent and sound of Elizabethan times upon them; that the song of forsaken love—

'My silks and fine array'—is sweet enough to recall the lyrics of Beaumont and Fletcher, and strong enough to hold its own even beside such as that one of Aspatia—'Lay a garland on my hearse'—which was cut (so to speak) out of the same yew; that Webster might have signed the *Mad Song*, which falls short only (as indeed do all other things of the sort) of the two great dirges in that poet's two chief plays; that certain verses among those headed *To Spring*, and *To the Evening Star*, are worthy even of Tennyson for tender supremacy of style and noble purity of perfection; but when we have to drop comparison and cease looking back or forward for verses to match with these, we shall hardly find words to suit our sense of their beauty. We speak of the best among them only; for, small as the pamphlet is (seventy pages long, with title-page and prefatory leaf), it contains a good deal of chaff and bran besides the pure grain and sifted honeymeal. But these best things are as wonderful as any work of Blake's. They have a fragrance of sound, a melody of colour, in a time when the best verses produced had merely the arid perfume of powder, the twang of dry wood and adjusted strings; when here the painting was laid on in patches, and there the music meted out by precedent; colour and sound never mixed together into the perfect scheme of poetry. The texture of these songs has the softness of flowers; the touch of them has nothing metallic or mechanical, such as one feels in much excellent and elaborate verse of this day as well as of that. The sound of many verses of Blake's cleaves to the sense long after conscious thought of the meaning has passed from one: a sound like running of water or ringing of bells in a long lull of the wind. Like all very good lyrical verse, they grow in pleasurable effect upon the memory the longer it holds them—increase in relish the longer they dwell upon the taste. These, for example, sound singularly plain, however sweet, on a first hearing; but in time, to a reader fit to appreciate the peculiar properties and merits of a lyric, they come to seem as perfect as well can be:

> Thou the golden fruit dost bear,
> I am clad in flowers fair ;
> Thy sweet boughs perfume the air,
> And the turtle buildeth there.
> There she sits and feeds her young :
> Sweet I hear her mournful song ;
> And thy lovely leaves among,
> There is love, I hear his tongue.

The two songs, *To Memory* and *To the Muses*, are perhaps nearer being faultless than any others in the book. This last especially should never be omitted in any professedly complete selection of the best English lyrics. So beautiful indeed is its structure and choice of language that its author's earlier and later vagaries and erratic indulgences in the most lax or bombastic habits of speech become hopelessly inexplicable. These unlucky tendencies do however break out in the same book which contains such excellent samples of poetical sense and taste; giving terrible promise of faults that were afterwards to grow rank and run riot over much of the poet's work. But even from his worst things here, not reprinted in the present edition, one may gather such lines as these:

> My lord was like a flower upon the brows
> Of lusty May : ah life as frail as flower !
> My lord was like a star in highest heaven,
> Drawn down to earth by spells and wickedness ;
> My lord was like the opening eye of day ;
> But he is darkened ; like the summer moon
> Clouded ; fall'n like the stately tree, cut down :
> The breath of heaven dwelt among his leaves.

Verses not to be despised, when one remembers that the boy who wrote them (evidently in his earlier teens) was living in full eighteenth century. But for the most part the blank verse in this small book is in a state of incredible chaos, ominous in tone of the future 'Prophetic Books,' if without promise of their singular and profound power or menace of their impenetrable mistiness, the obscurity of confused wind and cloud. One is thankful to see here some pains taken in righting these deformed limbs and planing off those monstrous knots, by one not less qualified to decide on such minor points of execution than on the gravest matters of art; especially as some amongst these blank verse poems contain things of quite original and incomparable grandeur. Nothing at once more noble and more sweet in style was ever written, than part of this *To the Evening Star*:

> *Smile on our loves ; and while thou drawest round*
> *The sky's blue curtains, scatter silver dew*
> *On every flower that closes its sweet eyes*
> *In timely sleep. Let thy west wind sleep on*
> *The lake* : speak silence with thy glimmering eyes,
> And wash the dusk with silver.

One other thing we may observe of these 'Sketches': that they contain, though only in the pieces rejected from our present collection, sad indications of the inexplicable influence which an early reading of the detestable pseudo-Ossian seems to have exercised on Blake. How or why such lank and lamentable counterfeits of the poetical style did ever gain this luckless influence—one, too, which in after years was to do far worse harm than it has done here—it is not easy to guess. Contemporary vice of taste, imperfect or on some points totally deficient education, may explain much and more than might be supposed, even with regard to the strongest untrained intellect; but on the other hand, the songs in this same volume give evidence of so rare a gift of poetical judgment, such exquisite natural sense and art, in a time which could not so much as blunder except by

322

precedent and machinery, that such depravity of error as is implied by admiration and imitation of such an one as Macpherson remains inconceivable. Similar puzzles will, however, recur to the student of Blake's art; but will not, if he be in any way worthy of the study, be permitted for a minute to impair his sense of its incomparable merits. Incomparable, we say advisedly: for there is no case on record of a man's being quite so far in advance of his time, in everything that belongs to the imaginative side of art, as Blake was from the first in advance of his.

BLAKE'S LIFE AND CHARACTER

In 1782 Blake married, it seems after a year or two of engaged life. His wife, Catherine Boucher, deserves remembrance as about the most perfect wife on record. In all things but affection, her husband must have been as hard to live with as the most erratic artist or poet who ever mistook his way into marriage. Over the stormy or slippery passages in their earlier life Mr Gilchrist has passed perhaps too lightly. No doubt Blake's aberrations were mainly matters of speech or writing; it is however said, truly or falsely, that once in a patriarchal mood he did propose to add a second wife to their small and shifting household, and was much perplexed at meeting on one hand with tears and on all hands with remonstrances. For any clandestine excursions or furtive eccentricities he had probably too much of childish candour and impulse; and this one hopeful and plausible design he seems to have sacrificed with a good grace, on finding it really objectionable to the run of erring men. As to the rest, Mrs Blake's belief in him was full and profound enough to endure some amount of trial. Practically he was always, as far as we know, regular, laborious, immaculate to an exception; and in their old age she worked after him and for him, revered and helped and obeyed him, with an exquisite goodness.

For the next eighteen years we have no continuous or available record under Blake's own hand of his manner of life; and of course must not expect as yet any help from those who can still, or could lately, remember the man himself in later days. He laboured with passionate steadiness of energy, at work sometimes valueless and sometimes invaluable; made, retained, and lost friends of a varying quality. Even to the lamentable taskwork of bad comic engravings for dead and putrescent 'Wit's Magazines' his biographer has tracked him and taken note of his doings. The one thing he did get published—his poem, or apology for a poem, called *The French Revolution* (the first of seven projected books)—is, as far as I know, the only original work of its author worth little or even nothing; consisting mainly of mere wind and splutter. The six other books, if extant, ought nevertheless to be looked up, as they can hardly be without some personal interest or empirical value, even if no better in workmanship than this first book. During these years however he produced much of his greatest work; among other things, the *Songs of Innocence and Experience*, and the 'Prophetic Books' from *Thel* to *Ahania*; of all which we shall have to speak in due time and order. The notes on Reynolds and Lavater, from which we have here many extracts given, we must hope to see some day printed in full. Their vivid and vigorous style is often a model in its kind; and the matter, however violent and eccentric at times, always clear, noble, and thoughtful; remarkable especially for the eagerness of approbation lavished on the meanest of impulsive or fanciful men, and the fervour of scorn excited by the best works, and the best intentions of others. The watery wisdom and the bland absurdity of Lavater's axioms meet with singular tolerance from the future author of the *Proverbs of Hell*; the considerate regulations and suggestions

324

of Reynolds's *Discourses* meet with no tolerance at all from the future illustrator of Job and Dante. In all these rough notes, even we may say in those on Bacon's Essays, there is always a bushel of good grain to an ounce of chaff. What is erroneous or what seems perverse lies for the most part only on the surface; what is falsely applied is often truly said; what is unjustly worded is often justly conceived. A man insensible to the perfect manner and noble matter of Bacon, while tolerant of the lisping and slavering imbecilities of Lavater, seems at first sight past hope or help; but subtract the names or alter the symbols given, and much of Blake's commentary will seem, as it is, partially true and memorable even in its actual form, wholly true and memorable in its implied meaning. Again, partly through ingrained humour, partly through the rough shifts of his imperfect and tentative education, Blake was much given to a certain perverse and defiant habit of expression, meant rather to scare and offend than to allure and attract the common run of readers or critics. In his old age we hear that he would at times try the ironic method upon objectionable reasoners; not, we should imagine, with much dexterity or subtlety.

The small accidents and obscure fluctuations of luck during these eighteen years of laborious town life, the changes of residence and acquaintance, the method and result of the day's work done, have been traced with much care and exhibited in a direct distinct manner by the biographer. Nothing can be more clear and sufficient than the brief notices of Blake's favourite brother and pupil, in character seemingly a weaker and somewhat violent *replica* of his elder, not without noble and amiable qualities; of his relations with Fuseli and Flaxman, with Johnson the bookseller, and others, whose names are now fished up from the quiet comfort of obscurity, and made more or less memorable for good or evil through their connexion with one who was then himself among the obscurest of men. His alliance

325

with Paine and the ultra-democrats then working or talking in London is the most curious episode of these years. His republican passion was like Shelley's, a matter of fierce dogmatic faith and rapid assumption. Looking at any sketch of his head and face one may see the truth of his assertion that he was born a democrat of the imaginative type. The faith which accepts and the passion which pursues an idea of justice not wholly attainable looks out of the tender and restless eyes, moulds the eager mobile-seeming lips. Infinite impatience, as of a great preacher or apostle —intense tremulous vitality, as of a great orator—seem to me to give his face the look of one who can do all things but hesitate. We need no evidence to bid us believe with what fervour of spirit and singleness of emotion he loved the name and followed the likeness of freedom, whatever new name or changed likeness men might put upon her. Liberty and religion, taken in a large and subtle sense of the words, were alike credible and adorable to him; and in nothing else could he find matter for belief or worship. His forehead, largest (as he said) just over the eyes, shows an eager steadiness of passionate expression. Shut off any single feature, and it will seem singular how little the face changes or loses by the exclusion. With all this, it is curious to read how the author of *Urizen* and *Ahania* saved from probable hanging the author of the *Rights of Man* and *Age of Reason*. Blake had as perfect a gift of ready and steady courage as any man: was not quicker to catch fire than he was safe to stand his ground. The swift quiet resolution and fearless instant sense of the right thing to do which he showed at all times of need are worth notice in a man of such fine and nervous habit of mind and body.

In the year after Paine's escape from England, his deliverer published a book which would probably have been something of a chokepear for the *conventionnel*. This set of seventeen drawings was Blake's first series of original designs, not meant to serve as merely illustrative work. Two of the 'Prophetic Books,' and the *Songs of Innocence*, had already been engraved; but there the designs were supplementary to the text; here such text as there was served only to set out the designs; and even these 'Keys' to the 'Gates of Paradise,' somewhat of the rustiest as they are, were not supplied in every copy. The book is itself not unavailable as a key to much of Blake's fitful and tempestuous philosophy; and it would have been better to re-engrave the series in full than to give random selections twisted out of their places and made less intelligible than they were at first by the headlong process of inversion and convulsion to which they have here been subjected.

The frontispiece gives a symbol of man's birth into the fleshly and mutable house of life, powerless and painless as yet, but encircled by the likeness and oppressed by the mystery of material existence. The pre-existent spirit here wellnigh disappears under stifling folds of vegetable leaf and animal incrustation of overgrowing husk. It lies dumb and dull, almost as a thing itself begotten of the perishable body, conceived in bondage and brought forth with grief. The curled and clinging caterpillar, emblem of motherhood, adheres and impends over it, as the lapping leaves of flesh unclose and release the human fruit of corporeal generation. With mysterious travail and anguish of mysterious division, the child is born as a thing out of sleep; the original perfect manhood being cast in effect into a heavy slumber, and the female or reflective element called into creation. This tenet recurs constantly in the turbulent and fluctuating evangel of

327

Blake; that the feminine element exists by itself for a time only, and as the shadow of the male; thus Space is the wife of Time, and was created of him in the beginning that the things of lower life might have air to breathe and a place to hide their heads; her moral aspect is Pity. She suffers through the lapse of obscure and painful centuries with the sufferings of her children; she is oppressed with all their oppressions, she is plagued with all the plagues of transient life and inevitable death. At sight of her so brought forth, a wonder in heaven, all the most ancient gods or daemons of pre-material life were terrified and amazed, touched with awe and softened with passion; yet endured not to look upon her, a thing alien from the things of their eternal life; for as space is impredicable of the divine world, so is pity impredicable of the daemonic nature. (See the *First Book of Urizen*.) For of all the minor immortal and uncreated spirits Time only is the friend of man; and for man's sake has given him Space to dwell in, as under the shadow and within the arms of a great compassionate mother, who has mercy upon all her children, tenderness for all good and evil things. Only through his help and through her pity can flesh or spirit endure life for a little, under the iron law of the maker and the oppressor of man. Alone among the other co-equal and co-eternal daemons of his race, the Creator is brought into contact and collision with Space and Time; against him alone they struggle in Promethean agony of conflict to deliver the children of men; and against them is the Creator compelled to fight, that he may reach and oppress those whose weakness is defended by all the warring hands of Time, sheltered by all the gracious wings of Space.

In the first plate of the *Gates of Paradise*, the woman finds the child under a tree, sprung of the earth like a mandrake, which he who plucks up and hears groan must go mad or die; grown under the tree of physical life, which is rooted in death, and the leaf of it is poisonous, and it bears as fruit the

328

wisdom of the serpent, moral reason or rational truth, which invents the names of virtue and vice, and divides moral life into good and evil. Out of earth is rent violently forth the child of dust and clay, naked, wide-eyed, shrieking; the woman bends down to gather him as a flower, half blind with fierce surprise and eagerness, half smiling with foolish love and pitiful pleasure; with one hand she holds other children, small and new-blown also as flowers, huddled in the lap of her garment; with the other she plucks him up by the hair, regardless of his deadly shriek and convulsed arms, heedless that this uprooting of the mandrake is the seal of her own death also. Then follow symbols of the four created elements from which the corporeal man is made: the water, blind and mutable as doting age, emblem of ignorant doubt and moral jealousy; the heavy melancholy earth, grievous to life, oppressive of the spirit, type of all sorrows and tyrannies that are brought forth upon it, saddest of all the elements, tightest as a curb and painfullest as a load upon the soul; then the air wherein man is naked, the fire wherein man is blind; ashamed and afraid of his own nature and its nakedness, surrounded with similitudes of severance and strife: overhung by rocks, rained upon by all the storms of heaven, lighted by unfriendly stars, with clouds spread under him and over; 'a dark hermaphrodite,' enlightened by the light within him, which is darkness—the light of reason and morality; evil and good, who was neither good nor evil in the eternal life before this generated existence; male and female, who from of old was neither female nor male, but perfect man without division of flesh, until the setting of sex against sex by the malignity of animal creation. Round the new-created man revolves the flaming sword of Law, burning and dividing in the hand of the angel, servant of the cruelty of God, who drives into exile and debars from paradise the fallen spiritual man upon earth. Round the woman (a double type perhaps at once of the female nature

329

and the 'rational truth' or law of good and evil) roar and freeze the winds and snows of prohibition, blinding, congealing, confusing; and in that tempest of things spiritual the shell of material things hardens and thickens, excluding all divine vision and obscuring all final truth with solid-seeming walls of separation. But death in the end shall enlighten all the deluded, shall deliver all the imprisoned; there, though the worm weaves, the Saviour also watches; the new garments of male and female to be there assumed by the spirit are so woven that they shall no longer be as shrouds or swaddling-clothes to hamper the newly born or consume the newly dead, but free raiment and fair symbol of the spirit. For the power of the creative daemon, which began with birth, must end with death; upon the perfect and eternal man he had not power till he had created the earthly life to bring man into subjection; and shall not have power upon him again any more when he is once resumed by death. Where the Creator's power ends, there begins the Saviour's power; where oppression loses strength to divide, mercy gains strength to reunite. For the Creator is at most God of this world only, and belongs to the life which he creates; the God of this world is a thing of this world, but the Saviour or perfect man is of eternity, belonging to the spiritual life which was before birth and shall be after death.

BLAKE AND HIS PATRON

Hayley's patronage of Blake is a piece of high comedy perfect in its way. The first act or two were played out with sufficient liking on either side. 'Mr Hayley acts like a prince' towards 'his good Blake,' not it seems in the direct way of pecuniary gifts or loans, but in such smaller attentions as he could easily show to the husband and wife on their first arrival close at hand. It must be remarked and remembered that throughout this curious and incongruous intercourse there is no question whatever of obligation on Blake's part for any kindness shown beyond the equal offices of friend to friend. It is for 'Mr Hayley's usual brotherly affection' that he expresses such ready gratitude. That the poor man's goodwill was genuine we need not hesitate to allow; but the fates never indulged in a freak of stranger humour than when it seemed good to their supreme caprice to couple in the same traces for even the shortest stage a man like Hayley with a man like Blake, and bracket the *Triumphs of Temper* with the *Marriage of Heaven and Hell*.

England, with a deplorable ingratitude, has apparently forgotten by this time what her Hayley was once like. It requires a certain strength of imagination to realize the assured fact that he was once a 'greatest living poet'; retrospection collapses in the effort, and credulity loses heart to believe. Such, however, was in effect his profession; he had the witness of his age under hand and seal to the fact, that on the death of his friend Cowper the supreme laurels of the age or day had fallen by inheritance to that poet's accomplished and ingenious biographer. There is something pathetic and almost piteous in his perfect complacency and his perfect futility. A moral country should not have forgotten that to Mr Hayley, when at work on his chief poem, 'it seemed to be a kind of duty incumbent on those who devote themselves to poetry to render a powerful and too often a perverted art as beneficial to life and manners as the limits of composition and the character of modern times will allow.' Although the ages, he regretted to reflect, were past, in which poetry was idolized for *miraculous effects*, yet a poem intended to promote the cultivation of good humour, and designed to unite the special graces of Ariosto, of Dante, and of Pope, might still be of service to society; or, he added with a chaste and noble modesty, 'if this may be thought

331

too chimerical and romantic by sober reason, it is at least one of those pleasing and innocent illusions in which a poetical enthusiast may be safely indulged'; who will deny it?

This was the patron to whom Flaxman introduced Blake as an available engraver, and, on occasion, a commendable designer. Hayley was ready enough to cage and exhibit among the flock of tame geese which composed his troop of swans this bird of foreign feather; and until the eagle's beak and claws came into play under sharp provocation, the Felpham coop and farm-yard were duly dignified by his presence and behaviour as a 'tame villatic fowl.' The master bantam-cock of the hen-roost in person fluttered and cackled round him with assiduous if perplexed patronage. But of such alliances nothing could come in the end but that which did come. 'Mr H.,' writes Blake in July 1803 to Mr Butts, his one purchaser (on the scale of a guinea per picture), 'approves of my designs as little as he does of my poems. I have been forced to insist on his leaving me, in both, to my own self-will; for I am determined to be no longer pestered with his genteel ignorance and polite dis-approbation. His imbecile attempts to depress me only deserve laughter.' Let a compassionate amateur of human poultry imagine what confusion must by this time have been reigning in the poor hen-roost and dove-cote of Eartham! Things, however, took some time in reaching the tragic pitch of these shrill discords. For months or years they appear to have run through various scales of very tolerable harmony. Blake, in the intervals of incessant en-graving and occasional designing, was led by his good Hayley into the greenest pastures of literature and beside the stillest waters of verse; he was solicited to help in softening and arranging for public inspection the horrible and pitiful narrative of Cowper's life; he was prevailed upon to listen while Hayley 'read Klopstock into English to Blake,' with

what result one may trust he never knew. For it was
probably under the sting of this infliction that Blake scratched
down in pencil a brief lyrical satire on the German Milton,
which modern humanity would refuse to read in public if
transcribed; although or because it might be, for grotesque
ease and ringing breadth of melodious extravagance, a scrap
saved from some tattered chorus of Aristophanes, or caught
up by Rabelais as the fragment of a litany at the shrine of the
Dive Bouteille. Let any man judge, from the ragged shred
we can afford to show by way of sample, how a sight or
handling of the stuff would have affected Hayley:

> *The moon at that sight blushed scarlet red,*
> *The stars threw down their cups and fled,*
> *And all the devils that were in hell*
> *Answered with a ninefold yell.*
> *Klopstock felt the intripled turn,*
> *And all his bowels began to churn;*
> *And his bowels turned round three times three,*
> *And locked in his soul with a ninefold key ;*
>
> *Then again old Nobodaddy swore*
> *He never had seen such a thing before*
> *Since Noah was shut in the ark,*
> *Since Eve first chose her hell-fire spark,*
> *Since 'twas the fashion to go naked,*
> *Since the old Anything was created ;*
> *And . . .*

Only in choice Attic or in archaic French could the rest be
endured by modern eyes; but Panurge could hardly have
improved on the manner of retribution devised for flaccid
fluency and devout sentiment always running at the
mouth.

333

into the keen outline of vision. He walked and laboured under other heavens, on another earth, than the earth and the heaven of material life:

> With a blue sky spread over with wings,
> And a mild sun that mounts and sings ;
> With trees and fields full of fairy elves
> And little devils who fight for themselves ;
> With angels planted in hawthorn bowers,
> And God Himself in the passing hours.

All this was not a mere matter of creed or opinion, much less of decoration or ornament to his work. It was, as we said, his element of life, inhaled at every breath with the common air, mixed into his veins with their natural blood. It was an element almost painfully tangible and actual; an absolute medium or state of existence, inevitable, inexplicable, insuperable. To him the veil of outer things seemed always to tremble with some breath behind it: seemed at times to be rent in sunder with clamour and sudden lightning. All the void of earth and air seemed to quiver with the passage of sentient wings and palpitate under the pressure of conscious feet. Flowers and weeds, stars and stones, spoke with articulate lips and gazed with living eyes. Hands were stretched towards him from beyond the darkness of material nature, to tempt or to support, to guide or to restrain. His hardest facts were the vaguest allegories of other men. To him all symbolic things were literal, all literal things symbolic. About his path and about his bed, around his ears and under his eyes, an infinite play of spiritual life seethed and swarmed or shone and sang. Spirits imprisoned in the husk and shell of earth consoled or menaced him. Every leaf bore a growth of angels; the pulse of every minute sounded as the falling foot of God; under the rank raiment of weeds, in the drifting down of thistles, strange faces frowned and white hair fluttered;

340

tempters and allies, wraiths of the living and phantoms of the dead, crowded and made populous the winds that blew about him, the fields and hills over which he gazed. Even upon earth his vision was 'twofold always'; singleness of vision he scorned and feared as the sign of mechanical intellect, of talent that walks while the soul sleeps, with the mere activity of a blind somnambulism. It was fourfold in the intervals of keenest inspiration and subtlest rapture; threefold in the paradise of dreams lying between earth and heaven, lulled by lighter airs and lit by fainter stars; a land of night and moonlight, spectral and serene. These strange divisions of spirit and world according to some dim and mythologic hierarchy were with Blake matters at once serious and commonplace. The worlds of Beulah and Jerusalem, the existence of Los god of Time and Enitharmon goddess of Space, the fallen manhood of Theotormon, the imprisoned womanhood of Oothoon, were more to him even than significant names; to the reader they must needs seem less. This monstrous nomenclature, this jargon of miscreated things in chaos, rose as by nature to his lips, flowed from them as by instinct. Time, an incarnate spirit clothed with fire, stands before him in the sun's likeness; he is threatened with poverty, tempted to make himself friends of this world; and makes answer as though to a human tempter:

> My hands are laboured day and night
> And rest comes never in my sight;
> My wife has no indulgence given
> Except what comes to her from heaven;
> We eat little, we drink less;
> This earth breeds not our happiness.

He beheld, he says, Time and Space as they were eternally, not as they are seen upon earth; he saw nothing as man sees: his hopes and fears were alien from all men's; and upon him

From A STUDY OF SHAKESPEARE

THE aim of the present study is simply to set down what the writer believes to be certain demonstrable truths as to the progress and development of style, the outer and the inner changes of manner as of matter, of method as of design, which may be discerned in the work of Shakespeare. The principle here adopted and the views here put forward have not been suddenly discovered or lightly taken up out of any desire to make a show of theoretical ingenuity. For years past I have held and maintained, in private discussion with friends and fellow-students, the opinions which I now submit to more public judgment. How far they may coin-cide with those advanced by others I cannot say, and have not been careful to inquire. The mere fact of coincidence or of dissent on such a question is of less importance than the principle accepted by either student as the groundwork of his theory, the mainstay of his opinion. It is no part of my project or my hope to establish the actual date of any among the various plays, or to determine point by point the lineal order of their succession. I have examined no table or catalogue of recent or of earlier date, from the time of Malone onwards, with a view to confute by my reasoning the conclusions of another, or by the assistance of his theories to corroborate my own. It is impossible to fix or decide by inner or outer evidence the precise order of production, much less of composition, which critics of the present or the past may have set their wits to verify in vain; but it is quite possible to show that the work of Shakespeare is naturally divisible into classes which may serve us to distinguish and determine as by landmarks the several stages or periods of his mind and art.

Of these the three chief periods or stages are so unmistakably indicated by the mere text itself, and so easily recognizable by the veriest tiro in the school of Shakespeare, that even were I as certain of being the first to point them out as I am conscious of having long since discovered and verified them without assistance or suggestion from any but Shakespeare himself, I should be disposed to claim but little credit for a discovery which must in all likelihood have been forestalled by the common insight of some hundred or more students in time past. The difficulty begins with the really debatable question of subdivisions. There are certain plays which may be said to hang on the borderland between one period and the next, with one foot lingering and one advanced; and these must be classed according to the dominant note of their style, the greater or lesser proportion of qualities proper to the earlier or the later stage of thought and writing. At one time I was inclined to think the whole catalogue more accurately divisible into four classes; but the line of demarcation between the third and fourth would have been so much fainter than those which mark off the first period from the second, and the second from the third, that it seemed on the whole a more correct and adequate arrangement to assume that the last period might be subdivided if necessary into a first and second stage. This somewhat precise and pedantic scheme of study I have adopted from no love of rigid or formal system, but simply to make the method of my critical process as clear as the design. That design is to examine by internal evidence alone the growth and the expression of spirit and of speech, the ebb and flow of thought and style, discernible in the successive periods of Shakespeare's work; to study the phases of mind, the changes of tone, the passage or progress from an old manner to a new, the reversion or relapse from a later to an earlier habit, which may assuredly be traced in the modulations of his varying verse, but can only be traced by ear and not by finger. I have busied myself with no

England has hitherto been erroneously described as written in blank verse; an error which I can only attribute to the prevalence of a groundless assumption that whatever is neither prose nor rhyme must of necessity be definable as blank verse. But the measure, I must repeat, which was adopted by the authors of *Gorboduc* is by no means so definable. Blank it certainly is; but verse it assuredly is not. There can be no verse where there is no modulation, no rhythm where there is no music. Blank verse came into life in England at the birth of the shoemaker's son who had but to open his yet beardless lips, and the high-born poem which had Sackville to father and Sidney to sponsor was silenced and eclipsed for ever among the poor plebeian crowd of rhyming shadows that waited in death on the noble nothingness of its patrician shade.

These, I suppose, are the first or the only plays whose names recur to the memory of the general reader when he thinks of the English stage before Marlowe; but there was, I suspect, a whole class of plays then current, and more or less supported by popular favour, of which hardly a sample is now extant, and which cannot be classed with such as these. The poets or rhymesters who supplied them had already seen good to clip the cumbrous and bedraggled skirts of those dreary verses, run all to seed and weed, which jingled their thin bells at the tedious end of fourteen weary syllables; and for this curtailment of the shambling and sprawling lines which had hitherto done duty as tragic metre some credit may be due to these obscure purveyors of forgotten ware for the second epoch of our stage: if indeed, as I presume, we may suppose that this reform, such as it was, had begun before the time of Marlowe; otherwise, no doubt, little credit would be due to men who with so high an example before them were content simply to snip away the tags and fringes, to patch the seams and tatters, of the ragged coat of rhyme which they might have exchanged for that royal robe of heroic verse wherewith he had clothed the ungrown limbs of limping and lisping tragedy.

SHAKESPEARE'S FIRST PERIOD

The briefest glance over the plays of the first epoch in the work of Shakespeare will suffice to show how protracted was the struggle and how gradual the defeat of rhyme. Setting aside the retouched plays, we find on the list one tragedy, two histories, and four if not five comedies, which the least critical reader would attribute to this first epoch of work. In three of these comedies rhyme can hardly be said to be beaten; that is, the rhyming scenes are on the whole equal to the unrhymed in power and beauty. In the single tragedy, and in one of the two histories, we may say that rhyme fights hard for life, but is undeniably worsted; that is, they contain as to quantity a large proportion of rhymed verse, but as to quality the rhymed part bears no proportion whatever to the unrhymed. In two scenes we may say that the whole heart or spirit of *Romeo and Juliet* is summed up and distilled into perfect and pure expression; and these two are written in blank verse of equable and blameless melody. Outside the garden scene in the second act and the balcony scene in the third, there is much that is fanciful and graceful, much of elegiac pathos and fervid if fantastic passion; much also of superfluous rhetoric and (as it were) of wordy melody, which flows and foams hither and thither into something of extravagance and excess; but in these two there is no flaw, no outbreak, no superflux, and no failure. Throughout certain scenes of the third and fourth acts I think it may be reasonably and reverently allowed that the river of verse has broken its banks, not as yet through the force and weight of its gathering stream, but merely through the weakness of the barriers or boundaries found insufficient to confine it. And here we may with deference venture on a guess why Shakespeare was so long so loth to forgo the restraint of rhyme. When he wrote, and even when he rewrote or at least retouched, his youngest tragedy he had not yet strength to walk straight in the steps of the mighty master, but two months older than himself by birth, whose foot never from the first faltered in the arduous path of severer tragic verse. The loveliest of love-plays is after all a child of 'his salad days, when he was green in judgment,' though assuredly not 'cold in blood'—a physical condition as difficult to conceive of Shakespeare at any age as of Cleopatra. It is in the scenes of vehement passion, of ardour and of agony, that we feel the comparative weakness of a yet ungrown hand, the tentative uncertain grasp of a stripling giant. The two utterly beautiful scenes are not of this kind; they deal with simple joy and with simple sorrow, with the gladness of meeting and the sadness of parting love; but between and behind them come scenes of more fierce emotion, full of surprise, of violence, of unrest; and with these the poet is not yet (if I dare say so) quite strong enough to deal. Apollo has not yet put on the sinews of Hercules. At a later date we may fancy or may find that when the Herculean muscle is full-grown the voice in him which was as the voice of Apollo is for a passing moment impaired. In *Measure for Measure*, where the adult and gigantic god has grappled with the greatest and most terrible of energies and of passions, we miss the music of a younger note that rang through *Romeo and Juliet*; but before the end this too revives, as pure, as sweet, as fresh, but richer now and deeper than its first clear notes of the morning, in the heavenly harmony of *Cymbeline* and the *Tempest*.

The same effusion or effervescence of words is perceptible in *King Richard II* as in the greater (and the less good) part of *Romeo and Juliet*; and not less perceptible is the perpetual

358

inclination of the poet to revert for help to rhyme, to hark back in search of support towards the half-forsaken habits of his poetic nonage. Feeling his foothold insecure on the hard and high ascent of the steeps of rhymeless verse, he stops and slips back ever and anon towards the smooth and marshy meadow whence he has hardly begun to climb. Any student who should wish to examine the conditions of the struggle at its height may be content to analyse the first act of this the first historical play of Shakespeare. As the tragedy moves onward, and the style gathers strength while the action gathers speed—as (to borrow the phrase so admirably applied by Coleridge to Dryden) the poet's chariot-wheels get hot by driving fast—the temptation of rhyme grows weaker, and the hand grows firmer which before lacked strength to wave it off. The one thing wholly or greatly admirable in this play is the exposition of the somewhat pitiful but not unpitiable character of King Richard. Among the scenes devoted to this exposition I of course include the whole of the death-scene of Gaunt, as well the part which precedes as the part which follows the actual appearance of his nephew on the stage; and into these scenes the intrusion of rhyme is rare and brief. They are written almost wholly in pure and fluent rather than vigorous or various blank verse; though I cannot discern in any of them an equality in power and passion to the magnificent scene of abdication in Marlowe's *Edward II.* This play, I think, must undoubtedly be regarded as the immediate model of Shakespeare's; and the comparison is one of inexhaustible interest to all students of dramatic poetry. To the highest height of the earlier master I do not think that the mightier poet who was as yet in great measure his pupil has ever risen in this the first (as I take it) of his historic plays. Of composition and proportion he has perhaps already a somewhat better idea. But in grasp of character, always excepting the one central figure of the piece, we find his hand as yet the unsteadier of the two. Even after a lifelong study of this as of all other plays of Shakespeare, it is for me at least impossible to determine what I doubt if the poet could him-self have clearly defined—the main principle, the motive and the meaning of such characters as York, Norfolk, and Aumerle. The Gaveston and the Mortimer of Marlowe are far more solid and definite figures than these; yet none after that of Richard is more important to the scheme of Shakespeare. They are fitful, shifting, vaporous: their out-lines change, withdraw, dissolve, and 'leave not a rack behind.' They, not Antony, are like the clouds of evening described in the most glorious of so many glorious passages put long afterwards by Shakespeare into the mouth of his latest Roman hero. They 'cannot hold this visible shape' in which the poet at first presents them even long enough to leave a distinct image, a decisive impression for better or for worse, upon the mind's eye of the most simple and open-hearted reader. They are ghosts, not men; *simulacra modis pallentia miris.* You cannot descry so much as the original intention of the artist's hand which began to draw and relaxed its hold of the brush before the first lines were fairly traced. And in the last, the worst and weakest scene of all, in which York pleads with Bolingbroke for the death of the son whose mother pleads against her husband for his life, there is a final relapse into rhyme and rhyming epigram, into the 'jigging vein' dried up (we might have hoped) long since by the very glance of Marlowe's Apollonian scorn. It would be easy, agreeable, and irrational to ascribe without further evidence than its badness this misconceived and misshapen scene to some other hand than Shakespeare's. It is below the weakest, the rudest, the hastiest scene attri-butable to Marlowe; it is false, wrong, artificial beyond the worst of his bad and boyish work; but it has a certain like-ness for the worse to the crudest work of Shakespeare. It is difficult to say to what depths of bad taste the writer of certain passages in *Venus and Adonis* could not fall before his genius or his judgment was full-grown. To invent an earlier play on the subject and imagine this scene a surviving fragment, a floating waif of that imaginary wreck, would in my opinion be an uncritical mode of evading the question at issue. It must be regarded as the last hysterical struggle of rhyme to maintain its place in tragedy; and the explanation, I would fain say the excuse, of its reappearance may perhaps be simply this; that the poet was not yet dramatist enough to feel for each of his characters an equal or proportionate regard; to divide and disperse his interest among the various crowd of figures which claim each in its place, and each after its kind, a fair and adequate share of their creator's attention and sympathy. His present interest was here wholly concentrated on the single figure of Richard; and when that for the time was absent, the subordinate figures became to him but heavy and vexatious encumbrances, to be shifted on and off the stage with as much of haste and as little of labour as might be possible to an impatient and uncertain hand. Now all tragic poets, I presume, from Aeschylus the godlike father of them all to the last aspirant who may struggle after the traces of his steps, have been poets before they were tragedians; their lips have had power to sing before their feet had strength to tread the stage, before their hands had skill to paint or carve figures from the life. With Shakespeare it was so as certainly as with Shelley, as evidently as with Hugo. It is in the great comic poets, in Molière and in Congreve,[1] our own lesser

---

[1] It is not the least of Lord Macaulay's offences against art that he should have contributed the temporary weight of his influence as a critic to the support of so ignorant and absurd a tradition of criticism as that which classes the great writer here mentioned with the brutal if 'brawny' Wycherley—a classification almost to be paralleled with that which in the days of our fathers saw fit to couple together the names of Balzac and of Sue. Any

Molière, so far inferior in breadth and depth, in tenderness and strength, to the greatest writer of the 'great age,' yet so near him in science and in skill, so like him in brilliance and in force—it is in these that we find theatrical instinct twin-born with imaginative impulse, dramatic power with inventive perception.

The example afforded by the *Comedy of Errors* would suffice to show that rhyme, however inadequate for tragic use, is by no means a bad instrument for romantic comedy. In another of Shakespeare's earliest works, which might almost be described as a lyrical farce, rhyme plays also a great part; but the finest passage, the real crown and flower of *Love's Labour's Lost*, is the praise or apology of love spoken by Biron in blank verse. This is worthy of Marlowe for dignity and sweetness, but has also the grace of a light and radiant fancy enamoured of itself, begotten between thought and mirth, a child-god with grave lips and laughing eyes, whose inspiration is nothing akin to Marlowe's. In this as in the overture of the play and in its closing scene, but especially in the noble passage which winds up for a year the courtship of Biron and Rosaline, the spirit which informs the speech of the poet is finer of touch and deeper of tone than in the sweetest of the serious interludes of the *Comedy of Errors*. The play is in the main a yet lighter thing, and more wayward and capricious in build, more formless and

competent critic will always recognize in *The Way of the World* one of the glories, in *The Country Wife* one of the disgraces, of dramatic and of English literature. The stains discernible on the masterpiece of Congreve are trivial and conventional; the mere conception of the other man's work displays a mind so prurient and leprous, uncovers such an unfathomable and unimaginable beastliness of imagination that in the present age at least he would probably have figured as a virtuous journalist and professional rebuker of poetic vice or artistic aberration.

fantastic in plot, more incomposite altogether than that first heir of Shakespeare's comic invention, which on its own ground is perfect in its consistency, blameless in composition and coherence; while in *Love's Labour's Lost* the fancy for the most part runs wild as the wind, and the structure of the story is as that of a house of clouds which the wind builds and unbuilds at pleasure. Here we find a very riot of rhymes, wild and wanton in their half-grown grace as a troop of 'young satyrs, tender-hoofed and ruddy-horned'; during certain scenes we seem almost to stand again by the cradle of new-born comedy, and hear the first lisping and laughing accents run over from her baby lips in bubbling rhyme; but when the note changes we recognize the speech of gods. For the first time in our literature the higher key of poetic or romantic comedy is finely touched to a fine issue. The divine instrument fashioned by Marlowe for tragic purposes alone has found at once its new sweet use in the hands of Shakespeare. The way is prepared for *As You Like It* and the *Tempest*; the language is discovered which will befit the lips of Rosalind and Miranda.

What was highest as poetry in the *Comedy of Errors* was mainly in rhyme; all indeed, we might say, between the prelude spoken by Aegeon and the appearance in the last scene of his wife: in *Love's Labour's Lost* what was highest was couched wholly in blank verse; in the *Two Gentlemen of Verona* rhyme has fallen seemingly into abeyance, and there are no passages of such elegiac beauty as in the former, of such exalted eloquence as in the latter of these plays; there is an even sweetness, a simple equality of grace in thought and language which keeps the whole poem in tune, written as it is in a subdued key of unambitious harmony. In perfect unity and keeping the composition of this beautiful sketch may perhaps be said to mark a stage of advance, a new point of work attained, a faint but sensible change of manner, signalized by increased firmness of hand and

363

clearness of outline. Slight and swift in execution as it is, few and simple as are the chords here struck of character and emotion, every shade of drawing and every note of sound is at one with the whole scheme of form and music. Here too is the first dawn of that higher and more tender humour which was never given in such perfection to any man as ultimately to Shakespeare; one touch of the by-play of Launce and his immortal dog is worth all the bright fantastic interludes of Boyet and Adriano, Costard and Holofernes; worth even half the sallies of Mercutio, and half the dancing doggerel or broad-witted prose of either Dromio. But in the final poem which concludes and crowns the first epoch of Shakespeare's work, the special graces and peculiar glories of each that went before are gathered together as in one garland 'of every hue and every scent.' The young genius of the master of all our poets finds its consummation in the *Midsummer Night's Dream*. The blank verse is as full, sweet, and strong as the best of Biron's or Romeo's; the rhymed verse as clear, pure, and true as the simplest and truest melody of *Venus and Adonis* or the *Comedy of Errors*. But here each kind of excellence is equal throughout; there are here no purple patches on a gown of serge, but one seamless and imperial robe of a single dye. Of the lyric or the prosaic part, the counterchange of loves and laughters, of fancy fine as air and imagination high as heaven, what need can there be for any one to shame himself by the helpless attempt to say some word not utterly unworthy? Let it suffice us to accept this poem as the landmark of our first stage, and pause to look back from it on what lies behind us of partial or of perfect work.

The second period is that of perfection in comic and historic style. The final heights and depths of tragedy, with all its reach of thought and all its pulse of passion, are yet to be scaled and sounded; but to this stage belongs the special quality of faultless, joyous, facile command upon each faculty required of the presiding genius for service or for sport. It is in the middle period of his work that the language of Shakespeare is most limpid in its fullness, the style most pure, the thought most transparent through the close and luminous raiment of perfect expression. The conceits and crudities of the first stage are outgrown and cast aside; the harshness and obscurity which at times may strike us us among the notes of his third manner have as yet no place in the flawless work of this second stage. That which has to be said is not yet too great for perfection of utterance; passion has not yet grappled with thought in so close and fierce an embrace as to strain and rend the garment of words, though stronger and subtler than ever was woven of human speech. Neither in his first nor in his last stage would the style of Shakespeare, even were it possible by study to reproduce it, be of itself a perfect and blameless model, but his middle style, that in which the typical plays of his second period are written, would be, if it were possible to imitate, the most absolute pattern that could be set before man. I do not speak of mere copyist's work, the parasitic knack of retailing cast phrases, tricks and turns of accent, cadences and catchwords proper only to the natural manner of the man who first came by instinct upon them, and by instinct put them to use; I speak of that faithful and fruitful discipleship of love with which the highest among poets and the most original among workmen have naturally been always the first to study and the most earnest to follow the footsteps of their greatest precursors in that kind. And this only high and profitable form of study and discipleship can set before itself, even in the work of Shakespeare, no pattern so perfect, no model so absolute, as is afforded by the style or manner of his second period.

To this stage belong by spiritual right if not by material, by rule of poetic order if not by date of actual succession, the greatest of his English histories and four of his greatest and most perfect comedies; the four greatest we might properly call them, reserving for another class the last divine triad of romantic plays which it is alike inaccurate to number among tragedies or comedies proper: the *Winter's Tale*, *Cymbeline*, and the *Tempest*, which belong of course wholly to his last manner, or, if accuracy must be strained even to pedantry, to the second manner of his third or final stage. A single masterpiece which may be classed either among histories or tragedies belongs to the middle period; and to this also we must refer, if not the ultimate form, yet assuredly the first sketch at least of that which is commonly regarded as the typical and supreme work of Shakespeare. Three lesser comedies, one of them in great part the recast or rather the transfiguration of an earlier poet's work, complete the list of plays assignable to the second epoch of his genius.

The ripest fruit of historic or national drama, the consummation and the crown of Shakespeare's labours in that line, must of course be recognized and saluted by all students in the supreme and sovereign trilogy of *King Henry IV* and *King Henry V*. On a lower degree only than this final and imperial work we find the two chronicle histories which remain to be classed. In style as in structure they bear witness of a power less perfect, a less impeccable hand. They have less of perceptible instinct, less of vivid and vigorous utterance; the breath of their inspiration is less continuous and less direct, the fashion of their eloquence is more deliberate and more prepense; there is more of study and structure apparent in their speech, and less in their general

366

scheme of action. Of all Shakespeare's plays they are the most rhetorical; there is more talk than song in them, less poetry than oratory; more finish than form, less movement than incident. Scene is laid upon scene, and event succeeds event, as stone might be laid on stone and story might succeed story in a building reared by mere might of human handi‑work; not as in a city or temple whose walls had risen of themselves to the lyric breath and stroke of a greater than Amphion; moulded out of music by no rule or line of mortal measure, with no sound of axe or anvil, but only of smitten strings: built by harp and not by hand.

The lordly structure of these poems is the work of a royal workman, full of masterdom and might, sublime in the state and strength of its many mansions, but less perfect in proportion and less aerial in build than the very highest fabrics fashioned after their own great will by the supreme architects of song. Of these plays, and of these alone among the maturer works of Shakespeare, it may be said that the best parts are discernible from the rest, divisible by analysis and separable by memory from the scenes which precede them or follow and the characters which surround them or succeed. Constance and Katherine rise up into remem‑brance apart from their environment and above it, stand clear in our minds of the crowded company with which the poet has begirt their central figures. In all other of his great tragic works—even in *Hamlet*, if we have grace and sense to read it aright and not awry—it is not of any single person or separate passage that we think when we speak of it; it is to the whole masterpiece that the mind turns at mention of its name. The one entire and perfect chrysolite of *Othello* is neither Othello nor Desdemona nor Iago, but each and all; the play of *Hamlet* is more than Hamlet himself, the poem even here is too great to be resumed in the person. But Constance is the jewel of *King John*, and Katherine is the crowning blossom of *King Henry VIII*—a funeral flower as

367

of 'marigolds on death-beds blowing,' an opal of as pure water as 'tears of perfect moan,' with fitful fire at its heart, ominous of evil and sorrow, set in a mourning band of jet on the forefront of the poem, that the brow so circled may, 'like to a title-leaf, foretell the nature of a tragic volume.' Not indeed that without these the ground would in either case be barren; but that in either field our eye rests rather on these and other separate ears of wheat that overtop the ranks, than on the waving width of the whole harvest at once. In the one play our memory turns next to the figures of Arthur and the Bastard, in the other to those of Wolsey and his king: the residue in either case is made up of outlines more lightly and slightly drawn. In two scenes the figure of King John rises indeed to the highest height even of Shakespearian tragedy; for the rest of the play the lines of his character are cut no deeper, the features of his personality stand out in no sharper relief, than those of Eleanor or the French king; but the scene in which he tempts Hubert to the edge of the pit of hell sounds a deeper note and touches a subtler string in the tragic nature of man than had been struck by any poet save Dante alone, since the reign of the Greek tragedians. The cunning and profound simplicity of the few last weighty words which drop like flakes of poison that blister where they fall from the deadly lips of the king is a new quality in our tragic verse; there was no foretaste of such a thing in the passionate imagination which clothed itself in the mighty music of Marlowe's burning song. The elder master might indeed have written the magnificent speech which ushers in with gradual rhetoric and splendid reticence the black suggestion of a deed without a name; his hand might have woven with no less imperial skill the elaborate raiment of words and images which wraps up in fold upon fold, as with swaddling-bands of purple and golden embroidery, the shapeless and miscreated birth of a murderous purpose that labours into light even while it

368

loathes the light and itself; but only Shakespeare could give us the first sample of that more secret and terrible knowledge which reveals itself in the brief heavy whispers that seal the commission and sign the warrant of the king. Webster alone of all our tragic poets has had strength to emulate in this darkest line of art the handiwork of his master. We find nowhere such an echo or reflection of the spirit of this scene as in the last tremendous dialogue of Bosola with Ferdinand in the house of murder and madness, while their spotted souls yet flutter between conscience and distraction, hovering for an hour as with broken wings on the confines of either province of hell. One pupil at least could put to this awful profit the study of so great a model; but with the single and sublime exception of that other design from the same great hand, which bares before us the mortal anguish of Bracciano, no copy or imitation of the scene in which John dies by poison has ever come near enough to evade the sentence it provokes. The shrill tremulous agony of Fletcher's Valentinian is to the sullen and slow death-pangs of Shakespeare's tyrant as the babble of a suckling to the accents of a man. As far beyond the reach of any but his maker's hand is the pattern of a perfect English warrior, set once for all before the eyes of all ages in the figure of the noble Bastard. The national side of Shakespeare's genius, the heroic vein of patriotism that runs like a thread of living fire through the world-wide range of his omnipresent spirit, has never, to my thinking, found vent or expression to such glorious purpose as here. Not even in Hotspur or Prince Hal has he mixed with more godlike sleight of hand all the lighter and graver good qualities of the national character, or compounded of them all so lovable a nature as this. In those others we admire and enjoy the same bright fiery temper of soul, the same buoyant and fearless mastery of fate or fortune, the same gladness and glory of life made lovely with all the labour and laughter of its full fresh days;

369

but no quality of theirs binds our hearts to them as they are bound to Philip—not by his loyal valour, his keen young wit, his kindliness, constancy, readiness of service as swift and sure in the day of his master's bitterest shame and shame‑fullest trouble as in the blithest hour of battle and that first good fight which won back his father's spoils from his father's slayer; but more than all these, for that lightning of divine rage and pity, of tenderness that speaks in thunder and indignation that makes fire of its tears, in the horror of great compassion which falls on him, the tempest and storm of a beautiful and godlike anger which shakes his strength of spirit and bows his high heart down at sight of Arthur dead. Being thus, as he is, the English masterwork of Shakespeare's hand, we may well accept him as the best man known to us that England ever made; the hero that Nelson must have been had he never come too near Naples.

I am not minded to say much of Shakespeare's Arthur; there are one or two figures in the world of his work of which there are no words that would be fit or good to say. Another of these is Cordelia. The place they have in our lives and thoughts is not one for talk; the niche set apart for them to inhabit in our secret hearts is not penetrable by the lights and noises of common day. There are chapels in the cathedral of man's highest art as in that of his inmost life, not made to be set open to the eyes and feet of the world. Love and death and memory keep charge for us in silence of some beloved names. It is the crowning glory of genius, the final miracle and transcendent gift of poetry, that it can add to the number of these, and engrave on the very heart of our remembrance fresh names and memories of its own creation.

There is one younger child in this heavenly family of Shakespeare's who sits side by side with Arthur in the secret places of our thought; there are but two or three that I remember among the children of other poets who may be named in the same year with them: as Fletcher's Hengo,

Webster's Giovanni, and Landor's Caesarion. Of this princely trinity of boys the 'bud of Britain' is as yet the most famous flower; yet even in the broken words of childish heroism that falter on his dying lips there is nothing of more poignant pathos, more 'dearly sweet and bitter,' than Giovanni's talk of his dead mother and all her sleepless nights now ended for ever in a sleep beyond tears or dreams. Perhaps the most nearly faultless in finish and proportion of perfect nature among all the noble three is Landor's portrait of the imperial and right Roman child of Caesar and Cleopatra. I know not but this may be found in the judgment of men to come wellnigh the most pathetic and heroic figure bequeathed us after more than eighty years of a glorious life by the indomitable genius of our own last Roman and republican poet.

We have come now to that point at the opening of the second stage in his work where the supreme genius of all time begins first to meddle with the mysteries and varieties of human character, to handle its finer and more subtle qualities, to harmonize its more untuned and jarring discords; giving here and thus the first proof of a power never shared in like measure by the mightiest among the sons of men, a sovereign and serene capacity to fathom the else unfathomable depths of spiritual nature, to solve its else insoluble riddles, to reconcile its else irreconcilable discrepancies. In his first stage Shakespeare had dropped his plummet no deeper into the sea of the spirit of man than Marlowe had sounded before him; and in the channel of simple emotion no poet could cast surer line with steadier hand than he. Farther down in the dark and fiery depths of human pain and mortal passion no soul could search than his who first rendered into speech the aspirations and the agonies of a ruined and revolted spirit. And until Shakespeare found in himself the strength of eyesight to read and the cunning of handiwork to render those wider diversities of emotion and those further complexities of

371

character which lay outside the range of Marlowe, he certainly cannot be said to have outrun the winged feet, outstripped the fiery flight of his forerunner. In the heaven of our tragic song the first-born star on the forehead of its herald god was not outshone till the full midsummer meridian of that greater godhead before whom he was sent to prepare a pathway for the sun. Through all the forenoon of our triumphant day, till the utter consummation and ultimate ascension of dramatic poetry incarnate and transfigured in the master-singer of the world, the quality of his tragedy was as that of Marlowe's, broad, single, and intense; large of hand, voluble of tongue, direct of purpose. With the dawn of its latter epoch a new power comes upon it, to find clothing and expression in new forms of speech and after a new style. The language has put off its foreign decorations of lyric and elegiac ornament; it has found already its infinite gain in the loss of those sweet superfluous graces which encumbered the march and enchained the utterance of its childhood. The figures which it invests are now no more the types of a single passion, the incarnations of a single thought. They now demand a scrutiny which tests the power of a mind and tries the value of a judgment; they appeal to something more than the instant apprehension which sufficed to respond to the immediate claim of those that went before them. Romeo and Juliet were simply lovers, and their names bring back to us no further thought than of their love and the lovely sorrow of its end; Antony and Cleopatra shall be before all things lovers, but the thought of their love and its triumphant tragedy shall recall other things beyond number—all the forces and all the fortunes of mankind, all the chance and all the consequence that waited on their imperial passion, all the infinite variety of qualities and powers wrought together and welded into the frame and composition of that love which shook from end to end all nations and kingdoms of the earth.

The same truth holds good in lighter matters; Biron and Rosaline in comedy are as simply lovers and no more as were their counterparts and coevals in tragedy: there is more in Benedick and Beatrice than this simple quality of love that clothes itself in the strife of wits; the injury done her cousin, which by the repercussion of its shock and refraction of its effect serves to transfigure with such adorable indigna- tion and ardour of furious love and pity the whole bright light nature of Beatrice, serves likewise by a fresh reflection and counterchange of its consequence to exalt and enlarge the stature of her lover's spirit after a fashion beyond the reach of Shakespeare in his first stage. Mercutio again, like Philip, is a good friend and gallant swordsman, quick- witted and hot-blooded, of a fiery and faithful temper, loyal and light and swift alike of speech and swordstroke; and this is all. But the character of the Bastard, clear and simple as broad sunlight though it be, has in it other features than this single and beautiful likeness of frank young man- hood; his love of country and loathing of the Church that would bring it into subjection are two sides of the same national quality that has made and will always make every Englishman of his type such another as he was in belief and in unbelief, patriot and priest-hater; and no part of the design bears such witness to the full-grown perfection of his creator's power and skill as the touch that combines and fuses into absolute unity of concord the high and various elements of faith in England, loyalty to the wretched lord who has made him knight and acknowledged him kinsman, contempt for his abjection at the foul feet of the Church, abhorrence of his crime and constancy to his cause for some- thing better worth the proof of war than his miserable sake who hardly can be roused, even by such exhortation as might put life and spirit into the dust of dead men's bones, to bid his betters stand and strike in defence of the country dishonoured by his reign.

The entrance to the third period of Shakespeare is like the entrance to that lost and lesser Paradise of old,

With dreadful faces thronged, and fiery arms.

Lear, Othello, Macbeth, Coriolanus, Antony, Timon, these are names indeed of something more than tragic purport. Only in the sunnier distance beyond, where the sunset of Shakespeare's imagination seems to melt or flow back into the sunrise, do we discern Prospero beside Miranda, Florizel by Perdita, Palamon with Arcite, the same knightly and kindly Duke Theseus as of old; and above them all, and all others of his divine and human children, the crowning and final and ineffable figure of Imogen.

Of all Shakespeare's plays, *King Lear* is unquestionably that in which he has come nearest to the height and to the likeness of the one tragic poet on any side greater than himself whom the world in all its ages has ever seen born of time. It is by far the most Aeschylean of his works; the most elemental and primeval, the most oceanic and Titanic in conception. He deals here with no subtleties as in *Hamlet*, with no conventions as in *Othello*: there is no question of 'a divided duty' or a problem half insoluble, a matter of country and connection, of family or of race; we look upward and downward, and in vain, into the deepest things of nature, into the highest things of providence; to the roots of life, and to the stars; from the roots that no God waters to the stars which give no man light; over a world full of death and life without resting-place or guidance.

But in one main point it differs radically from the work

374

and the spirit of Aeschylus. Its fatalism is of a darker and harder nature. To Prometheus the fetters of the lord and enemy of mankind were bitter; upon Orestes the hand of heaven was laid too heavily to bear; yet in the not utterly infinite or everlasting distance we see beyond them the promise of the morning on which mystery and justice shall be made one; when righteousness and omnipotence at last shall kiss each other. But on the horizon of Shakespeare's tragic fatalism we see no such twilight of atonement, such pledge of reconciliation as this. Requital, redemption, amends, equity, explanation, pity, and mercy, are words without a meaning here.

> *As flies to wanton boys are we to the gods;*
> *They kill us for their sport.*

Here is no need of the Eumenides, children of Night everlasting; for here is very Night herself.

The words just cited are not casual or episodical; they strike the keynote of the whole poem, lay the keystone of the whole arch of thought. There is no contest of conflicting forces, no judgment so much as by casting of lots: far less is there any light of heavenly harmony or of heavenly wisdom, of Apollo or Athene from above. We have heard much and often from theologians of the light of revelation: and some such thing indeed we find in Aeschylus: but the darkness of revelation is here.

For in this the most terrible work of human genius it is with the very springs and sources of nature that her student has set himself to deal. The veil of the temple of our humanity is rent in twain. Nature herself, we might say, is revealed—and revealed as unnatural. In face of such a world as this a man might be forgiven who should pray that chaos might come again. Nowhere else in Shakespeare's

375

work or in the universe of jarring lives are the lines of character and event so broadly drawn or so sharply cut. Only the supreme self-command of this one poet could so mould and handle such types as to restrain and prevent their passing from the abnormal into the monstrous: yet even as much as this, at least in all cases but one, it surely has accomplished. In Regan alone would it be, I think, impossible to find a touch or trace of anything less vile than it was devilish. Even Goneril has her one splendid hour, her fire-flaught of hellish glory; when she treads under foot the half-hearted goodness, the wordy and windy though sincere abhorrence, which is all that the mild and impotent revolt of Albany can bring to bear against her imperious and dauntless devilhood; when she flaunts before the eyes of her 'milk-livered' and 'moral fool' the coming banners of France about the 'plumed helm' of his slayer.

On the other side, Kent is the exception which answers to Regan on this. Cordelia, the brotherless Antigone of our stage, has one passing touch of intolerance for what her sister was afterwards to brand as indiscretion and dotage in their father, which redeems her from the charge of perfection. Like Imogen, she is not too inhumanly divine for the sense of divine irritation. Godlike though they be, their very godhead is human and feminine; and only therefore credible, and only therefore adorable. Cloten and Regan, Goneril and Iachimo, have power to stir and embitter the sweetness of their blood. But for the contrast and even the contact of antagonists as abominable as these, the gold of their spirit would be too refined, the lily of their holiness too radiant, the violet of their virtue too sweet. As it is, Shakespeare has gone down perforce among the blackest and the basest things of nature to find anything so equally exceptional in evil as properly to counterbalance and make bearable the excellence and extremity of their goodness. No otherwise

376

could either angel have escaped the blame implied in the very attribute and epithet of blameless. But where the possible depth of human hell is so foul and unfathomable as it appears in the spirits which serve as foils to these, we may endure that in them the inner height of heaven should be no less immaculate and immeasurable.

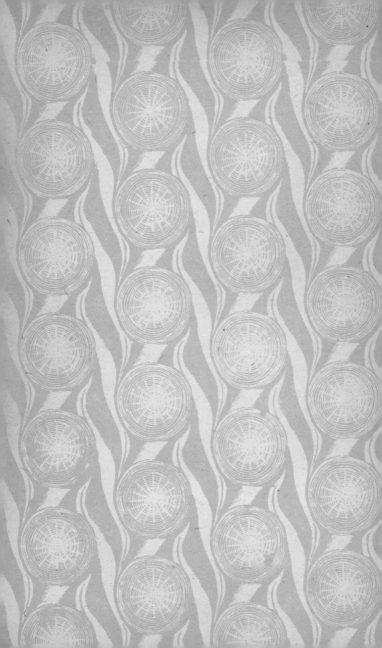